Goin' Railroading

TWO GENERATIONS OF COLORADO STORIES

BY MARGARET COEL, AS TOLD BY SAM SPEAS

PRUETT

PRUETT PUBLISHING COMPANY
BOULDER, COLORADO

©1991 by Margaret Coel

Printed in the United States

10 9 8 7 6 5 4 3 2 1

Library of Congress Cataloging-in-Publication Data

Speas, Sam, 1900–1981.
  Goin' Railroading : two generations of Colorado stories / Margaret Coel as told by Sam Speas.
     p.   cm.
  Originally published: ©1985.
  Includes bibliographical references and index.
  ISBN 0-87108-821-5 (paperback) : $14.95
  1. Speas, Sam, 1900–1981. 2. Locomotive engineers—Colorado—Biography. 3. Colorado and Southern Railroad—History. 4. Speas family. 5. Como (Colo.)—Social life and customs. I. Coel, Margaret, 1937–   II. Title.
[HD8039.R322U57   1991]
625.2'7'092—dc20
[B]   91-31038
                                                                                CIP

Contents

Acknowledgments

Many people helped to make this book a reality: Colorado and Southern railroaders C.B. Clark, Ed Boyle, John Dietz, and Doug Schnurbusch; railroad buffs Mike Trent and Carl Schneider; and Bernard Duffy, son of Engineer J.T. Duffy. Photos are due to the generosity of Mike Trent, R.A. Ronzio, Ed Haley, George Champion, Mrs. George Lundberg, Marjorie Oshier Garcia, Mary Dyer, John Dietz, Lawrence Paddock, and the Climax Molybdenum Company. I thank them all.

Preface

This is the story of a unique group of Colorado pioneers—the railroaders. Like other pioneers, such as homesteaders, gold seekers, farmers, ranchers, miners, and merchants, railroaders came west in the last decades of the nineteenth century seeking opportunity and adventure. Their work, their contributions, and the force of their personalities shaped the communities developing on the plains and in the mountains of Colorado.

Theirs was the golden age of railroading when trains touched the lives of everyone. The trains whistling into Colorado's small, isolated towns connected them to one another and to the rest of the country. Trains took people wherever they wished to go, and everybody traveled by train. Trains carried goods of all kinds—timber, wheat, corn, hay, clothing, food, furniture, tools, machinery. Over the span of a century, trains were a unifying and civilizing force.

Running the trains was an important job that the railroaders took seriously. They never forgot that mountain towns marooned in January snows depended upon the trains for food and supplies; that people waiting at the station had no other way to travel; that mines, factories, and businesses would shut down if the trains didn't get through.

But making sure that the trains got through was more than a job. It was an adventure—the great adventure of the age, just as space is the great adventure of today. Railroaders saw themselves as an elite group, "brotherhoods" partaking in the adventure, racing downtrack with the fire hot in the boiler, steam spouting overhead, whistle blowing, and the horizon receding far into the distance. All the dangers—and there were dangers, more than in any other occupation—paled in comparison to the sheer thrill of adventure.

It was our wish, my father's and mine, to tell you what it was like to be a railroader in Colorado, especially on the Colorado and Southern

Railway, during this golden age. I hope that in telling the story of the
pioneer railroaders, we've captured some of the excitement and danger,
and some of the glory.

—Margaret Coel
1991

Preface to First Edition

Stories happen to those who can tell them, Thucydides said, which may explain why my father, Sam Speas, had such an enormous stock of railroading tales. Some he had heard from his father, who went railroading in Colorado in 1883 when the railroads were little more than a decade old, and who spent thirty-five years as an engineer on the narrow gauge Denver, South Park and Pacific line. Other tales came from his own experiences—growing up among railroaders in the railroad town of Como, riding through the mountains in the cabs of narrow gauge engines with his father at the throttle, and working forty-six years as a fireman and engineer on the Colorado and Southern, eventually becoming the railroad's senior engineer. His brothers, Clarence and Neil, were also engineers on the Colorado and Southern.

Dad loved nothing more than to spin yarn after yarn about railroading to a captive audience at the kitchen table over a pot of coffee. No trip on the railroad was dull or routine, or like any other, he claimed. Railroading was exciting, with moments "when the hair stood up on the back of your neck."

For years, I said, "Dad, you should write a book." He always replied, "You're the writer in the family."

"But you're the storyteller," I would say.

Not until he had retired from the Colorado and Southern and could take the time to look at a family railroading career in Colorado that had spanned nearly a century did we reach an agreement. He would tell the stories, I would write them down—which is how this book came to be.

We spent three years on the project and countless hours reminiscing, researching, and sifting through reams of railroad documents and memorabilia he had collected. His memory was prodigious and accurate. Several times I questioned the dates of certain events, pointing out different dates in some history book. "The history book is wrong," he would announce, and, after checking other sources, I would find that the history book was wrong and he was right.

When he couldn't put his finger on some detail, we would pick up a bag of hamburgers at a drive-in and head to George Champion's house for lunch. George and his son George, Jr. always supplied the beer. Around the dining room table, Dad, then eighty years old, and George, in his ninety-seventh year, jogged each other's memory about the people and events in Como when they were young. On one occasion we brought along a photo of the Como bridge club. Dad had identified everybody except two women, and he was hoping George would remember their names. After studying the photo under a magnifying glass for some time, George said, "Darned if I can remember who they are, Sam. Guess we'll have to ask some of the oldtimers."

"But George," Dad replied, "there's nobody around older than us."

Working on this project gave me a chance to know my father in a new and different way. I had always been aware that railroading was more than just a job to him. It was a way of life that took him from home long hours, sometimes days and, in busy seasons, weeks at a time. It kept him coming and going at all hours. And when he was home, he was usually resting for the next trip, his snores shaking the rafters in the middle of the day.

What I had not known was how much he loved railroading. He was a lucky man who had found his life's work and relished it. Everything, it seemed, had conspired to make him a railroader—his father's influence, his own taste for adventure, even the influenza outbreak of 1919 that nearly took his life but allowed him to save face while dropping out of the University of Colorado Engineering School where he had been awarded an academic scholarship, and to do what he really wanted to do all along—go railroading.

He seemed in good health, the years we worked on this project, but I sensed we should hurry to record everything. As we worked through each chapter, he made notes for corrections and changes. Rather than rewriting at that point, we pushed on to the end of the manuscript. We had finished the first draft and had begun rewriting chapter one the last day I saw him. "So far, so good," he told me. Late that afternoon, October 20, 1981, he suffered a heart attack and died.

In an odd turn of fate, the Colorado and Southern Railway, where he had worked most of his life, also ceased to exist that year. On January 5, 1982, the railroad was absorbed into the Burlington Northern system, ending an era of Colorado railroading.

With Dad's notes at hand, I was able to complete the project we had started together. Here and there the notes admonished me, as he had when explaining some complicated detail of the workings of a steam locomotive, "Get it straight, or the reader will think I don't know what I'm talking about."

Any errors that may have crept past his notes and into this manuscript are mine, not his. He knew what he was talking about.

CHAPTER ONE

Goin' Railroading

When the Kansas Pacific passenger train pulled into Denver Union Station near the end of May 1883, my father, the first Sam Speas, was aboard. Twenty-six years old, standing just under six feet tall, with broad shoulders and bright red hair, he had come to Colorado to go railroading.

He had left Kansas City thirty-six hours earlier, riding across the plains in a red plush chair, his gripsack bouncing in the rack overhead. Fine woods lined the coach interior, and brass lanterns with green glass swung from the clerestory. A coal stove in the middle of the car took off the chill at night.

As the train rolled the 638 miles from Kansas City to Lawrence, Topeka, Brookville, Kit Carson, and, finally, Denver, Sam watched herds of wild antelope graze alongside the track. From time to time, he caught sight of coyotes chasing jackrabbits. The train stopped for meals at four stations along the way, including Wallace Station in western Kansas, where Sam and the other passengers dined on buffalo steak. Fare for the trip was forty-four dollars, a bargain compared to ten cents per mile, the usual fare western railroads charged at the time.

Sam was the first member of his family to go railroading. In the

1

hundred years since his great grandfather had emigrated from Germany, the Speas family had been farmers. Sam's father, Peter Heronymous Speas, had wrested a meager living out of the infertile soil in Cass County, Missouri, near the town of Freeman. When I asked Sam later what crops his father had grown on the farm, he told me, "rocks, mostly."

Cass County also happened to sit in the center of the Missouri-Kansas border wars that flared around the time of the Civil War. William Quantrill, the Younger brothers, and Jesse James, who lived down the road from the Speas farm, terrorized the county, stealing cattle and crops and burning houses and barns. One day, Peter spotted Cole Younger and four men galloping toward the farm. When they reached the house, Peter jumped from the porch, rifle raised, and shouted, "Cole Younger, you ride out of here or you're a dead man." They turned their horses and galloped off. Sam was a young boy at the time, hiding with his mother and sisters in the kitchen, but he remembered asking his father, "Would you have shot him?" and his father's reply, "I would have had to."

He also remembered the day he was helping his father load supplies into the wagon in Freeman when the Missouri Pacific passenger train whistled into the station. He watched the engineer oil the valves and check the wheels and running gear on the locomotive while the passengers disembarked and the baggagemen unloaded trunks, suitcases, and mailbags. Then he watched the train pull out of town, smoke pouring from the stack, whistle screeching, and bell clanging, until the last car shrunk to a small black speck down the track as the sounds faded away and Peter called for him to finish loading the bags of flour so they could return to the farm. On that day, my father told me later, he decided to become a railroader, and not just any railroader. He decided to become an engineer.

The nineteenth century was the golden age for America's railroads, a time when almost every young boy watched the trains rumble by and dreamed of going railroading. Trains were new and wonderful, even fantastic. As railroads spread inland from the eastern seaboard in the 1830s and 1840s, they changed the way Americans lived, connecting towns and regions, hauling trade goods and raw materials from here to there, and allowing ordinary people to travel greater distances than they had ever dreamed possible. When the Missouri Pacific laid the first tracks west of the Mississippi River in the 1850s, railroads started for the frontier. By 1869, the year the transcontinental railroad flung itself from Omaha to California, they had girded the entire continent. The transcontinental line led to feeder railroads throughout the West, which needed railroaders to run them. They attracted men like Sam who had grown up thinking nothing could be more exciting than working on the railroad.

Sam worked on the family farm until 1881, however, when he finally got a chance at a railroading job. The Missouri Pacific was hiring new men in Freeman that year, and Sam caught on as fireman and brakeman. For the next two years, he worked up and down the line from Arkansas and north central Texas to Kansas City, St. Louis, and Omaha—wherever the railroad sent him.

Some railroaders on the Missouri Pacific had gone west to work on the narrow gauge railroads built in the mountains of Colorado. After sampling the long hours, brutal work, and bitter winters, they had hurried back to the Missouri Pacific with tales of their experiences. Thirty-hour trips without rest were usual, they said. Open engine cabs with no protection from freezing blizzards, back-breaking labor shovelling coal or working the locomotives on steep grades, brakes that often didn't work, and trains that wrecked on the mountainside—all were part of the job.

Despite such hazards, Sam wondered about the opportunities. He learned that a fireman on Colorado's railroads could move up to engineer in three or four years, while the seniority list on the Missouri Pacific was so long a man could spend a lifetime shoveling coal. By working every day in the month, an engineer in Colorado could take home $100, at a time when carpenters and bricklayers drew $40. In 1883, $100 went a long way. An engineer could stay in a boardinghouse for $4.50 a week or rent a furnished room for $15 a month. He could buy a ready-made suit for $15 or have a tailor-made suit for $35. He could buy boots for $3 or shoes for $1.25. He could take himself to the Tabor Grand Opera House and sit in the dress circle for $3. He could have a wagon and two horses for $160, a frame bungalow for $850, or a brick home for $1,000. After working on a farm that produced barely enough crops to keep his family alive, and after shoveling tons of coal up and down the Missouri Pacific line with little hope of doing anything else, Sam decided that the opportunities on Colorado's railroads looked good. He handed in his resignation on the Missouri Pacific and headed west.

He was not the only man who heard about opportunities in the West. Thousands of people were streaming into Colorado at the time. Between 1870 and 1880, Denver's population had jumped from 4,700 to 35,000, and it was growing by 10,000 new residents every year. One newcomer, who also arrived in 1883, wrote "The city is full of sightseers and fortune hunters, many seeking employment, a great many more than can obtain it." Those who couldn't afford the train fare west rode across the plains in ox-drawn wagons. But most came on the train. Every day carriages lined up in front of Union Station to ferry the incoming passengers to hotels and boardinghouses.

After Sam disembarked from the train, he made his way through the crowds in Union Station, past the carriages in front, and set out on foot for the Union Pacific offices at Fortieth and Blake streets, two miles away. He said later that he thought he had come to a major metropolis, so many people were rushing along the wooden sidewalks and dodging carriages and wagons in the unpaved, dusty streets. With new houses and buildings going up on every street, the banging hammers and clanging trowels could be heard all over town. Six-story buildings stood along Fifteenth and Sixteenth streets, the heart of Denver's business district. Nearby were neat residential neighborhoods with painted frame bungalows and brick homes, as well as the mansions of Denver's new millionaires. Everywhere wild roses poked through the wrought iron fences and trailed down the sidewalks.

In twenty-five years, Denver had grown from a collection of tents and log cabins on the banks of Cherry Creek and the South Platte River to a prosperous, modern community with a municipal gas works and irrigation system. Gas was manufactured from coal, stored in tanks, and piped to Denver's homes and buildings. Homeowners irrigated gardens with well water that flowed in ditches along the sides of the streets. The Denver City Railroad Company had forty-five horse cars that carried citizens from one part of town to another over fifteen miles of track. On the north edge of town, black smoke belched from the stacks of the Boston and Colorado Smelting Company, a sure sign of progress.

But signs of Denver's frontier origins were also visible. Every morning young boys drove the day herds down Fifteenth Street to the pasture at Broadway and Colfax, near the corner where the Brown Palace Hotel would later stand. Alongside the new six-story buildings stood squat, ramshackle saloons with two-story false fronts where professional gamblers rolled the dice and stacked the cards. Not far from Sixteenth and Curtis streets, site of the Tabor Grand Opera House which had opened two years earlier, Soapy Smith worked his con games, exhorting crowds to step right up, pay one dollar, and fish a lucky fifty-dollar bar of soap from the basket. No one ever fished the lucky bar because Soapy made sure it never reached the basket. According to the *Rocky Mountain News,* which warned of the "bunko steerers and sneak thieves coming into town daily," Soapy was not the only con artist in Denver that spring.

But Denver citizens, with sights set on the future, paid little attention to cattle grazing downtown or gamblers and con artists from the frontier past. By 1883, Denver had become the hub of the rich mining region in the mountains. Railroad tracks extended like spokes in every direction from Denver. Trains from the east rolled into town carrying machinery, tools, and supplies for the mines. Other trains, loaded with ore and bullion, lumbered into Denver from the mountains.

Fifteen years earlier, when the transcontinental railroad was built across southern Wyoming, bypassing Colorado, doomsayers predicted that Denver would dry up and blow into Kansas. General Grenville M. Dodge, the Union Pacific's chief engineer, stated publicly that Denver would become a deserted village with grass growing in the streets. Those predictions seemed to come true as people packed up and moved away. The price of lots in the center of town plummeted to a few dollars, if anyone wanted them. Few did.

Rather than accept Denver's demise, a band of citizens, led by former territorial governor John Evans, decided to build the Denver Pacific Railway and Telegraph Company, connecting Denver to the transcontinental line at Cheyenne and to all points between California and New York. On June 22, 1870, the first Denver Pacific passenger train rolled into Denver, with engineer Sam Bradford at the throttle of the locomotive. People began moving back to town, causing real estate that had gone begging for a few dollars to soar to several hundred dollars.

Two months later, on August 15, 1870, the Kansas Pacific opened its line, linking Denver to Kansas City and St. Louis and to the Kansas farmlands, insuring food for Colorado's citizens until they established their own farms. That fall the Colorado Central completed the first section of track from Golden to Jersey, north of Denver, and the Boulder Valley Railroad built from Hughes Station (now Brighton) on the Denver Pacific line to the coalfields of Erie and Marshall and on to Boulder.

That was just the beginning. In the 1870s, the Atchison, Topeka and Santa Fe started across southern Colorado, while the Burlington and Colorado started west, finally connecting Denver to Nebraska in 1882. Like the first railroads, these railroads built east of the mountains were standard gauge, with rails laid four feet, eight and one-half inches apart. The measurement was first adopted by the ancient Romans as the width between wheels on chariots and carts. The Romans transplanted the gauge to Britain, where, centuries later, inventors of the first steam locomotives adopted it for the tracks. By 1883, standard gauge had become standard in the United States, although early railroads had laid rails everywhere from two feet to six feet apart.

Narrow gauge railroads, with rails laid three feet apart, were built into the mountains. The Colorado Central reached the mines around Idaho Springs, Black Hawk, and Central City, while the Denver and Rio Grande and the Denver, South Park and Pacific raced each other to the mining districts of Leadville and Gunnison. Well suited to the mountains, narrow gauge track could be laid through rockbound canons and over steep grades more quickly and for less cost than standard gauge track. The lightweight narrow gauge locomotives and small cars could wind around the mountainsides better than the narrow gauge in the mountains that it became known as "Colorado standard gauge," a fact that led Colorado's railroaders to refer to the actual standard gauge as "broad gauge."

The trains rolled on iron rails that were thirty feet long and weighed 300 pounds—thirty pounds per yard. They were bolted together with fish-plates, causing a clickety clack sound as wheels passed over the joints. Laid quickly, often without proper grading or ballast, the rails dipped in the middle, resulting in low centers and high joints and making the trains sway sideways and lurch forward and backward.

But those swaying, lurching trains insured Denver's future and made it possible for Colorado's mines to expand and prosper. From the discovery of gold in Colorado in 1858 until the first railroad arrived in 1870, the mines produced $32 million in gold, silver, copper, and lead. In the next twelve years, with railroads crisscrossing Colorado, mining production leaped to $163 million. Before the railroads arrived, it took one wagon four months to haul one stamp mill from the Hendrie and Balterhoff shops in Burlington, Iowa, to the mines of Colorado. After the railroads reached Colorado, one train could haul dozens of stamp mills, hoists, pumps, and drilling rigs to the mines in three days. Railroads also carried such things as stationary steam engines that were so heavy no wagon team of mules or horses could have hauled them into the mountains. They shipped loads of ore for eighty cents to $2.80 per one hundred pounds, compared to the wagon rate of $20 to $25 for the same hundred pounds. They brought the laborers from farms, villages, and cities to work in the mines and operate the smelters in Denver, Leadville, Black Hawk, and Golden, and they brought the railroaders, like Sam, to run the trains.

When Sam reached the offices of the Union Pacific, which had gained control of the railroads in northern Colorado in 1881, the master mechanic took a look at his service letter from the Missouri Pacific. Service letters were proof that railroaders had experience. Sam's letter stated that he was "honest, sober, and attended strictly to his business" and "cheerfully recommended him for employment." What railroaders did not know at the time was that certain kinds of water-marked paper alerted a new employer that the railroader's work or behavior left something to be desired, no matter what the letter said. Companies used the water-marked code to blackball railroaders across the country.

No fireman's jobs were available that May of 1883, but the master mechanic told Sam that he expected some to open up in the summer. Rather than lose an experienced man with a good service letter to the Bur-lington or Rio Grande, he offered Sam a job as wiper, with the promise that he would have one of the first fireman's jobs available. The next day, Sam started work in the Union Pacific's Fortieth Street yards, wiping gobs of grease and soot from the boiler jackets and rubbing graphite on the smoke boxes of the locomotives. Nothing was more important in the railroading world of the nineteenth century than a shiny, beautiful locomotive. Sam worked as a wiper twelve hours a day, seven days a week, for $1.75 per day.

That summer, four firemen were "set up" or promoted to engineer: M.J. Murphy, Joe Allen, J.H. Nixon, and C.N. Woodward. On August 18, 1883, two and one-half months after Sam had arrived in Colorado, he was promoted to fireman on the Union Pacific and was on the way to becoming an engineer.

CHAPTER TWO

The Big Smoke

In August 1883, the Union Pacific assigned Sam to the Denver Yards District as fireman on engine 128 for M.J. Murphy, an engineer set up that summer. Yard crews made up and broke up the long trains pulling into Denver every day. A train from Kansas City, for example, could have cars destined for Boulder, Colorado Springs, or Pueblo. Crews had to uncouple the cars, shunt them to other tracks, and couple them into trains being made up for those towns. Other cars, with freight for the mountains, had to be shunted into position for unloading and reloading the freight into narrow gauge cars.

It was stop and go, push and pull in the yards, slow and tedious work that railroaders tolerated only at certain points in their careers. Engineers past their prime, whose failing eyesight and impaired hearing kept them off the main line, tolerated yard work in preference to retiring. New engineers and firemen tolerated it while waiting for jobs on the main line. For Sam, used to blasting down the Missouri Pacific track with the horizon receding far ahead, it was like hitching a racehorse to a milk wagon.

In the late fall, both Sam and Engineer Murphy were sprung from the yards and assigned to the main line, working wherever they were needed in the Union Pacific's other five districts: the Julesburg, Fort Collins, Clear

Creek, Platte Canon, or Highline. In the Julesburg District, where Sam fired for Murphy, they streaked across the plains at sixty miles per hour on track built ten years earlier by the Colorado Central. In the Fort Collins District, he fired for C.N. Woodward over rolling hills and along straightaways that ran miles ahead. In the days before speedometers, railroaders calculated the speed by counting the number of telegraph poles they passed in one minute. There were forty poles per mile, which meant that trains were traveling sixty miles per hour if they passed forty poles in one minute. Twenty poles meant that the speed was thirty miles per hour, eight poles meant twelve miles per hour. They also judged the speed by clocking the time between mileposts. Sixty seconds between posts meant sixty miles per hour, while 120 seconds meant thirty miles per hour.

The narrow gauge locomotives that Sam fired in the Clear Creek District lumbered uphill at a top speed of fifteen miles per hour. On the downgrade, the engineer held the speed to five miles per hour to keep the train from running away. Even with thirty-seven-inch driver wheels, which meant the locomotives could run safely at a maximum speed of thirty-seven miles per hour, there were few straightaways in Colorado's mountains where trains got up to that speed.

By the winter of 1884, Sam had landed a regular fireman's job on the Clear Creek, then the busiest district in the Union Pacific's Colorado system. Every day, a stream of trains followed one another out of Denver Union Station, heading up Clear Creek Canon. At Forks Creek, a siding and station twenty miles from Denver, the trains either continued another twenty-one miles to Idaho Springs and Georgetown or followed North Clear Creek eleven miles to Black Hawk and Central City.

Those eleven miles covered some of the steepest, most rugged mountain terrain on the Union Pacific. The locomotives climbed along the mountainside to the switchback at Hidden Treasure Mill and doubled back, gaining altitude above Clear Creek, before rumbling across Gregory Street in Black Hawk on a steel trestle. Still climbing, they curved around the mountainsides, over other trestles, and back and forth on another switchback before pulling into Central City, named for its location in the center of one of Colorado's richest gold districts.

After unloading the freight destined for the mines in the Clear Creek District, the trains started down the canon with loaded ore cars bound for smelters in Black Hawk, Golden, or Denver. The tracks either hugged the creek bed or climbed along high, narrow roadbeds blasted and hacked out of the rock wall.

A train trip through Clear Creek Canon was a hair-raising experience in the 1880s, especially for passengers from the flatlands. One passenger wrote: "The train followed a continuous serpentine course of twenty-five miles along the creek, crossing the same some dozen times, winding around huge boulders, running under cliffs, shutting out the light of the sun, then going through the same ordeal again, and on, on until we arrived at the Springs."

The return trip was even more exciting. "It was near 6 p.m. when we left Idaho, with brakes on and steam all off," he wrote. "For twenty-five miles we sped down through the canon at a rate that made my head giddy, often dodging for fear of coming in contact with some huge boulder on some short curve, of which there were hundreds."

But in the engine cab, the engineer and fireman usually had everything under control. Thirty-ton locomotives, built by Brooks, Cooke, or Porter-Bell and designed for hairpin curves, worked in the Clear Creek District. Under the pilots were two pony truck wheels that guided the locomotive along the tracks. Beneath the boilers were six powerful drivers that gripped the tracks, pulling the locomotive uphill and holding it on the downgrade. The drivers also carried the locomotive's weight, which was evenly distributed on spring riggings. Since there were no wheels under the engine cabs, the locomotives carried the 2-6-0 designation—two pilot wheels, six drivers, and no engine cab wheels.

The fireman's job on the Clear Creek tested a man's mettle. Sam was constantly on the move, shoveling coal as fast as he could to keep the steam pressure in the boiler betwteen 130 and 150 pounds and the locomotive chugging uphill. He scooped a load of coal, yanked the overhead chain to open the firebox door, threw the coal into the firebox, and yanked the chain again to close the door before the fire jumped into the engine cab. Then he scooped the next load of coal and started over again. Automatic firebox doors operated by a foot pedal were unknown in the 1880s.

Firing a locomotive was not simply a matter of throwing coal into the firebox. Sam had to "lay the fire" by spreading the coal a uniform thickness of three inches so that air could circulate freely and keep the coal burning. Temperatures in the firebox reached a white heat of 2,200 degrees —hot enough to melt steel—yet firemen wore no protective goggles. Like all firemen, Sam protected his eyes by throwing the first shovelful of coal near the door to create a black hole upon which he could focus while he laid the fire. Each fireman had his own shovel, and he knew by the heaviness of the coal in the shovel the number of scoops it would take to cover the fire. If he closed the door too fast, oxygen was choked off and black smoke poured from the stack, a fact that earned firemen the nickname "the big smoke."

Sam also had to keep an eye on the steam gauge, making sure that it registered the right amount of pressure. And since locomotives were not yet equipped with glass water gauges that showed the level of water in the boiler, both the fireman and engineer checked the water level from time to time by opening the gauge cocks—called try-cocks by railroaders. Three or four try-cocks were located in a vertical slant on the boiler. If the top cock let off steam when it was opened, and the second cock let off water, the fireman knew that the water level in the boiler was somewhere between the two. If steam came from the second cock and water from the third, the water level was between those two cocks. If the lower valves hissed steam, the enginemen knew they had trouble.

Nothing was more important in operating a rolling steam power plant than keeping the water at the correct level in the boiler. In fact, the lives of the enginemen depended upon it. Water always had to cover the crown sheet—the roof of the firebox. If it dropped below, cool water injected through the line from the tender to the boiler would hit the crown sheet and blow the locomotive sky high.

On the other hand, high water in the boiler could also cause an explosion. It washed into the cylinders like a fountain, pulling water out of the boiler faster than new water could be injected. When this happened, the fireman had seconds to open the blow-off cocks and drain the excess water before everything was blown to pieces.

Besides shoveling coal to keep up the steam, watching the steam gauge, opening the try-cocks, and injecting water into the boiler, Sam also had to keep one eye on the left side of the track for rocks, livestock, or anything else that could derail the locomotive and which the engineer could not see from the right side. He performed these chores, walking around the engine deck that vibrated, undulated, swayed, and shook as the locomotive rolled along.

Every ten miles the locomotive stopped to take on water at a tank alongside the track and Sam climbed on top of the tender to take care of the outside chores. The tender's U-shaped tank, wrapped around the center coal space, held 2,500 gallons of water, most of which the locomotives used in a ten-mile uphill pull. Sam threw open the hatch door at the far end, pulled the spout from the water tank, and jerked the rope to open the valve and start the water flowing. At any moment the spout could kick upward and thrash about, shooting water everywhere while the fireman dodged this way and that, trying to close the valve and keep from being knocked off the tender. Many years later, after I had followed my father railroading in the 1920s, I saw a young, inexperienced fireman open the water valve while standing on the spout. The spout flew upward, launching him off the tender and into a clump of bushes fifteen feet away. He was shaken but unhurt.

After filling the tank, Sam swung back into the engine cab to clean the firebox before the locomotive got underway again. He shook the ashes and clinkers from the grate into the ashpan below. Then he leapt to the ground and opened the gate under the ashpan to let the red hot clinkers drop onto a metal plate between the rails. If they did not drop, and usually they did not, he took a long iron ash hook and pulled them down, all the while getting a strong whiff of sulphurous gases. When he had finished this chore, he closed the gate and fastened it with a chain so that it would not open en route, drop hot ashes, and set the wooden ties and trestles on fire. Taking care of the locomotive's waste was a big part of the fireman's job. On a one-day trip, a locomotive could leave behind as much as a ton of ashes.

On trips up Clear Creek Canon and back, the locomotive burned six tons of coal, which meant that Sam did not have to take on more coal en route. But on trips in Platte Canon, or on the broad gauge, he would have to take on coal at least once. The engineer would give five blasts with the whistle to signal "coaling up" and spot the tender at the coal platform. Sam would climb out onto the tender and shovel coal from the platform into the tender's coal space. Sometimes the brakeman or shovelers who worked at the coaling platforms would help the fireman take on coal, but usually he shoveled the entire six tons alone.

Sam did these chores in all kinds of weather, with the tender slick as glass in the rain, crusted with ice in winter, and hot enough to fry a slab of bacon in the summer. But working outdoors wasn't much different from working inside the engine cab. The engineer could close the door on his side, shutting out some of the weather, although wind and snow still blew through the thin wooden walls and floor. The fireman's door had to be latched open to give him access to the coal. Canvas curtains were supposed to be hung on the sides between the engine cab and tender, but few locomotives had them. Those that were in place were torn and shredded after one winter. The fireman's side of the engine was like an icebox in the winter. His clothes would stiffen in the cold, and ice would form on his eyelashes. He would hover around the boiler, the only source of heat, as much as possible in the winter, but in the summer, there was no escaping the heat from the boiler. The hardships of the fireman's job resulted from the fact that the mechanical engineers who designed locomotives for the manufacturing companies never actually rode in them. They were concerned with designing a powerful, efficient steam power plant, not with making life easier for railroaders.

Two hours before the locomotive rolled out of the Denver yards, Sam was on the job, building the fire the hostler had started, checking the coal and water in the tender and the sand in the dome on top of the boiler, and lifting the headlight from its tapered tongue to replenish the oil in the dispenser, even though firemen considered the headlights useless. They joked that they had to light a match at night to see if the headlights were burning.

Sam also washed windows, shined the steam gauge, swept the floor, wiped the soot and dirt from the boiler jacket, and polished it to a high sheen, completing the job the wiper had started. Early engineers were particular about the way their engines looked, and the fireman had to answer for a locomotive that wasn't spotless.

Union Pacific officials also expected the locomotives to sparkle in the sun as they rolled down track. One day while Sam was still firing in the yards, a company official paid an unannounced visit. He dabbed his silk handkerchief on a boiler jacket, spotted a speck of dirt, and let out a bellow that could be heard across the yards. Any man who left a dirty boiler, he shouted, would lose his job, or his head.

By the time Sam came in from a trip firing, he had put in two hours cleaning the engine and sixteen or more hours on the road. He had shoveled between six and twenty tons of coal, tended the gauge and try-cocks, and replenished the oil. He had hopped onto the tank a dozen times to take on either coal or water and had cleaned the ashpan more times than he wanted to remember. He had also watched his side of the track. And if he didn't keep up the steam pressure, or if the water started to drop, or if he took too long performing some chore, he caught the wrath of the engineer who expected a perfect job. Long after Sam's days as a fireman, he remembered pulling into Denver Union Station, tired enough to fall asleep in his boots. Still, he would not have traded the thrill of riding down track on a steam locomotive with the sounds of smoke pouring from the stack, steam gusting, whistle wailing, bell clanging, and fire roaring in the firebox, and the smells of coal and grease and hot metal, for any other job in the world. In the nineteenth century, nothing compared to the excitement of railroading.

He collected two dollars for every 100 miles, which were calculated in various ways. On passenger trains, 110 valley miles or 44 mountain miles equaled 100 miles. On freight trains, it took 85 valley miles, or 44 mountain miles to equal 100. The rate of pay in the early days did not take into account the number of hours railroaders worked. Sam was lucky to collect two dollars for a sixteen-hour trip.

In March 1884, he was one of the first railroaders to ride a locomotive over the Georgetown Loop. Before building the Loop, the railroad had stopped at Georgetown, two miles below Silver Plume. No locomotive could have climbed the 6 percent grade between the two mining towns, but the Loop spiraled up the canon on four and one-half miles of curves and trestles that reduced the grade to 3.5 percent. That meant that locomotives gained three and one-half feet in altitude for every 100 feet traveled. The highest trestle, Devil's Gate, rose on spidery iron legs ninety-six feet above the creek and seventy-five feet above the lower track.

Soon after it opened, the Loop began attracting excursionists from across the country, eager to ride a passenger coach over the high Devil's Gate. That summer at least one excursion train pulled out of Denver every day bound for the Loop, and on weekends, the number jumped to seven trains a day. They whistled out to the middle of Devil's Gate and stopped, letting passengers clamber out of the coaches and stroll along the two-foot walkway, suspended between Clear Creek and 14,000-foot mountain peaks. Sometimes the trains stopped at the approach to Devil's Gate to let passengers walk across the trestle. The trains followed, picking up the passengers on the other side and continuing their journey.

Nothing endeared Colorado's railroads to the public like excursion trains. Before the railroad arrived, most people traveled no farther than a day's walk from home. A twenty-mile trip in a buggy or wagon took all day and was a major event in most lives. With excursion trains, people could climb into the coach for a day's outing, traveling almost 120 miles roundtrip. They pulled out of Denver in the morning and, four hours later, rode across the Loop and arrived at Graymont, a short distance above Silver Plume. They had fifteen minutes to stretch their legs before reboarding the train for the return trip. Most brought picnic baskets or purchased a picnic lunch at the lunch room at Forks Creek.

Excursions on the Georgetown Loop were still popular in the 1920s when I started railroading. On one trip, I fired the engine on the point of a doubleheader, hauling a six-car train of tourists who had come from Chicago to see the Loop. The engineer was Al Russell, an old hoghead in the Clear Creek District who was then nearing retirement. He had started firing about 1900 and had been set up to engineer in 1905. We had orders to cut off at the approach and cross Devil's Gate light, rather than run both locomotives and the train on the trestle at the same time. We started across, chugging along at two miles per hour, half the speed limit, with the trestle swaying and groaning beneath us, and the clickety-clack of the wheels echoing in the mountain stillness. When we reached the far side, we stopped and waited for the other engine to bring the train across. Then we coupled up and continued to Silver Plume and Graymont, just as my father had done forty years earlier.

My father worked on the Clear Creek until midsummer of 1884, firing the locomotives on excursion trains and on freight trains between Denver and Graymont and between Denver and Central City. Just when he thought he had found a permanent job, the master mechanic called him into the office and ordered him to take the next passenger train to Boulder, and report for work on the Greeley, Salt Lake and Pacific.

CHAPTER THREE

The 10 Spot

In the summer of 1884, Sam rode the passenger train on the old Boulder Valley Railroad to Boulder. At the depot at about Ninth and Water streets, he left the coach and walked northeast. Horse-drawn wagons and buggies rolled along the dirt streets, raising clouds of dust, and townspeople jostled one another on the narrow plank sidewalks. Sam crossed Pearl Street with its two-story false front stores and made his way to a boardinghouse for railroaders run by Joe and Nellie McCabe at Fifteenth and Pine streets.

In the twenty-five years since its founding, Boulder had grown from a clump of log cabins where a few prospectors lived to a town of 3,000 that included businessmen, teachers, doctors, lawyers, miners, and railroaders. Neighborhoods of frame bungalows and brick mansions, with hitching posts in front, stretched north and east from the Pearl Street business district. Maple, locust, and cottonwood trees grew everywhere. Around the trunks were sturdy wooden boxes that protected the bark from the town's horses. Every evening a light keeper strolled through town to light the kerosene lamps on the corners, and at dawn, he retraced his route, snuffing them out. South of town, on a sagebrush-studded hill, stood Old Main, the brick building that housed the University of Colorado. Nearby was University Hill, where the townspeople grazed their cattle.

From its beginning, Boulder had been a supply center for the gold diggings in the mountains. Wagons had rolled up Boulder Canon, carrying food and tools to the miners in places like Magnolia, Gold Hill, Caribou, Ward, Nederland, Eldora, Hessie, Sunshine, and Sunset. By 1884, Boulder had a smelter and ore sampling works, two flour mills, a foundry, brewery, brickyard and wood yard, blacksmith and harness shops, several general stores, and two banks, all of which depended upon the mines for business.

And the mines depended upon the railroads. Two railroads, the Boulder Valley and the Colorado Central, had built to Boulder in 1873, making it possible to haul mining machinery from factories in the East and Midwest to the foot of Boulder Canon. In the railroad yards at Ninth and Water streets, freight was transferred to horse-drawn wagons for the final leg of the journey to the mines.

In the spring of 1883, the Union Pacific built the narrow gauge Greeley, Salt Lake and Pacific west of Boulder. An unusual railroad, it was made up of three disjointed sections—the narrow gauge line out of Boulder and standard gauge lines between Greeley and Fort Collins and between Fort Collins and Stout. Although the Union Pacific had intended to build through the canons, cross the Rocky Mountains, and continue to the Pacific Ocean, accounting for the railroad's name, the farthest point west that any of the sections reached was Sunset, fourteen miles from Boulder.

With the Greeley, Salt Lake and Pacific in operation, mining machinery could move by rail all the way to the mines. The crews and motive power for the new railroad came from the Clear Creek District. Standard gauge trains carried freight as far as the Boulder yards, where it was off-loaded and put on Greeley, Salt Lake and Pacific cars.

Sam fired the Number 10—called the 10 spot—a 2-6-0 Brooks mogul that hauled a mixed passenger and freight train fourteen miles between Boulder and Sunset. The train ran to Orodell, Two Brothers, Crisman, Black Swan Mill, and Gold Hill Station, later Salina, where most of the freight was unloaded. It then continued to Tambourine, Wall Street, Wood Mountain, Freese, Copper Rock, and Shale before pulling into Sunset, the end of the line. On the return trip it picked up heavy cars of ore at Gold Hill Station.

The engineer on the run was Squire Thorne, twenty-eight years old, five-feet six-inches tall, and built like a block of granite with a pill-box cap usually stuck on his head. Friendly and gregarious, Thorne was well liked by the railroaders. Forty years later, long after he had left the Greeley, Salt Lake and Pacific and was running locomotives in the Clear Creek District, I often chatted with him in Denver Union Station while he got ready to take the morning passenger train to Silver Plume. He told me he had started working on the Union Pacific as a conductor, but he soon found that riding in the caboose and walking up and down the coach aisles collecting tickets was not to his liking. After one trip, he walked into the master mechanic's office, threw his conductor's cap on the counter, and announced he wanted to be an engineer. The Union Pacific needed good engineers for its expanding system in Colorado at the time, and the master mechanic, recognizing Thorne's ability, gave him the job. Thorne was set up to engineer on May 18, 1881, without working as a fireman or passing the engineer's examinations.

He loved the job. Watching the track stretch ahead, listening to the steam gusting and the wheels clickety-clacking was just to his liking, except for the day in 1891 when the locomotive jumped the track and rolled into Boulder Creek, giving Thorne and his fireman, named Monroe, the fright of their lives. But the early engineers always said they ran the engines "by a-guessing," never knowing when an old steamer was "likely to lie down on the track, roll over the bank, and kick up her heels."

Thorne's accident happened long after he and Sam worked together on the Greeley, Salt Lake and Pacific. In the summer of 1884, they made two round trips daily between Boulder and Sunset. On weekends, they hauled the excursion trains that the railroad had started running to increase business and offset any slowdown in the mining industry. Excursions, sponsored by church groups, social clubs, and the railroad, were as popular in Boulder as they were in Denver. On Saturday and Sunday mornings, the Boulder depot filled with families heading for a day's outing in the mountains.

The excursion trains chugged into Boulder Canon, climbing a 4 percent grade through tunnels of aspen and pine trees, doubling back around hairpin curves, and crossing from side to side on sixty-six bridges and trestles. At Sunset, the excursionists hurried off the train with their picnic baskets.

Since there was no wye or turntable at Sunset at that time, the locomotive was moved to the rear of the train. Running backward, it pulled the train to Boulder with Thorne hanging out the right window and Sam leaning from the left gangway trying to spot any obstacles on the track ahead. On top of the 10 spot was a headlight that faced backward to light the downhill journey at night. A pilot, or cowcatcher, was also attached to the rear of the tender.

One warm summer afternoon, Sam and Thorne had just backed out of Sunset when a young mother stepped onto her porch to call her daughter. The five-year-old child was nowhere in sight and soon everyone in town took up the search. Someone got the idea that she may have climbed aboard the train while it stood in the station. The telegrapher wired the Boulder stationmaster to look for the child as soon as the train pulled into Boulder. The stationmaster found her, but not in the coach. She had climbed onto the cowcatcher and ridden it down the mountain.

In the early 1920s, I was deadheading on passenger train 30 from Denver to Cheyenne when one of the senior conductors on the North End, Johnny Mans, sat down beside me for a chat. He told me that his wife had been that little girl. She had hung onto the cowcatcher for her life, he said, too terrified to scream.

While working on the 10 spot, Sam lived at Joe and Nellie McCabe's boardinghouse. Railroaders came and went at McCabes', eating hearty meals and resting on clean beds in between trips. On summer evenings, they gathered on the wide, sagging front porch, smoking, joking, and trading railroading yarns. The McCabes still ran the boardinghouse in 1921 when I was working out of Boulder. Railroaders still sprawled lazily across the porch on summer evenings, until Mrs. McCabe stormed through the front door, threw us some towels, and ordered us to shoosh the flies from her kitchen, just as she had in my father's day.

At the boardinghouse, Sam met Anna, Nellie McCabe's sister, who helped serve the meals. Most of the unmarried women the railroaders got to know were part of the railroading world themselves—as sisters, daughters, widows of railroaders, or as serving girls in the boardinghouses. Railroading's long, irregular hours left little time for courtships, however. Sam was lucky to have a regular schedule on the 10 spot that gave him some free time to court Anna. In the summer they took long walks through town, donned roller skates at the rink, and caught the acts of traveling entertainers. In the winter they went sledding on Mapleton Hill. Two years after they met, Sam and Anna were married.

On November 4, 1887, Sam passed the engineer's examinations and was promoted. Only those firemen selected by company officials were allowed to take the exams. Except for the requirement of three or four years experience as a fireman, selection was arbitrary. The officials simply chose those men they believed would make good engineers. For the firemen, selection was a risk. If they failed the exams, they were fired, unlike brakemen who could take the conductor's exams again and again and continue working as brakemen until they passed.

It was a risk Sam took eagerly. From the time he had watched the Missouri Pacific train pull out of Freeman, he had longed to be an engineer. After four years firing on the Union Pacific, he knew the material on the examinations cold.

The examinations were oral, lasted two days, and were tough. They covered the operation of the steam locomotives and the company rule book. Engineers not only had to know how to run the locomotive, they had to know how every valve, flue, eccentric, piston, and cylinder worked. If any part broke down en route, the engineer had to fix it and get the locomotive and train safely to the next terminal.

Engineers also had to know the company rules covering such things as which trains had right of track and which engines went on the point of a double header. The rules also covered the flag, whistle, bell, lantern, and hand signals that the railroaders used to communicate with one another in the day before radios. Lamps swung across the track meant stop, up and down meant move ahead. Bells had to be rung a quarter of a mile ahead of every crossing. One short whistle while moving meant apply brakes and stop, but a short whistle while standing still meant "test brakes." Two long whistles when stopped meant throw off brakes and proceed. While moving, two long whistles meant proceed. One long and one short meant approaching curve. Several short whistles meant obstacle on the track ahead. On long freights, with as many as four locomotives, each whistle repeated the signal, making a chorus of sounds.

The day Sam was promoted to engineer, November 5, 1887, the master mechanic called him into his office in Denver. He told him that the company needed another engineer in the Highline District, working on the Denver, South Park and Pacific, and ordered Sam to take a freight train to Como the following day. "If you like it there," he told him, "you've got a new job. If not, come on back."

Sam left the Denver yards with a Baldwin 2-8-0 on the head of the freight train and a helper engine coupled in front of the caboose. Years later, the conductor on the train, Jim Earley, told me how they had gathered speed as they rolled through Sheridan Junction and Littleton and into Platte Canon. They climbed through the canon, rumbling past Baileys, named for the owner of a nearby ranch, and stopped to take on coal at Grant, sixty-six miles from Denver. By then, Sam's fireman had shoveled six tons of coal and was set to shovel six more before the train reached Como, and Sam was glad to be at the throttle. With steam billowing around the boiler, the locomotive pulled the train to the top of 9,991-foot Kenosha Pass along track that followed an old Ute trail.

On the other side of the pass lay South Park, fifty miles long and twenty-five miles wide, with the town of Como nestling against Silver Heels Mountain in the Park Range. After the helper engine cut off, turned on the wye, and headed back to Denver, the train wound downhill along a narrow shelf cut into the mountainside and drifted across the Park, past Jefferson. Sam was struck by the beauty of the area. He told me later that he decided then to stay in Como and work on the Denver, South Park and Pacific.

CHAPTER FOUR

Pretty Rough Riding

In November 1887, Sam brought the freight train into Como, the busy division point on the Denver, South Park and Pacific. At least ten trains rumbled in and out of town every day, with the number often climbing as high as twenty-six. Either they traveled between Como and Leadville over the Highline or they rolled to Gunnison through the Alpine Tunnel. They also steamed back and forth in the Platte Canon between Como and Denver.

Next to the track at the northeast corner of town stood the Como depot, the thirteen-stall stone and wood roundhouse and machine shops, and the stately two-story Pacific Hotel where passengers dined and rested on layovers. The town spread southward, its wide, dusty roads lined with small frame houses, boardinghouses, general stores, liveries, confectionaries, Chinese laundries, and saloons. Almost every man in the population of 400 worked on the railroad, including about twenty-two engineers, dozens of firemen, and 100 machinists, roundhouse employees, office clerks, and section gang laborers. Brakemen and conductors lived in Leadville or Denver and laid over in Como in the boardinghouses or in the railroad's tenement buildings near the track.

Como was a company town. In the mid 1870s, some 300 laborers laying the DSP&P track across South Park had pitched their tents where Como was later built. In 1879, the railroad bought the land and sold the lots to railroaders. The new town adopted the name that the local miners from the area of Lake Como in Italy had given their community at the King mines, about three miles southeast. When the Union Pacific gained control of the DSP&P, it also gained control of Como, keeping the rule that only company employees could buy lots or build houses there. Shortly after Sam arrived, he arranged to buy a house on Broadway next door to Dunbar's Livery. Then he sent for Anna, who arrived several days later on the passenger train, their household belongings in the baggage car.

There was no shortage of work for railroaders in Como. Freight trains hauled the drills, rigs, shovels, picks, black powder, hoists, pumps, wire ropes, and stationary engines to the mining districts and carried the ore from the mines to smelters in Leadville and Denver. Long coal trains rumbled out of Como every day, hauling the coal needed to keep the steam engines running at the mines and to supply the DSP&P locomotives. The coal came from the King mines and from the Baldwin mines near Gunnison, both owned by the Union Pacific. Merchandise trains carried the flour, fruits, vegetables, calico, pots and pans, and furniture needed by the miners and their families.

But not all DSP&P trains served the mining districts. Hay trains hauled the timothy hay from South Park ranches. In the summer, stock trains also rolled across South Park, hauling sheep to grazing lands near Gunnison. In the fall, the trains brought the sheep to Denver, where they were loaded onto trains bound for eastern Colorado. DSP&P trains also carried sheep and cattle from South Park ranches to Denver on the first leg of their journey to eastern markets. Passenger trains carried the people who shuffled back and forth between Denver and the mountain towns.

With the coming of the railroad, South Park was transformed from a quiet valley where the buffalo grazed to a busy thoroughfare. Ed Pike, the proprietor of Pike's Market, liked to entertain the kids in Como with tales of his experiences driving a stagecoach between Denver and Leadville in the 1860s. From the stage stop on top of Kenosha Pass, he had watched buffalo herds roll across the park like waves of some brown ocean. He had even seen Ute and Arapaho hunting parties stalking the herds.

By 1887, when Sam came to Como, the stagecoaches, buffalo, and warriors had given way to locomotives that clanged across the park with steam billowing, smoke pouring from the stacks, and trains bound for some of Colorado's most rugged mountain country. To conquer that country, the DSP&P, headed by Governor Evans, had built a railroad that climbed 11,493-foot Boreas Pass, the highest railroad pass in the nation. It had pulled into Leadville, the nation's highest city at 10,208 feet, and burrowed

11,612-foot-high Alpine Tunnel, the nation's highest railroad tunnel. DSP&P trains twisted around twenty-five-degree hairpin curves and climbed 4.49 percent grades, some of the sharpest curves and steepest grades in railroad history. No challenge had been too great for the builders of the DSP&P, and, in 1887, no obstacles seemed to stand in the way of a prosperous future as a feeder line in the Union Pacific system.

Sam considered it a great stroke of luck to work for such a railroad, especially as an engineer. Engineers in my father's day considered themselves the aristocrats of the railroading world. They were in charge of the locomotives, a fact that made them indispensable. The conductor had charge of the train, but his authority stopped at the back of the tank. Without the engineer, the conductor had charge of a train going nowhere.

From 1815, when Englishman Robert Stephenson invented the first steam locomotive, engineers were called "drivers" after the men who drove the horses on stagecoaches. Transplanted to the United States, the name was used until the Union Pacific built across the West. Then engineers came to be called after the construction engineers. Railroaders called them hogheads, heads, or hoggers.

As a new engineer in Como, Sam went to work in the freight pool. Senior engineers held the scheduled passenger runs to Gunnison and Leadville, while the others took turns running the freight trains. The first engineer in from a trip went to the bottom of the list in the freight pool as "last out." The engineer at the top was "first out" and would be called for the next freight. Every engineer hoped to get a good rest and decent meal under his belt before he worked up to first out, and sometimes he managed to do so.

The engineer first out had no idea where he was going until the notice went up on the blackboard in the roundhouse. Sam could make a trip to Leadville followed by a trip to Gunnison. He could get a call for an extra to Breckenridge or a regular freight to Denver. Sometimes he was lucky enough to draw the same run for a long period, always an advantage. When he was familiar with the route, the engineer knew when to open the throttle, when to set the brakes, and what to expect around the next curve.

Like other Colorado railroads in the 1880s, the DSP&P assigned locomotives to the runs. For example, the 216, a Baldwin 2-8-0, had the Como-Hancock run; the 198, a Cooke 2-8-0, went to Leadville on freight; and the smaller 110 and 111, both Cooke 2-6-0s, hauled the Leadville passenger trains. It was an inefficient way to run railroads, with locomotives standing on the track waiting for the departure of certain trains when they could have been hauling other trains. Nevertheless, Colorado railroads did not change the system until 1920.

The system encouraged the engineers' belief that the locomotives they ran trip after trip belonged to them. This was especially true of passenger engineers who ran the same locomotives for years. Every engineer knew his locomotive as well as if he had built it himself from the blueprints, which he was capable of doing. The clanking rods, swooshing steam, and roar in the firebox where the air whipped around like a cyclone at 150 miles per hour told him how his locomotive was working. If it broke down en route, the engineer got out the tools he always carried and fixed it, substituting one part for another if necessary to get it to the next terminal. After every trip, he filed a report on the locomotive's condition with the superintendent and pointed out any major repairs that had to be done in the machine shops.

But it was up to him to make the minor repairs on his own time, in between trips. He checked each part carefully, tightened the bolts, oiled the valve gear, replenished the grease in the cups, and made sure everything was working right. He took such good care of his locomotive that, if he got sick or had to lay off for some reason, he couldn't sleep for worrying over how another engineer was treating it.

Every engineer also had his own whistle which he altered to a sound suiting his fancy by inserting plugs of wood in the holes. Some whistles sounded low and melodious, others were high and shrill. Everyone in Como knew which engineer was on the train pulling in or out of town by the sound of the whistle. Kids stopped their games to sing ditties like "Here comes Ed Haight and the 58." If the engineer laid off, or the locomotive went into the shops, he detached his whistle from the top of the steam dome and took it home for safekeeping.

All through the day and night in Como, callers could be heard calling the railroaders to work. They walked through town, rapping on front doors and shouting "441 on time," "extra west, 4 a.m.," or "415 on time." Most of the callers were young office clerks who later worked up to other jobs on the railroad. Tom Gibbony, later an engineer on the Colorado and Southern, started railroading as a caller in Como. He remembered rapping on the bedroom windows to waken the railroaders and sometimes going inside the houses to start the fire in the coal stoves. Usually the callers in Como trusted the railroaders to show up on time, rather than having them sign the call book to prove they had been called. The railroader who did not show up was fired.

When Sam got a call for the Leadville freight, he had about an hour and a half to pack his grip, eat lunch, and walk to the depot. Years later, my brothers, Clarence and Neil, and I would walk with him and hang around, watching the railroaders bustle about the depot while Dad took care of the things he had to do before the trip.

First, he picked up his orders. There were two types: train orders and work messages. Train orders gave the engineer and conductor authority to move the train from one terminal to another, and no train moved without them. They gave the train's destination, told when it had right of track, and stated the time it had to take the siding to let an oncoming train pass. Work messages specified the work to be done during the trip, such as "pick up two ore cars in Breckenridge, drop off six empties at Dickey, switch ten cars at Kokomo."

The dispatcher wrote the orders making sure every locomotive hauled the heaviest load possible and did the maximum work along the way. He dispatched ten to twenty-six trains a day from Como, sending them to Leadville or Gunnison and points in between, while at the same time other trains were chugging back toward town. He performed this amazing feat with only the help of his ledger, where he copied the orders for each train. By referring to the ledger, he figured the location of the trains. Since every town and station on the DSP&P had an open telegraph line, he could check on moving trains if he wanted to, but usually he just relied on the ledger. Taking into account such things as departure and arrival times, distance between stations and locations of sidings, he wrote the orders for the next outward bound train.

Two copies went to the conductor, one for him and one for the engineer. A third copy went to the telegrapher, called the operator or brass pounder, to be wired to the stations on the line.

After getting the orders, Sam set his pocket watch by the standard clock in the dispatcher's office in the depot. Then he compared time with the conductor and signed the register that he had done so. To insure that their watches kept correct time, engineers and conductors had to have them inspected quarterly and prove they had done so by filing certificates of inspection with the superintendent. If orders called for a train to be in the siding exactly at 9:25 a.m., it had to be there because another train was bearing down track.

By 1887, the DSP&P, like all railroads in the United States, operated on standard time, which was telegraphed daily at 11 a.m. central time from the Washington Observatory in St. Louis to railroad offices across the country. Every depot had an official standard clock which was set by the telegraphed time. This had not always been the case, however. Four years earlier, when Sam started firing on the Union Pacific, railroads operated on local time, which varied from town to town and caused endless confusion and hazards. Noon in Denver could be 12:18 in Longmont; 6 p.m. in Cheyenne could be 6:16 or 6:15 ten miles away. Finally, on October 11, 1883, the railroads adopted standard time with four time zones across the country, putting everyone else on time. The 4 p.m. train rolled out of the station at 4 p.m. sharp, and the passenger who got to the station at 4:02 watched the last car recede down track. Gradually, federal and local governments followed the railroads' example and adopted standard time, but Congress did not pass the Standard Time Act, making it official nation-wide, until 1918.

After setting his watch, Sam hurried to the track where his locomotive stood on the point of the train, fired up and ready to go. Grabbing the long-snouted oilcan he kept in the cab, he oiled the valves, rods, bearings, and every other part that moved. He tested the rod keys, looked over the wheels for cracks, and made sure the screws, locks, nuts, and bolts were tight. He checked the headlight, lamps, and gauge lights and saw that there was enough sand in the dome and oil stored in the cab to last the trip. He was as particular as the other early engineers about how his locomotive looked, and the fireman had the boiler shining and the cab swept clean if he valued his job.

Not until Sam was satisfied that everything on the locomotive was in peak condition did he climb into the cab. Behind stretched the train with sixteen cars and three helper engines for the trip to the top of Boreas Pass. He waited for the conductor to give the highball—by waving his lantern in a wide semi-arc. Then Sam blew the whistle twice, signaling the engineers in the helpers that it was time to go. They each responded with two whistle blasts of their own. Then they opened the throttles, and, with the Johnson Bars down in the corner, the train started rolling down track. After it rolled about 100 feet, Sam whistled three times and set the brakes. The other engineers also set the brakes, testing to see that they worked. No engineer wanted to start over Boreas Pass without some brakes, even though the fact that they worked on the straightaways did not mean they would hold on the downgrade. After the test, the train started off again. My brothers and I would run alongside for half a mile waving to Dad as the freight rolled out of town.

It took all his skill as an engineer to get a sixteen-car freight train to the top of Boreas Pass, even with three helpers pushing. Keeping a steady hand on the throttle, he notched up the Johnson Bar as the locomotive blasted uphill. The throttle regulated the amount of steam that moved from the steam dome on top of the boiler into the valve chests above the cylinders. As the steam entered the cylinders, it pushed against pistons that were connected to rods on the driving wheels, causing the wheels to turn.

The Johnson Bar, named for a designer at the Baldwin Locomotive Works, worked like a transmission. Set in a half-moon quadrant, it controlled the amount of steam entering the cylinders. It also controlled which end of the cylinders got the steam first, thus moving the locomotive forward or backward. To start up a train, the engineer opened the throttle and moved the Johnson Bar down, letting as much steam as possible into the cylinders. As the train got underway, he pulled back on the throttle and notched back the Johnson Bar, using less steam. Laborious chuffing from the locomotive meant that the Johnson Bar was down in the corner, but a continuous roar of steam from the locomotive meant that the engineer had notched up the bar. By adjusting the throttle and bar together, the engineer worked the locomotive, always trying to get the most power with the least amount of steam.

The engineers in my father's day ran the locomotives "by the seat of their pants." They judged the performance by the sound of the steam, the feel of the throttle in hand, and the way the engine rocked down track. The job demanded skill, intelligence, a high degree of alertness, and the ability to make constant adjustments, all of which made it interesting. But even the best engineer, who knew how to get the best performance from the locomotive, could not keep 93 percent of the energy in the coal from disappearing up the smokestack.

While working the locomotive on Boreas Pass, Sam had to keep an eye ahead for wild animals, cattle, and rocks on the track. He also had to watch the steam gauge and test the try-cocks to make sure water stayed at the correct level in the boiler. Since water rolled to the back of the boiler on the upgrade, less water was needed to cover the crown sheet. But on the downgrade, with water rolling toward the front, more water was needed.

The freight train lumbered to the top of Boreas Pass at about twelve miles an hour. After it pulled into the station, the helper engines cut off, turned on the wye, and returned to Como to push the next outward bound freight. Before the train started down the other side, Sam set the brakes on the engine and blew the whistle three times, signaling the brakemen to set the retainer, or partial, brakes on the train. In the late 1880s, DSP&P trains were still equipped with Eames vacuum brakes, a system that set the brakes by siphoning air out of the hoses between the engine and cars. Since the Eames brakes seldom worked, the engineer was lucky to set the brakes on the first two cars behind the tank before the power gave out. If a train broke in two, disconnecting the brake hoses, rear cars careening downhill with no brakes would push the front cars and locomotive off track.

In the 1890s, DSP&P passenger trains were equipped with Westinghouse air brakes, designed to stop cars even on break-in-twos. Still, freight trains kept the Eames brakes until the early 1900s. The Westinghouse brakes, which required air pressure to set the brakes, featured an air reservoir, usually located on top of the boiler, auxiliary reservoirs on each car, and air hoses that ran the length of the train. An ingenious invention, the triple valve, operated the braking system. Triple valves were located between the hoses and reservoirs. By turning the brake valve in the engine cab to the right, the engineer cut off the flow of air from the main reservoir and created a vacuum in the hoses. This caused the triple valves to open automatically, allowing the compressed air in the auxiliary reservoirs to move into the brake cylinders and set the brakes. When the engineer turned the valve to the left, air reentered the hoses, causing the triple valves to close and releasing the brakes.

While the Westinghouse brake marked an improvement over the Eames vacuum brake, it also had drawbacks. The hoses usually leaked, cutting down on the efficiency. And ninety pounds of air pressure in the reservoirs was not enough to stop downhill trains on the DSP&P's 4 percent grade. It took as much power to brake a train creeping downhill at five miles per hour as it would take to lift it into the air several feet.

DSP&P engineers depended upon the brakemen to set the hand brakes most of the time. Before starting downgrade, the brakemen would set the brakes on some of the cars to slow the train. If the train started accelerating en route, the engineer turned the valve to set the rest of the brakes, but if they didn't hold, he whistled "down brakes." Then the brakemen hoisted themselves onto the car tops and ran across the moving train, leaping over the chasms between cars. Using oak brake clubs, they turned the brake wheel on top of each car. Each turn wound an iron chain around a vertical shaft, pulling the brake shoes against the car wheels. If the brakes were set too tightly, the car wheels slid along the rails, or the chains snapped, releasing the brakes altogether. A good brakeman knew by the feel of the brake wheels when he had set the brakes exactly right. He also knew he had only moments to slow the train. An accelerating train down a 4.49 percent grade with sixteen loaded cars doubled its speed in sixteen seconds, eventually blasting off track around a curve.

The engineer did everything he could to keep the train under control on the downgrade without having to rely on the undependable braking system. He followed the unwritten rule: the locomotive should not run faster than a man can walk, or five miles per hour. Without speedometers, he judged the speed by the sway of the cab and his own instincts. The challenge of holding trains on the downgrade after coaxing them uphill earned the DSP&P Railroad its nickname: Damned Slow Pulling and Pretty Rough Riding.

How any trip went on the DSP&P depended on the quality of coal in the tender. In the 1880s and 90s, the railroad used coal from either the King mines near Como or the Baldwin mines near Gunnison. After 1896, when the King mines were closed, the locomotives burned Baldwin coal most of the time. A tank of Baldwin coal meant a full head of steam and few stops to clean the firebox and dump the clinkers. But it sent sparks out the smokestack that set hay and timber fires en route.

At times when the Gunnison route was closed by winter storms, the railroad company sent Trinidad coal to Como. Trinidad coal did not give off hot sparks, but neither did it build a good head of steam in the small narrow gauge boilers. It burned slowly, piling up ashes and clinkers that clogged the firegrates and choked the air. Even though better quality coal meant faster trains and easier trips, the DSP&P was not disposed to spend more money to transport good coal to Como just to make the railroader's life easier.

One of the boomer engineers who traveled across the country working on different railroads in busy seasons took matters into his own hands while working on the DSP&P. When he saw the mixture of lump and slack coal in the tender, he moved the locomotive under the water tank at Como, pulled down the spout, and washed the slack to the ground. Then he spotted the tender at the coal bin and ordered the fireman to take on more coal. Back and forth he went between the water tank and the bin until the tender was filled with lump coal and slack littered the ground. He had an easier trip than usual on the DSP&P, but it was his last.

Sam and the other DSP&P engineers were always asking for better coal, but they made do with whatever the company provided for each trip. The truth is that they were just as ready for a hot meal and long rest after sixteen hours on the road with a tank of Baldwin coal as they were with a tank of Trinidad coal. Whether the trip took sixteen hours or thirty, was hard or easy—and few were easy on the DSP&P—engineers were paid about $3.40, based on the pay rate at the time of $3.40 per 100 miles.

Sam collected his pay once a month when the pay train came rumbling down track with number 283, a Dawson and Bailey 4-4-0 on the point and engineer Jim Burke and fireman Mike Keefe in the engine cab. The special train consisted of the pay car, which resembled a miniature bank furnished with tables, chairs, a safe, and money cage, and the caboose, where the paymaster lived en route. The train stopped along the line at stations and sidings, wherever it came upon railroaders. Each man's pay was determined in advance at the Denver office from time reports turned in daily to the superintendent. The paymaster doled out the pay in gold coins.

Sam spent three years in the DSP&P freight pool, with no scheduled time off and no free weekends for fishing or hunting. Vacations were unheard of in the 1880s and 90s. He worked every day, except for the short period when he laid off sick and the company gave his job to another engineer. He had recuperated and was ready to go to work two weeks before the company called him back. As far as the DSP&P was concerned, railroaders had to be on the job when there was work to be done, and no excuse for absence was tolerated.

Despite the steady workload in the late 1880s, the DSP&P found itself moving toward bankruptcy. Historians have attributed its financial troubles to the high costs of constructing and operating the narrow gauge over the mountains, especially in the winter, to keen competition with the Rio Grande Railroad for the Gunnison and Leadville mining traffic, and to inefficient operations. On August 29, 1889, the DSP&P was reorganized as the Denver, Leadville and Gunnison Railway Company, still under the control of the Union Pacific. Sam and the other railroaders got service letters from the old DSP&P and kept on working for the new company. For them, nothing had changed. They still called the railroad "the South Park."

CHAPTER FIVE

Fast Freight to Leadville

ocomotive number 265, a 2-8-0 Rhode Island, was ready to go, fire building in the firebox, steam rising in the boiler, the tender full of coal and water. Coupled ahead of the 265 was a helper engine. Behind stood sixteen loaded boxcars. Each car weighed ten tons empty and carried another ten tons in freight. At the rear of the cars stood two more helper engines and, at the very end of the train, the caboose.

It was 2:05 a.m. in the early summer of 1893 when train number 499 left the Como depot. Sam was at the throttle of the 265. The fireman was Tom McGrath and the train conductor a man named Kissic. The trip they made that day was typical of trips on the fast freight to Leadville.

With the oil-fed headlight playing feebly across the track in the early morning darkness, the train gathered speed before starting up Boreas Pass. After rounding Peabody's Curve, Sam began working the locomotive on the steady uphill climb. Behind, the other engines groaned and hissed, smoke pouring from the stacks, as the train wound through tunnels of ponderosa, lodgepole pine, and aspen before reaching the summit.

There, the two helper engines in front of the caboose cut off to return to Como and help the next westbound freight, while the 265, still part of the doubleheader, got ready for the downhill run. The firemen took on water and cleaned the ashpans, while the brakemen ran across the tops of the cars setting the brakes. Slowly, the train began to roll downhill, dropping 600 feet in altitude in three miles.

With the throttle barely open and the Johnson Bar notched back, Sam watched the track ahead as the 265 cut around Rocky Point, the train swaying behind. Still dropping in altitude, it looped around short, snakelike curves before turning into the giant curve of all—168-foot-long Engineer's Curve. Then it drifted across Illinois Gulch on Gold Pan Trestle and bent back upon itself around Hookeye Curve. Curves were routine on the Highline. The distance between Como and Leadville was 63.83 miles, 58.53 of which were curves. Uncoiling out of Hookeye, the train made a dash for Breckenridge, pulling into the station at Main and Watson streets with bell clanging and brakes screeching.

Breckenridge owed its existence to the old South Park railroad, now the Denver, Leadville and Gunnison. Trains stopped there at all hours of the day and night to take on coal and water, pick up passengers, and load and unload freight. In 1882, when the railroad built over Boreas Pass, Breckenridge was a rough mining camp with more saloons than anything else and a transient population of miners, gamblers, and ruffians. The gold ore mined from the riverbeds near Breckenridge was shipped by wagon over Boreas and Kenosha passes, sometimes taking several weeks to reach the smelters in Denver.

After the railroad arrived, freight trains hauled the ore to Denver in one day and returned the next with supplies and machinery. By the 1890s, Breckenridge had become Colorado's richest placer mining district, producing $35 million in gold by 1900. Enormous dredges worked in the Swan and Blue rivers, in French Gulch, and in the gulches north and east of town. A fifty-mile network of flumes and ditches carried water to the gulches. The Great Flume alone was twenty-one miles long and was built with two million feet of timber.

The growth of dredge mining brought respectability to Breckenridge. Miners built houses and moved their families to town, bringing the population to 2,000. Breckenridge became the seat of Summit County and the location of three smelters, a sawmill and stamp mill, as well as numerous businesses. When the railroaders laid over, they could get a meal and clean room at Breckenridge's hotels and see a performance at the opera house. If they got sick, or needed the services of a lawyer, Breckenridge had both doctors and lawyers, including one law firm with the name of Breeze and Breeze.

But Sam and the crew on the fast freight had stopped in Breckenridge that morning in 1893 to replenish the coal and water. Rolling out of town, the train headed down the Blue River valley, past the looming shadows of the dredges in the riverbed. This was Sam's favorite leg of the trip, an easy run, with the train drifting on the downgrade as the faint light in the sky outlined the rugged peaks of the Ten Mile Range to the west. At Dickey, they stopped to take on more water while two helper engines coupled in for the climb over Fremont Pass.

Dickey was the busy junction between the Ten Mile and Montezuma districts. Westbound trains pulling into Dickey either turned into Ten Mile Canon or switched over to the Dillon-Keystone branch. Across from the depot stood a two-stall engine house, each stall long enough to hold two of the helper engines stationed here. Dickey also had a wye and enough sidetracks for 188 cars waiting to be hauled one place or another. One cold December night in 1887, six loaded ore cars tied up at Breckenridge took a walk, breaking loose and thundering down the line, sparks flying from the wheels. When they reached Dickey, they jumped the track at the curve, flew through the air, and landed in the depot, destroying half the building. It was probably Dickey's most exciting moment.

But all was quiet at Dickey when train 499 pulled out at 4:25 a.m. Three miles down the line, the train rumbled around the edge of Frisco with whistle blowing and bell jangling to let the town's 250 residents know that the fast freight to Leadville was coming through on time.

Just beyond, the train started up Ten Mile Canon. The jagged peaks of the Ten Mile Range were now to the east with the southern edge of the Gore Range on the west. High above the tracks, tailings from the district's silver mines spilled down the mountainside. In winter, avalanches, often set off by the sounds of the locomotives, ran down the steep gullies and closed the route, bringing the rotary and shovelers to dig out the track. The worst slides occurred at Curtin.

At Wheeler station, later called Solitude, six miles through the canon, the locomotives took on more water before beginning the toughest part of the climb over Fremont Pass. In the next six miles, the train gained 800 feet in altitude. By the time it pulled into Kokomo on the eastern slope of Sheep Mountain, the locomotives had almost drained their tanks of water. McGrath and the other firemen jumped on top of the tenders to take on more water as the eastern sky turned red with the dawn.

Two miles farther and 94 feet higher, the fast freight reached the outskirts of Robinson, the Ten Mile District's largest town. Ore from hundreds of mines scattered across the nearby mountains was shipped to Robinson's two smelters, and trees felled in the surrounding forest were cut in Robinson's four sawmills. About 850 people lived in this prosperous town which counted two hotels, a bank, and the *Summit County Times* among its businesses.

Rumbling through the sleeping town of Robinson, the train continued on its way to Leadville. Three miles farther, and 460 feet higher, it inched over the top of Fremont Pass at 11,320 feet and stopped at Climax, another busy station with a turntable, engine house, and sidings. Even though molybdenum had been discovered fourteen years earlier, no one had figured out what to do with it by 1893. (It would not be accurately identified until 1900, or put to use as an alloy for strengthening steel until World War I.) When the train pulled into Climax, silver was still the most important mineral in the area.

After taking on more coal, the train started downhill, past French Gulch and Birds Eye stations, swaying in and out around curves on a high, narrow shelf with Mount Massive ahead and the Arkansas River headwaters below. In fourteen miles, the train descended 1,000 feet, pulling into the Leadville yards on East Ninth Street at 7 a.m.

Brakemen and yard crews went to work uncoupling the cars and shunting them to sidetracks next to the docks to be unloaded. Link and pin couplers made coupling and uncoupling railroading's most dangerous job. The brakemen stood between two cars as the locomotive shoved one toward the other. Just as the link on the end of one car slid into the hole on the drawbar of the other, he dropped the iron spike—called the pin—into the hole. To uncouple the cars, he had to nudge the pin out of the hole, running between moving cars to do so. In the process, he stood every chance of losing his fingers, mangling his hands, and smashing his legs, but link and pin couplers remained on the South Park freight trains until 1900, even though the Safety Appliance Act passed by Congress in March 1893 required railroads engaged in interstate commerce to install automatic couplers. The railroad managed to evade the law with the argument that, since it did not cross state lines, it was not engaged in interstate commerce.

At Leadville, Sam turned over the 265 to the hostler whose job it was to dump the ashes and clinkers, keep the fire going in the firebox, and make sure the locomotive was ready for the return trip to Como at 12:40 p.m. Sam, McGrath, Kissic, and the brakemen had a few hours to find a boardinghouse, eat breakfast, and take a rest.

They set out through streets crowded with miners hurrying to the day shift and other residents heading toward offices and stores. As one historian has observed, everyone was in Leadville in the early 1890s—miners, merchants, freighters, gamblers, bullwhackers, bankers, postal clerks, grocers, butchers, lawyers, doctors, and newspapermen. The population has been put everywhere from 14,000 to 35,000, with the exact figure hard to pin down. Hoping to strike it rich, people moved to town. But when working in the mines at four dollars a day didn't turn them into millionaires, they moved on.

The promise of wealth kept people coming to Leadville, however. Ninety mines were operating in the foothills of the Mosquito Range on Iron, Rock, Fairview, Yankee, White, Carbonate, Fryer, and Breech hills, and Stray Horse Ridge. Shafts had been sunk 1,000 feet into the earth with spokes stretching under the town itself. The names of some of Leadville's mines still evoke images of riches: the Little Pittsburg, the Chrysalite and Little Grant, the Yankee Doodle, A.Y. Minnie, Pendery, Iron Silver, the Robert Emmet and Robert E. Lee, the Highland Chief, Double Decker, Wolfe Tone and Ready Case, the Matchless, and the Little Johnny—all of which produced 2,000 tons of silver, gold, and lead ore every day with a value of twenty-five dollars per ton. By 1891, $160 million worth of minerals had been mined in Leadville.

Horse-drawn wagons lumbered through the streets in an endless circle, carrying ore across town from the mines to the smelters, hauling bullion from the smelters to the railroad loading docks, and ferrying supplies from the docks to the mines. Not until 1900 did the Mineral Belt Railway appear with spurs between the main tracks and the mines. To feed the thousands of horses working in Leadville, the South Park ran two sixteen-car hay trains every week.

Leadville was booming in early 1893, but it had been busted too. When the placer gold, discovered in 1859, had played out a few years later, miners had packed up and moved on, leaving Leadville with fading hopes. With the discovery of silver in 1873, a few miners came straggling back, but when the mines began producing the rich carbonate of lead-bearing silver, another boom was on. In May 1879, 1,500 people were living in Leadville. Six months later, there were 18,000 people in town sinking mining shafts and raiding the forests for timber to build houses, shops, hotels, sidewalks, and railroads. As one historian observed, Leadville's hills were disemboweled and denuded at the same time.

The railroads built to Leadville as fast as possible to get in on the boom. Both the DSP&P and the Rio Grande reached town by way of Buena Vista in 1880, and in 1884, the DSP&P completed the Highline route from Como to Leadville.

Together, the mines and railroads made an unbeatable team. Before the railroads came, costs of freighting ore to Denver were higher than the value of the ore. The railroads offered lower freight rates, and, at the same time, brought in the heavy machinery needed to reach the ore embedded deep in the earth. In the first year after the railroads arrived, Leadville's mining production grew from $11 million to $15 million.

Even the boardinghouses thrived in Leadville. Those that catered to railroaders like Sam and the crew on the fast freight were usually run by the wives, widows, daughters, and sisters of railroad men. They understood the railroaders' nomadic life, and since there were no regular hours in rail-roading, there were no regular hours in these boardinghouses. For one dollar, paid from the railroaders' pockets, the boardinghouses offered a hearty meal and a clean bed at any time of day or night.

After a meal and a couple hours rest, Sam and his crew were back in the Leadville yards getting ready to take the train to Como. The fast freight had become number 488, a workhorse made up of about ten ore cars that stopped at stations on the way to pick up more loaded cars and shunt others into the sidings. For the crew, it was stop and go, couple and uncouple cars, shunt cars back and forth—slow, hard work.

Five hours after leaving Leadville, the train tied up at Dickey while the locomotive switched onto the Keystone branch and headed toward Dillon, three miles down the line. After shoving empties into sidings there, it kept going another four miles to the Keystone railhead. There, waiting to roll to Denver, were cars loaded with cattle, sheep, and hay from ranches all around, flatcars filled with lumber from the nearby sawmill, and other cars loaded with ore from the silver mines in the Montezuma District—the Saints John, Wild Irishman, General Teller, and Pennsylvania. Before the DSP&P had reached Keystone, the wagons that hauled the ore down from the mines had kept on going over Argentine and Boreas passes to Denver, a trip that took a week in the summer and several weeks in the winter.

Coupling up with a new train, the 265 headed back to Dickey. Ore cars destined for Leadville's smelters were shoved onto the sidetracks to wait for the next westbound freight. Others, destined for Denver, stayed in the train. The ten cars the 265 had hauled out of Leadville also coupled in, along with two helper engines for the trip over Boreas Pass.

Back through the Blue River valley rolled train 488. At Breckenridge, more work had to be done. Cars had to be dropped off, others picked up, still others shunted to the siding. By the time the train started over Boreas Pass, night had fallen.

When the train pulled into Como at 10 p.m., it was two hours and twenty minutes late, which didn't leave much time for the crew to eat and rest before going out again at 2:05 a.m. Years later, I saw my father come in late from a trip, lie down on the living room sofa, pull an afghan over himself, and barely shut his eyes before the caller was at the door, shouting "81 on time." Dad would get up, eat the sandwich and apple pie and drink the milk mother had set out for his lunch, and without time even to change clothes, leave for the depot.

But he still considered it a marvelous stroke of luck to be an engineer on the old South Park. And, in early 1893, it seemed the luck would hold forever. The work would always last, the mines would always produce, the trains would always run. Given the fact that most railroaders, like

Sam, were working every day, month in and month out, it's no wonder they didn't see the crash before it came.

And it came with a fury. Later in that summer of 1893, Leadville's mines lost one of their biggest customers when the British mints in India stopped coining silver. That October, Congress repealed the Sherman Act, taking the country off the silver standard. As depression spread across the country, the value of silver plummeted and Leadville was busted again. Only eighteen mines managed to stay open, and those with skeleton crews. Ninety percent of Leadville's miners were thrown out of work. "Ruin and bankruptcy stared every mining man, every smelting man and every businessman in the face," declared the *Leadville Herald Democrat*.

It also stared the railroad companies in the face. The three freight trains and one passenger train that ran every day between Denver and Leadville were cut back to occasional runs. With most of the mines closed, there was little reason to go to Leadville, and with the depression deepening, little reason to go anywhere.

By the end of 1893, the mighty Union Pacific and its subsidiary, the Denver, Leadville and Gunnison, declared bankruptcy. To shore up an increasingly bleak financial picture, the company cut wages across the board by 10 percent. Work was cut even further. Sam had worked every day during the first six months of 1893, averaging $160 a month. During the next year, he worked only a few days each month, lucky to make between $40 and $50 a month. Railroaders who had thought about leaving the old South Park because of the long hours and relentless work resigned that year for lack of work.

But Sam stayed. Time off for him was an unaccustomed luxury during which he built a porch and shingled the wellhouse. He and Anna managed on their savings. Like most railroaders in Como, he considered the financial panic an inconvenience, a temporary ripple in the stream of progress, and he waited for business to return as usual.

CHAPTER SIX

The Road to Everywhere

T he number 26, a mixed freight and passenger train bound for the Chalk Creek District, left Denver every evening, steamed up Platte Canon, heaved itself over Kenosha Pass, and dropped into South Park. Turning on the wye at Como, it backed into the station shortly after midnight, its engine and crew ready to return to Denver with an eastbound train.

In the mid-1890s, Sam and his fireman, John Olson, often hauled the mixed freight between Como and the Chalk Creek District. The conductor was Pete Newbury, George Burris, Montag, Tyler, Burrows, or Steinmetz.

On one trip in March 1895, the dispatcher assigned the 273, a 2-8-0 Baldwin locomotive, to the Chalk Creek run even though it usually pulled freights across the Highline. The 273 coupled onto the front of the train while yard crews uncoupled the cars destined for Como and shunted other cars, bound for the Chalk Creek District, into the train. Some passengers had climbed from the coach, gathered belongings at the baggage car, met friends on the platform, and started for town in wagons or on foot. Everyone knew when the passenger trains arrived in Como by the strangers wandering along the roads, carpetbags in hand.

Passengers going to Chalk Creek took advantage of the layover in

37

Como to stretch their legs on the platform or eat a meal in the Pacific Hotel's dining room before resettling themselves in the red plush seats of the coach. Passengers boarding at Como stowed bags and coats in the overhangs, plopped into vacant seats, or made their way through the sliding doors to the smoker. Coaches were fine affairs with wood-paneled walls trimmed in gold leaf and oil-burning lamps with fancy glass shades hanging from the green enameled ceilings. Potbellied coal stoves kept the passengers warm even on cold March nights when the wind howled and the snow drifted across South Park.

Como's depot and railroad yards still hummed with activity during the slow years that followed the financial panic of 1893. While the number of trains had been cut back, railroaders still picked up orders, checked watches, oiled valves, and swept cabs, getting ready to run the trains that were scheduled. The caller's knock on the door was always welcome in those years. It meant a trip on the Highline as far as Dickey or Climax, and occasionally a trip to Leadville. For Sam, it often meant a trip to the Chalk Creek District where the mines were still operating, although production had dropped two-thirds since 1893.

At 2:15 a.m., the conductor gave the high sign and Sam blew the whistle, letting everyone in Como know the Chalk Creek mixed train was pulling out. It drifted five miles through wide, empty South Park. Some nights the train seemed suspended in darkness, with the headlight flickering dimly on the track ahead. Other nights, the moon and stars bathed South Park in silver light.

After pulling over Red Hill, the number 26 rolled about eleven miles to Garos, where it stopped to take on coal and water. Stock pens and loading chutes lined the track at Garos, a major cattle and hay station for South Park ranches. On one trip in 1890, Sam had steamed into Garos past hay stacks close to the track. Sparks from the smokestack started one of South Park's biggest bonfires. After watching his crops go up in smoke, the rancher sued both Sam and the railroad. At that time, engineers were held responsible for anything that went wrong en route, even mechanical failures or broken parts on the locomotives. Not long after the haystack fire, Sam made several monthly payments of thirty dollars each to the company for the misfortune of having a driving wheel crack during a trip over the Highline. But when he appeared in court at Fairplay to answer for the hay fire, the judge refused to hold him responsible for sparks from the smokestack. Neither was the railroad company responsible. After all, the track was there first, the judge told the rancher.

From Garos, the trains either continued to the Chalk Creek District or turned on the wye and headed toward the mines around Fairplay and Alma. Both had been mining camps in the 1860s with prospectors, fortune seekers, gamblers, and ne'er-do-wells moving in and out, setting up tents and log cabins here and there. By the 1890s, they had both become respectable towns, but Fairplay, the seat of Park County, considered itself more respectable. The three-story stone courthouse stood in the center of Fairplay surrounded by churches, schools, and comfortable Victorian homes. Down the road from the courthouse were the offices of the Fairplay *Flume,* which, ten years earlier, *Crofutt's Guide of Colorado* had called a "live newspaper that dishes up all the news weekly." What's more, trains pulled into the Fairplay passenger and freight depot on the outskirts of town, while they stopped at London Junction, one mile south of Alma. There, they connected with the South Park and Leadville Short Line, a spur that continued up Mosquito Gulch to the London Mine. Wagons brought ore from the mines above Alma to the junction. Still another spur cut off at Hilltop, below Fairplay, and ran west to the Leavick mines.

But since the number 26 was on its way to the Chalk Creek District that March of 1895, a helper engine coupled in at Garos for the climb over Trout Creek Pass. The train rumbled past the sleepy station of Cohen's Spur, called Weston in the 1860s when wagon trains had been made up there for the trek over Weston Pass to Leadville.

With the 273 steaming forward and the helper engine pushing, the train rolled to the summit of Trout Creek Pass at 9,483 feet. The helper engine cut off and Sam whistled for brakes before starting down the mountain. In thirteen miles, the train crossed Trout Creek twenty-seven times on wooden trestles and dropped 1,659 feet in altitude.

Before pulling into Schwanders, the number 26 rounded Deadman's Curve, where another mixed train had run away and jumped the track in 1884. After staring down an empty track waiting for the train to arrive that night, the station master at Schwanders had telegraphed the dispatcher in Como, who sent a light engine and crew down the line to search for the missing train. When they reached the bottom of Trout Creek Pass, the crew spotted the pile of twisted metal and splintered wood in the creekbed. Four DSP&P crew members lay crushed in the wreckage—the engineer, fireman, conductor, and brakeman. The railroaders never forgot that wreck. Long afterward, when the subject came up among Dad and his engineer friends as they drank coffee around our kitchen table, someone was always sure to shake his head and remark: "In this business, you're either careful or dead."

At Schwanders, the locomotive took on coal and water before starting up Chalk Creek Canon. Olson had to jump out on the tender to shovel the coal from the bin into the coalspace. Two helper engines coupled into trains at Schwanders to push them through Chalk Creek Canon or over Trout Creek Pass. Al Kroll, one of the engineers assigned to the helpers, had been an engineer on the Rio Grande, running helper engines between Gunnison and Marshall Pass. On one trip, Al was returning to Gunnison light when the tank hose between the tender and engine fell off and water began pouring out of the tank. Kroll stopped the engine while the fireman crawled inside the tank to plug the hole with wads of canvas, hoping to save enough water to get the locomotive to the next station. Just as Kroll climbed into the tank to give him a hand, a Rio Grande freight train rounded the curve and crashed into the locomotive, sending it and the tender off track and downslope several feet with the crew bouncing around inside. Bruised, but otherwise unhurt, both Kroll and the fireman were fired for leaving the engine unattended.

Kroll sent a wire to Walt Parlin, an engineer on the South Park in Como: "Fired. Get me a job." Kroll and Parlin had been friends since schooldays in Gunnison when Parlin's family owned the ranch across which the DSP&P had built on the way to Gunnison. The station on the ranch bore the family's name. When Parlin got the wire, he went to see the superintendent in Como about a job for his friend, with the result that Kroll found himself working on the helper engines out of Schwanders.

Leaving Schwanders, with the helpers coupled in, the number 26 rumbled south and crossed the Arkansas River on a 150-foot-long steel trestle before pulling into Nathrop. A busy junction where South Park track met the Rio Grande track between Pueblo and Leadville, Nathrop had a depot, hotel, and stores that served nearby ranchers as well as railroad crews. After stopping at Nathrop, the train headed west, steaming through peaceful Chalk Creek valley with the timbered slopes and snow-covered peaks of Mounts Princeton and Antero ahead and the creek meandering close by the track.

One historian has called Chalk Creek Canon the "road to everywhere," and in the 1860s and 1870s, miners, prospectors, drifters, and adventurers by the thousands had traveled in wagons and stagecoaches or on the backs of burros up the canon to St. Elmo. From there, they followed toll roads over Tincup Pass to the mines around the town of Tincup, or kept going to Taylor Park and the mines near Ashcroft and Aspen. Another road out of St. Elmo led to Hancock at the creek's headwaters and continued over Williams Pass in the Sawatch Range to the mining districts of Gunnison and Crested Butte.

At the foot of Mount Antero, the train rolled past Heywood Springs and the four-story Mount Antero Hotel with verandas, mansard roof, and two front towers. Begun in 1877, the hotel had been planned as a spa, close to the mineral waters of the springs. By 1895, it was still a gaping shell, but sporadic construction dragged on until it finally opened for business as the Mount Princeton Hotel in 1917.

A mile farther up the line, the train pulled into Hortense, where the engines took on more coal and water. Close by the station was the Hortense Hotel and Springs, where water boiled out of the earth at 183 degrees, the hottest natural spring water in Colorado. Before the mines and railroads had brought settlers to Chalk Creek, the Utes had regarded the springs as a sacred place. By 1895, miners, ranchers, and tourists came to Hortense to soak stiff and arthritic limbs in the water, cooled to a comfortable temperature by water from the creek.

Pulling out of Hortense, train number 26 chugged along the narrow, twisting shelf that had been blasted out of the slope of the mountain. Across the creek rose the chalky white granite cliffs that gave both the creek and the canon their name. According to legend, the Spanish had buried treasure in the caves among the cliffs in 1779 during the only Spanish expedition to South Park. Every kid in Como dreamed about finding that Spanish treasure. In the early 1900s, when I made trips to Chalk Creek in the engine cab with my father, he would wave toward the cliffs, shouting above the hissing steam and clanking rods, "See, right there, in that cave there, you can see it can't you? That's where the treasure is."

After gaining 829 feet in altitude in the next six miles, the number 26 rumbled into Alpine station, also known as Fisher. Two years earlier, the Alpine smelter had belched black smoke into the clear mountain air, but the 1893 panic had closed it down, leaving Alpine with only a frame depot, its roof steeply pitched to let the snow slide off. Sam and the engineers in the helpers took turns spotting the tenders under the water tank.

Five miles farther up the line, the train rolled into St. Elmo, smoke and steam curling from the locomotives and steam whistles blowing. One of the miners living in St. Elmo at the time later wrote that the train whistling through the canon was the most welcome sound in the world.

St. Elmo was the center of the Chalk Creek Mining District with fifty gold and silver mines scattered across the mountains. The town included a hotel, several stores and saloons, a grammar school, and about 300 residents, most of whom worked on the railroad or in the mines. But on Saturday nights, hordes of other miners in the district crowded the main street, gold coins in hand, ready for the saloons and gambling tables. Most of the passengers on the number 26 disembarked at St. Elmo, the usual destination in the Chalk Creek District.

On the road now for ten hours, Sam turned over the locomotive to the watchman and he, Olson, and the rest of the crew walked down the mountain slope from the station to the hotel on St. Elmo's main street. While they rested, the watchman tended the locomotives, a job John Olson had held in St. Elmo in the 1880s after he had first gone to work on the DSP&P and before he became a fireman. Although he had been promoted to engineer in 1893, he was still working as a fireman during the slack years of 1894 and 1895. Like Andrew Nelson, another DSP&P engineer, Olson had immigrated from Sweden at the age of sixteen. Both had worked in shipyards and factories in the East before drifting West and hiring out on the DSP&P. Not until they found themselves on the same railroad did they meet, although they had followed parallel paths halfway around the world.

It was evening when the number 26 left St. Elmo and, with the helper engines still coupled in, inched its way uphill toward Murphy's Switch, which was called Romley after 1897. High on the south slope of the mountain gaped the four main openings of the Mary Murphy Mine, the district's richest and largest producer. In its forty-four-year lifetime, the Mary Murphy produced $60 million in gold and silver. According to legend, the prospector who discovered gold here in 1875 had named the mine after an Irish nurse in a Denver hospital who had nursed him back to health from a serious illness.

From the railroad track to the top level of the mine ran a 4,996-foot-long tramway with buckets of ore screeching and clanking along heavy metal ropes on their way down to the empty railroad cars. The noise of the tramway and the whistle of the train echoed off the mountains as the number 26 pulled into the station.

Below the track, scattered on the downslope of the mountainside, were square, frame buildings painted a deep red color that housed the mining offices. Farther below were the boardinghouses where forty miners lived. Some of those miners, who had boarded the train at St. Elmo, scrambled off the coach and headed for the offices to report back to work. Others went to the offices hoping to find jobs. The helper engines uncoupled from the train to start pushing empties into the siding while Sam and the 273 started up the canon pulling a coach and two loaded cars destined for Hancock. Later the helpers ran to Hancock to turn on the wye.

Between Murphy's Switch and Hancock, the mountainsides were covered with the tailings of the Flora Bell, Alie Bell, Rarus, Treasury, Pittsburg, and Comstock mines. A line of mules and horses treaded down the narrow dirt roads bringing ore to the empty railroad cars sitting in the siding. End of the line for number 26 was Hancock, in the windswept valley at the edge of timberline, 11,027 feet high. In the west loomed the peaks of the Sawatch Range.

In 1895, when the number 26 pulled into Hancock, the depot, freight house, coal bin, and water tank stood next to the track. Nearby were the stone foundations of buildings from Hancock's heyday in the early 1880s when the Alpine Tunnel was under construction three miles up the line.

Hordes of laborers and loads of construction material had landed first at Hancock before making their way on the backs of burros to the tunnel site. Miners working the nearby mines—the Stonewall, Warrior, Kentucky, and Old Dog Tray—had come through Hancock. Fifteen houses had stood here, along with sawmills, a store, hotel, restaurants, and saloons.

But in 1895, the old South Park trains made only occasional trips to Hancock to drop off a few supplies for the miners still working in the area and pick up a few passengers. Most of the time, the engines ran light from Murphy's Switch to Hancock to turn on the wye before starting the downhill run.

On the way down, Sam stopped at every spur to pick up loaded ore cars and shunt empties into the sidings. By the time he reached Murphy's Switch, where other cars waited to be moved or picked up, he and Olson had worked fifteen hours straight. They tied up and walked down the mountainside to one of the boardinghouses to eat and sleep a few hours.

After resting, they climbed back into the engine for the return trip. Pulling a coach, eleven ore cars, and a caboose, they rolled into St. Elmo. Como-bound passengers were waiting at the station to board the train, but before it got underway, other cars had to be coupled in. Now number 27, the train finally left St. Elmo. With bell clanging and whistle screaming, it chugged down the canon to Hortense and Heywood and out across the valley to Nathrop and beyond to Schwanders. The helpers coupled into the train to push it to the top of Trout Creek Pass. There, they uncoupled and returned light to Schwanders. Engine 273, with Sam still at the throttle and Olson tending the fire, hauled the train the rest of the way to Como. When they pulled into the station, the crew had been on the road three days.

Later, when Dad was working short turnarounds from Buena Vista to Romley, my brothers and I often went along, lugging berry pails and picnic baskets. One of us got to ride in the engine cab each leg of the journey, while the others sat in the coach, noses pressed to the window, watching the cattle and horses grazing on the ranches, the rushing waters of Chalk Creek, and the snowcapped peaks in the distance, and waving to the people at every station as the train rolled by.

Two miles above Hortense, where Raspberry station had stood in the 1880s, Dad stopped the train long enough for us to jump out. While we scrambled over the mountainside, looking for the low, straggly bushes loaded with clusters of ripe, red raspberries, the train steamed up the canon out of sight. We climbed for hours, picking berries, and ate a picnic on one of the rock outcroppings that overlooked the track below. About the time the berries began to spil over in the pail, we would hear the train whistling down the canon, and we would run to the track. After Dad had stopped the train, we tumbled on while he hung out the cab window, making sure we got on safely. Whoever got to ride up front kept busy watching Dad run the engine and staying out of the fireman's way when he picked up the coal shovel. The other two boys settled into the coach seats and fell asleep.

CHAPTER SEVEN

Through the Mountain

I n 1895, the DL&G management decided to reopen the Alpine Tunnel three miles beyond Hancock, a decision that Como's railroaders greeted with less than enthusiasm. Most of them had worked on the mixed trains that rolled through the tunnel to Gunnison during the 1880s, before rockslides closed the portals in 1890. And they preferred a fifteen-hour trip on the Highline to a fifteen-minute trip through the tunnel.

The 1,805-foot-long Alpine Tunnel, longer than six football fields strung together, had been punched through the mountain under the Continental Divide. In places it was so narrow that crews would touch the walls from the engine cab, yet it had been constructed without ventilation systems. Black smoke, carbon monoxide, and other gases from the head locomotives spilled out the smokestacks, flumed along the train, seeped into the coaches, and engulfed the open cabs of the helper engines, forcing crews to the decks with neckerchiefs clutched to their mouths and noses. Blowers in the locomotives had to be kept open at full blast to prevent downdrafts from bursting the firebox doors and spilling the fire into the engines.

The engineer worked the steam going into the tunnel and set the brakes coming out. Any brakeman caught outside when the train darted into the tunnel had to flatten himself on the cartop at certain places to keep from being knocked off by the low ceiling. The moment the train shot out the other end, plummeting downgrade from the apex, the tunnel's highest spot, the brakeman had to jump up and run along the cartops, setting the brakes as fast as possible.

Despite its hazards, the Alpine Tunnel had connected South Park to the Gunnison Coal District. In a race with the Rio Grande to tap into the lucrative coal-hauling business, the DSP&P had begun construction on the tunnel in the blizzards, drifting snow, and freezing temperatures of January 1880 rather than wait for spring. In the next two years, ten thousand workers trekked to the construction site, lured by the railroad's advertisements in Eastern newspapers that extolled the scenic wonders of the Rocky Mountains and the high wages—$3.50 per day for laborers who hacked through the granite with picks and shovels and $5.00 per day for those brave enough to blast through the granite with black powder.

The Union Pacific provided free train rides wherever the railhead happened to be located as the DSP&P built over Trout Creek Pass and up Chalk Creek Canon. The rest of the way to the tunnel site the workers walked with tools and belongings strapped on their backs.

They bunked in drafty cabins near the construction site and crawled to work in the blizzards, roped together to keep from getting lost or falling off the mountain. They swung picks and shovels and shook over hand drills, wheezing and gasping in the thin mountain air, and they stalked off the job, whole crews at a time, when they had enough.

But new crews followed, and the work continued until the Alpine Tunnel had been cut through the sliding rock and decomposed granite and shored up with 500,000 feet of California redwood. Selected because of its fire-resistant qualities, which reduced the chances of ashes and clinkers setting the tunnel on fire, the redwood arrived at the site via the Central Pacific, the Union Pacific, and DSP&P, and finally, the backs of burros.

In December 1882, the first DSP&P locomotive steamed through the bore on the way to Gunnison. For seven years, trains ferried passengers and coal to Denver and returned with machinery and supplies for the mines and other passengers bound for the Gunnison District. Some passengers, including mine owners and railroad executives, traveled first class in the Pullman car, outfitted with twenty upper and lower berths, plush seats, fancy curtains, and parquet walls and described in the *Rocky Mountain News* as "altogether up to the degree of excellence for which this company—Pullman—is famed."

When cave-ins closed the east portal in 1890, Union Pacific executives, ensconced in paneled boardrooms in Omaha far from the day-by-day operations of the Colorado railroad, decided not to reopen the tunnel, even though trains had been running daily between Gunnison and Denver. That decision left a DSP&P skeleton crew and equipment in Gunnison hauling coal from the mines to town where Rio Grande freights picked it up and carried it over Marshall Pass to Denver.

By 1895, with Rio Grande trains still hauling coal out of Gunnison and the DL&G in bankruptcy, that decision struck the company receiver, Frank Trumbull, as foolish if not downright stupid. Bejowled, with deep-set eyes, thinning hair, and a bushy mustache, Trumbull had a reputation as a practical, hardheaded businessman. According to William Byers, editor of the *Rocky Mountain News,* Trumbull attained "all his liberal education as well as other acquirements in the world of business." On his own at the age of twelve, he had gone to work as a bookkeeper in Arcadia, Missouri, and two years later had worked up to a clerk's position in the Pleasant Hill, Missouri, post office. By age sixteen, he was embarked on a railroading career as a clerk on the Katy—The Missouri, Kansas and Texas Railroad. Later he hired on the Missouri Pacific, where he was working as a bookkeeper and traveling auditor at the same time Sam was firing Missouri Pacific locomotives.

By 1888, Trumbull was in Denver working in the wholesale coal business while serving as a consultant on western railroads for New York and London investors. As receiver for the bankrupt DL&G, he set out to increase the railroad's business and profits by reopening the Alpine Tunnel and claiming a share of the coal-hauling business. It also happened that Trumbull held an interest in the Kubler mines near Gunnison which would benefit from access to DL&G freights.

In May 1895, the DL&G crew working the short haul trips between the mines and Gunnison was assigned the task of repairing the track and pulling out rocks and debris from the tunnel's west portal. Nathan Martinis was the engineer, Mike Byrnes the fireman, Mike Flavin the conductor, and Elmer England the brakeman. Every morning, the crew ran the locomotive and caboose to the west portal from the siding three miles below, where they lived in a coach converted to a bunkhouse. While they worked in the west portal, laborers began hacking through the rocks and debris in the east portal.

By Saturday, June 8, Martinis and his crew had knocked a large enough opening in the rockslide for the locomotive and caboose to run inside. Using the locomotive's power, the crew went to work siphoning water trapped by rocks and timber. With no ventilation in the tunnel, the men were soon overcome by carbon monoxide. Martinis died at the throttle,

Flavin was dead in the caboose, and Byrnes, who had tried to get out, fell into a stream of water a few feet from the engine. The only survivor was England, who realized what was happening soon enough to drop to the ground and crawl out of the tunnel. The carbon monoxide also seeped through the holes in the cave-in and killed Oscar Cammann, one of the laborers in the east portal.

The four deaths confirmed the worst fears of Como's railroaders about the tunnel. But the company dispatched another crew to the west portal and work went forward. By July 4, DL&G trains were again steaming into Gunnison. Mixed train number 3 left Denver on alternate days for the twenty-hour trip. At Como, the Denver-based locomotives turned on the turntable and coupled into the eastbound train. Locomotive number 114, a Cooke 2-6-0, went on the point of the Gunnison-bound train with Sam often at the throttle. The fireman was jovial Patrick Colligan, known as Curly, who had gone to work on the DL&G in 1890. Two years after the tunnel reopening, he was set up to engineer.

Train number 3 crossed South Park, climbed over Trout Creek Pass, and continued through Chalk Creek Canon after coupling in a helper at Schwanders. Leaving Hancock, it pulled uphill three miles to the tunnel, winding along the mountainside, threading through groves of aspen and ponderosa, and rolling past open clearings that overlooked Chalk Creek valley below. After looping around the sharp curve outside the east portal, it plunged into the darkness of the tunnel and continued climbing to the apex. Overhead hung a red oil-burning lantern that signaled engineers to slow for the downgrade. Sam shut back on the throttle, set the air, and, with brakes screeching and cars swaying, the number 3 rumbled out of the tunnel and through the snowshed and stopped at Alpine Tunnel Station.

Located near the top of the mountain above timberline, where the wind howled constantly, Alpine Tunnel Station was a busy waystop with a boardinghouse, engine house, telegraph station, coal platform, and water tank. The helper engines uncoupled, turned on the table, and started light for Schwanders. After taking coal and water on locomotive 114, Sam and the crew and passengers ate dinner in the boardinghouse before continuing to Gunnison.

Leaving Alpine Station, the number 3 rolled down the 4 percent grade along a shelf cut into the mountainside, 1,500 feet above Quartz Valley. At the Palisades, a granite wall as high as a fifty-story building, the train crawled along the top of a narrow stone ledge. Rather than attempt the formidable task of blasting a roadbed out of the Palisades, the railroad had imported stone masons from Wales to build a thirty-foot-high ledge from stones quarried in the area and fitted together without mortar. The ledge sat on rock outcroppings below. As the train crawled over the top, passengers were treated to views of the valley and the blue peaks of the Wasatch Range in Utah.

The number 3 continued downhill, rounding curve after curve, bending back upon itself at Sherrod Curve, where Sam could watch the caboose almost side by side with the locomotive. Still descending, train number 3 eased into Woodstock, where an eastbound freight train was waiting on the siding.

In March 1884, an avalanche had crashed down the mountain here, ripping through Woodstock Station and tearing up the track and all the buildings only moments after the passenger train had rumbled by. The slide left thirteen people dead, including J.S. Brown, the telegraph operator, and the six children of Marcella Doyle, the Irish widow who ran the boardinghouse. The town of Woodstock was never rebuilt. Even the water tank was relocated one-fourth mile downgrade.

Six miles farther down the line, train number 3 steamed past Quartz, a jumping off point in the 1880s for the mines in the Gold Brick and Tincup districts. Once a busy station with a hotel, post office, stores, saloons, and dance hall, Quartz was little more than a siding by 1895.

After sweeping through Missouri Gulch, the train stopped at Pitkin for water. Starting off again, it rolled down track past Parlins, named for the family of Walt Parlin, and into Gunnison, where it stopped at the ornate, four-story La Veta Hotel to let the passengers disembark. Built in 1883, in Gunnison's heyday, the hotel still attracted most of the passengers arriving in town. When they had collected their baggage, the train continued the short distance to the depot at New York and Ninth streets. Sam turned over the locomotive to the watchman and, with the rest of the crew, set out for a boardinghouse.

Surrounded by farm and ranch lands and near rich coal deposits at the Baldwin mines and Crested Butte, as well as a smattering of gold mines and limestone deposits, Gunnison had evolved into the transportation center of the Western Slope. Governor Evans had foreseen its potential in 1879 when he and a partner, Sylvester Richardson, formed the Gunnison Town Company. They named the new town for Captain John W. Gunnison, who had led the Union Pacific survey through the area two decades earlier when the land still belonged to the Utes. Gunnison was platted and surveyed in 1879 at the same time Evans was building the DSP&P across the mountains, intent upon reaching the Pacific Ocean. As it turned out, Gunnison and the track to the Baldwin Mine marked the farthest point west the railroad reached.

After spending the night in Gunnison, the crew boarded the train, now the number 4, and started for Como. The train whistled back to the La Veta Hotel to pick up passengers and rumbled out of town. Pulling upgrade, it stopped for coal and water at Pitkin and continued to Alpine Tunnel Station, where it took on more water. After the helpers cut off, the train rolled through the tunnel and started down Chalk Creek Canon. It crossed Trout Creek Pass, chugged across South Park, and pulled into Como. Sam had been gone thirty-six hours and was $11.90 richer, less a couple of dollars for meals along the way and a night's lodging in Gunnison.

Excursion trains were also popular on the Gunnison route. For ten dollars, excursionists from around the country boarded the mixed train at Denver Union Station, spent twenty hours sitting upright in the coach (since the Pullman had not been put back on after the tunnel's reopening), and viewed the "scenic wonders of mountainside and meadow" advertised by the DL&G. Despite the popularity of the Gunnison route, passenger fares accounted for a small part of the company's business, most of which came from the coal mines, as Trumbull had foreseen.

In a short time, Trumbull had not only reopened the Alpine Tunnel and increased the company's mileage, he had also improved the railroad's equipment and turned the DL&G into a "splendid working organization," attractive enough for Eastern investors to purchase in the final days of 1898. In January 1899, they consolidated the DL&G with the Union Pacific, Denver and Gulf Railway Company to form a new railroad in Colorado named the Colorado and Southern Railway. Through consolidations that had taken place in the last two decades, the new company consisted of parts of the Union Pacific, the Colorado Central, and the Denver, South Park and Pacific lines. It also gained control of the Fort Worth and Denver City, giving Colorado access to the Gulf states.

Grenville M. Dodge, who had overseen construction of the transcontinental Union Pacific in 1868 and had confidently predicted Denver's demise, was named chairman of the board. Since Denver had flourished in the intervening years as the transportation hub for the mining districts, despite Dodge's prediction, he had the good sense to place the railroad in the hands of Frank Trumbull, the man who understood the mutual dependence between Colorado's mines and railroads. Trumbull became the first president of the Colorado and Southern Railway. He immediately began upgrading and streamlining the railroad's operations. The narrow gauge engines were renumbered from 1 to 99, while the numbers of broad gauge engines started at 100. By 1900, the C&S had built a forty-stall roundhouse in Denver at Seventh Street on the banks of the South Platte River. In 1901, the company built coal chutes at Como, Pine Grove, and Pitkin and one at Dickey in 1902. With coal chutes, engineers could spot the tender under one pocket of the chute while the fireman had only to pull a chain that opened the pocket, allowing the coal to rush into the tank. The chutes saved both time and effort, since the fireman no longer had to shovel coal into the tank at these stops. But section paddies still had to shovel coal from coal cars into the chutes.

One summer in the early 1900s, the C&S scheduled an excursion train to Gunnison for the railroaders and their families in Como. Almost everyone in town showed up at the depot early the morning of the excursion, jostling one another as they boarded the coaches and hurried along the aisles to claim a window seat and stow wicker picnic baskets in the overhangs. As the train rolled out of town, I watched Como's landmarks slip by—the roundhouse, the town hall, the school perched on the hillside—proud that my father was the engineer taking the whole town on a trip. It was mid-July and hot as a firebox as we rolled through South Park, but as we steamed over the high mountain passes and through Chalk Creek, it turned pleasantly cool. By the time we rumbled through Hancock, with the wind whipping across the open mountain meadow, most passengers had pulled on sweaters and jackets. After climbing uphill, we rounded the curve outside the east portal with Dad blowing the whistle to let us know we were entering the tunnel. Suddenly, we were rolling through darkness, the clickety-clack of the wheels on the tracks filling the coach. Even though we had closed the windows to keep out the gases, the air was close and foul during the twenty minutes it took to roll through the tunnel before stopping at Alpine Tunnel Station. After taking on coal and water, we plunged downhill, cars swaying, brakes screaming, and daylight flooding the coach.

Out along the high roadbed overlooking Quartz Valley the train steamed. When we reached the Palisades, everyone crowded around the windows on the right side to see the view of the valley below and the mountains on the horizon. We descended slowly around the curves past Quartz, Pitkin, and Parlins, and finally into Gunnison, where we pulled up at the depot. The trip had taken six hours.

Everyone jumped from the coaches and walked to the park, lugging picnic baskets. Dad left the engine for the fireman to look after and, within moments, he and the other men had organized games of baseball, tag, and hide-and-seek, while the women laid out the picnics and ladled out the lemonade.

As soon as the sun dropped behind the mountains, he walked back to the engine to check it over before starting the return trip. We gathered up the bats and balls and picnic leftovers and, when we heard the whistle blowing, hurried for the train, the kids running ahead, men carrying the belongings, and women lifting their skirts around their ankles to keep from tripping in the rocky, dust-blown streets. When everyone was on board, Dad opened the throttle, and the excursion train rolled out of town, bound for Como, bell clanging and whistle blowing in the gathering darkness.

CHAPTER EIGHT

Buckin' the Snow

I n the mountains of South Park, winter arrived in October and stayed into May, burying the track in snowdrifts thirty feet high and dropping temperatures thirty degrees below zero. The wind never stopped howling, a fact that prompted a standard joke in Como: "Newcomer: Does the wind always blow this way? Oldtimer: No, sometimes it blows the other way."

The railroad was faced with waging a continuous battle against winter or giving up the struggle and operating a summer railroad. From a financial point of view, neither option was good. Summer excursion and freight trains did not generate enough revenue to cover the railroad's costs. Yet, the enormous expenses of keeping the line open in winter had helped to drive both the DSP&P and DL&G into bankruptcy.

The Colorado and Southern Railway Company, like its predecessors, chose to fight the winter and operate year-round. Every September, Como's locomotives went into the shops for winter outfitting. Pilots were removed from the front of locomotives and in their place went steel wedge plows, capable of pushing snow off the track. Commonly called "butterfly" plows, they could be raised with a block and tackle, making it easier to withdraw from snowdrifts. Later, the raising mechanisms were removed, probably because the automatic couplers always had to be taken off before the plows could be raised. Priest flangers—knives that scraped the inside edges and tops of the rails to keep ice from derailing the trains—were mounted ahead of the pony-truck wheels. These were operated by air.

But nothing was done to outfit the engine cabs to make winter more tolerable for the railroaders. The fireman's side was still exposed, except for the usually ragged canvas curtains. By the late 1890s, some locomotive cab sides had been rebuilt with steel. Ice crusted over the metal walls, snow piled on the deck, cold air blew across the floors, and the wind howled through the gangway, blowing the coal off the shovel before the fireman could throw it into the firebox.

The railroaders fought the winter by dressing for it. Sam left for winter trips swathed in two sets of long heavy wool underwear, two pairs of pants, two woolen shirts, two overalls, two pairs of wool socks, and heavy leather boots. On top of all this he buttoned a hip-length mackintosh, wrapped two wool scarves around his neck, pulled a wool cap over his ears, and pulled on fur-lined gloves.

He never knew when he would reach his destination or when he would return home. In the age before weather forecasting, he often left Como under clear skies, expecting good weather for the trip, and pulled onto the summit of Boreas Pass in a blizzard so fierce he couldn't see the front of the locomotive and had to guess whether it was headed uphill or down.

Avalanches were a constant danger. The whistling, clanging locomotives sent snowslides crashing down the mountain, blocking the track with ice, rocks, and uprooted trees and sweeping boxcars in their path. And if avalanches didn't sweep the cars off track, the winds did. More than once, Sam found himself up front in the cab with a helper engine and caboose somewhere behind and a long gap where, moments before, a string of boxcars had been rolling along.

Below-zero temperatures could cause the water to freeze in the tank. To prevent this, the fireman had to inject hot water from the boiler. Sometimes he shoveled snow into the tank and injected hot water to melt it.

When snowdrifts piled across the track—often as high as a three-story building and as long as a football field—railroaders "bucked the snow." After placing the train in a siding, two or three locomotives coupled together, with throttles open and Johnson Bar down, rammed into the drift, pushing as far as possible without getting stuck. Then the engineers threw the Johnson Bars into reverse and the locomotives shot backwards, like balls out of a cannon. Throwing the Johnson Bar into reverse with the throttle wide open demanded the strength of Hercules. It was also hard on the locomotives, accounting for part of the reason narrow gauge locomotives often went to the shops for repair. To get through a drift, they hammered the snow hour after hour until they had finally punched a hole. Often in the winter, Sam spent twelve hours at a time bucking the snow.

Several years later, when I was firing for my father in Chalk Creek, I watched him buck the snow using the techniques gained from years of experience. On one trip, we were on the head locomotive, with two helpers behind. After uncoupling the train, the engines rammed the snow, plunging in and pulling out like mad bulls battering a wall. Each time we hit the snow, lumps of ice, rocks, and tree branches crashed inside the engine's cab, which shook so hard I expected it to collapse around us. Foot by foot we powered through the drift until suddenly we were free, racing out the other side. Snow covered the deck, mounded around the boiler, and piled over the tender. Grinning with success, Dad looked like a snowman sitting at the throttle.

When no amount of bucking the snow could clear the track, the rotary was called out. In 1880, DL&G was one of the first railroads in the nation to purchase a rotary snowplow, number 064, later numbered 99200, built by Cooke Locomotive and Machine Company. The next year, the rotary, with its steel blades, bested the Jull Plow, which had a front-end augur, in snow trials in Chalk Creek. Later the Jull Plow, number 99210, worked out of Trinidad, and the C&S bought another rotary, the 99201, which was stationed at Cheyenne. But the 99200 worked out of Como. Resembling a giant boxcar, it did not run on its own power. The boiler produced the steam to power the steel blades. The throttle and Johnson Bar operated the blades, with the Johnson Bar controlling the direction. The rotary also had brakes and a flanger that could be raised or lowered by air pressure. It took four locomotives and sometimes six to push one rotary through a snowdrift.

The rotary plunged into the snow, blades whirling, churning through the snow and spitting it to one side of the track. But it could not clear avalanches because the rocks and branches broke the blades. With the rotary went a special train made up of a bunk car and dining car. It carried a crew of as many as sixty shovelers hired from the labor pools in Denver every fall and brought to Como for the winter. Out on the snow-clogged track, they shoveled from dawn to dark until their clothes turned to ice and fingers numbed in their gloves. At night, they ate hot meals in the dining car, dropped onto cots in the bunk car, and, after breakfast in the early morning darkness, started back to work. They worked days, even weeks at a stretch, shoveling snow so the trains could run.

On one trip with train number 3, Sam hit a drift in Chalk Creek Canon a short distance beyond St. Elmo. He and the rest of the crew spent several hours trying to buck the snow while drifts piled behind, trapping the locomotives and train. With snow falling, temperatures hovering at zero, and the only food a few sandwiches and pieces of cake in their grips, they waited eight hours until the rotary arrived and cleared the track behind. Then they backed to St. Elmo, where they took rooms in the hotel and waited for the rotary crew to dig out the track ahead.

Locomotives waiting at the station for track to be cleared ahead had to be kept alive, with fire roaring in the firebox so the water wouldn't freeze and burst the flues. Part of the railroad's winter costs went up in the black smoke that poured out of the stacks of waiting locomotives.

When a train was blocked and had to back to the nearest station, certain things had to be done quickly. The engineer blew one long blast and three short blasts of the whistle, signaling the brakeman to protect the rear. Railroaders never worried about opposing trains—it was the dispatcher's job to make sure another train wasn't coming toward them—but there was always danger of being rammed by a following train. Until the conductor could send a telegram, the dispatcher had no way of knowing that the train he had sent west had run into a snowdrift and was now backing east. And if the dispatcher didn't know, neither did the following train.

When the brakeman heard the signal to protect the rear, he set a red flag in the center of the platform on the caboose. (If it was night, he set out a red lantern.) With the train backing up, he grabbed his flag kit and ran ahead of the caboose. If he spotted an oncoming train, he waved his lantern or flag back and forth across the track to signal the engineer to stop. As soon as the train was stopped, he told the engineer of the backing train. That meant that the following train also had to back up, with its brakeman running down track to protect the rear. Often the brakeman laid fusees and torpedoes on the track. The light of the fusees, which burned like a Roman candle, and the explosion of the torpedoes when the engines hit them, signaled the engineer to slow down and look for trouble ahead.

Probably the worst winter in the history of mountain railroading fell in 1898 and 1899, during the months the C&S was formed and began taking over operations of the old South Park line. By November of that winter, so much snow had fallen on the Highline that the sidings at Kokomo were clogged with stalled freight trains waiting for the rotary crew to dig out the tracks over Fremont Pass. Storm followed storm across the mountains through December, blanketing South Park in deep snows and keeping the rotary at work days on end.

In early January, Sam got a call to take the mixed train to Gunnison. The rotary had been through Chalk Creek Canon and, as far as anyone knew, the track was clear, even though the skies were leaden and snow was still falling. The mixed train rumbled across South Park, over Trout Creek Pass, and into Chalk Creek Canon with the wedge plow and the locomotive pushing snow off the track. Just outside St. Elmo, a ten-foot drift blocked the way. Sam set the train in a siding and, with the helper engines, bucked through. Coupling back with the train, he continued to St. Elmo, Romley, and Hancock, the wedge plow slicing the snow that grew heavier and deeper. Had the track been laid along the northern wall of the canon, the railroad would have gotten some help from the sun in keeping it clear. As it was, the track ran in the shade of the southern wall.

Rounding out of Hancock, the train started for the Alpine Tunnel, creeping along at three miles per hour with the locomotives balking in icy weather that congealed the oil and turned the valves and running gear cold and brittle. It was the last train to pull through the tunnel before snows closed the track in Chalk Creek Canon. At Alpine Tunnel Station, Sam got orders to wait while the rotary cleared the line to Gunnison.

Alpine Tunnel Station was a good place to wait. The larder in the station house was full, and the stone bunkhouse was tightly constructed and warmed by a coal stove. The crew and a few passengers passed the first day talking and playing cards. On the second day, they waited for word that the track was clear and the mixed train could continue to Gunnison. When no word had come by the third day, they decided to ration the food.

It was still snowing on the fifth day when the operator handed Sam a telegraphed message that his mother had died in Freeman, Missouri. Sam had not seen his family since 1883, when he had boarded the Kansas Pacific passenger train to go railroading in Colorado. He was now the experienced engineer he had then hoped to become, with seniority and a steady job, but he was also snowed in on top of a mountain, 160 miles from Denver and the nearest train to Missouri. He wired his father: "Hold funeral without me."

Word did not come until five days later that the track was clear. By then, the unexpected guests at Alpine Tunnel Station had eaten all the food in the larder, fed the engines the coal in the bin to keep them alive, burned the rest of the coal to stay warm, and were making wagers on how long they could hold out.

While Sam was stuck in the blizzard at Alpine Tunnel Station, blizzards were also closing the Highline. By the end of January, the railroad faced thirty-foot-high drifts on Boreas Pass and avalanches in Ten Mile Canon. Westbound trains waited at Como while the rotary and shovelers went to work digging out the track over the pass. On February 5, the first train in three weeks blasted into Breckenridge. The next day, another freight loaded with supplies made its way from Como to Dickey. It was the last train to cross the Highline for seventy-eight days. The mining towns were cut off from food, fuel, feed for the horses and livestock, and supplies of every kind.

With the Ten Mile District locked in snowslides, Leadville was also isolated. Emergency food and supplies, shipped on C&S freights to Grant, were off-loaded and sent into Leadville on horse-drawn sleighs. Not until the first days of April did the storms abate enough for the railroad to attempt to reopen the Highline. For three weeks, the rotary and shovelers chopped through the snow over Boreas Pass. Finally, on April 26, 1899, the first train rolled into Dickey. Sam was at the throttle of the lead locomotive—the 211 (later renumbered the 50), and John Olson was the engineer on the 66, coupled behind. It was another month before the rotary crew cleared the track through Ten Mile Canon and locomotive number 22 on the head of a freight steamed between high banks of snow into Leadville.

One winter several years later, Roy Rash, a Como fireman who later became an engineer on the C&S North End, turned the winter snows to his advantage during a hard trip. Rash had drawn a trip on a freight train to Gunnison with engineer Mike O'Hare, a big, robust Irishman who had gone to work on the DSP&P in 1889, stayed a few years, went booming around the country, and returned in 1902. Making sure the fireman earned every penny of his pay, O'Hare liked to throw open the throttle, drop the Johnson Bar in the corner, and work the engine full blast, setting up a draft that lifted lumps of coal off the firegrate and blew them out the stack. Gases blew out, too, before they could heat the water into steam. O'Hare was not the only South Park engineer who ran the locomotives this way. Curly Colligan and "Hardboiled" G.W. Williamson would also "hang the fireman's hide on the coal gate." No matter how hard the most conscientious fireman worked, he could not keep up with an open throttle and Johnson Bar.

The trip started out as Rash had feared with O'Hare highballing across South Park, throttle wide open, Johnson Bar down, and Rash shoveling as fast as he could. On Trout Creek Pass, Rash had no choice but to speed up, scooping coal, throwing it into the firebox, and scooping it again, swinging back and forth on the deck like a pendulum. All the time, O'Hare kept shouting, "Hurry up, you numbskull. Shovel faster. Get up the steam."

Through Chalk Creek Canon the train rumbled past Romley and Hancock, and on toward the Alpine Tunnel where the snow alongside the track was as high as the deck. When Rash saw the portal ahead, he decided he had had enough. As the engine darted into the tunnel, Rash stepped out of the cab onto the snow. When the caboose came by, he stepped in.

The train rolled out of the tunnel with O'Hare alone in the engine.

He blew the whistle, stopped the train, jumped down and ran back to the caboose with arms flailing, shouting "me fireman, me fireman." He heaved himself into the caboose, tears rolling down his cheeks. "I lost me fireman," he cried. "The poor lad must be laying back there somewhere on the track. Sure and he was the finest lad to ever pick up a shovel. How me heart aches," he moaned.

About then he saw the grin spreading across the conductor's face. He also saw that the man sitting next to the conductor was not the brakeman, but Rash himself, and he went for him, intent on administering the thrashing of a lifetime. But the conductor stepped in the middle, risking his own health to hold off the furious Irishman. With some coaxing, the conductor got Rash to agree to go back to work. But he got no concession from O'Hare, who spent the rest of the trip running the locomotive at full tilt and hollering that Rash was the lousiest fireman ever to pick up a shovel.

When they grew weary of winter, and they often did, Como's railroaders asked for transfers somewhere else in the C&S system. Engineer Dal Tompkins went to work out of Denver. Engineer Jim Morgan moved to Cheyenne to work on the Cheyenne-Wendover line where he was later killed in a wreck. Sam also had the chance to transfer, which would have meant a promotion in terms of working conditions, but he turned it down. Winters were hard on the old South Park, but summers on the Highline and in Chalk Creek Canon were beautiful, and life in Como was good.

CHAPTER NINE

Como Days

Railroading was an all-inclusive way of life that left little time to do other things. When Sam set out on a trip, he had no idea when he would return home, or even where he might be the next day. Bucking the snow, shunting cars at the mines, hauling heavy drags, waiting at stations en route could mean delays of hours, sometimes days, which made it impossible to plan ahead. Railroaders probably missed more holiday, birthday, and anniversary celebrations than any other group of men.

But the very hardships of the job were what they took the most pride in. The lack of routine, the excitement of living at the edge of danger, of never knowing what lay around the next curve, the sense of being a part of some great adventure—all of these things set the railroaders apart, in their minds, from ordinary men doing ordinary work in shops or factories or on farms.

While Como's railroaders were at work, miles down the line, their women coped with the daily chores back home. When the railroaders might find the time to chop the wood or milk the cows was anyone's guess, but the work had to be done and the women did it. They turned out meals day or night, whenever the men appeared. They cared for the children during the long summer days and the dark, cold days of winter. There probably wasn't a housewife in Como who, at one time or another, didn't look up from her chores when the passenger train whistled out of town and wish she could climb aboard.

Even more difficult were the lives of women married to men on the section gangs stationed at Grant, Pine Grove, or Boreas Pass. Each gang had one boss over ten men who worked up and down the line, tamping and replacing ties, tightening bolts, and making sure the track was in good condition. Single men lived in railroad bunkhouses, but married men and their families lived in drafty frame shacks somewhere along the track. While the men moved about, the women saw other people only when the train stopped to throw off the mail or the mail-ordered household goods. Most of the children could only dream of attending school.

Just after the turn of the century, one of the section bosses arrived home to find the shack dark, the fire out, and the children crying and hungry. His wife had flagged down the passenger train earlier in the day and climbed aboard. With no way of caring for the children and keeping his job, he wired an unmarried sister in Denver to "come immediately." The next day, the passenger train stopped long enough for her to disembark and collect her baggage. With the kind of stalwartness the job demanded, she set about the task of keeping the household together.

One day in 1894, Anna, who had married Sam in Boulder and followed him to Como, also climbed aboard the passenger train and rode away, leaving behind a scandal that rocked Park County. She had found the loneliness and isolation of Como, surrounded by the openness of South Park, unbearable. Como was a long way from anywhere, almost a full day from Denver or Leadville, and no one made the trip often. After working every day of the month, railroaders weren't eager to get back on the train on a rare day off.

In the seven years they had lived in Como, Anna and Sam had three children, each of whom had died in infancy. The death of children from such diseases as diphtheria, whooping cough, scarlet fever, and, especially, pneumonia, which descended like a plague over Como's frame houses, was the hardest burden the early railroaders and their wives had to bear. While the men had their work to keep them busy, the women were left at home to cope with grief and depression as best they could.

After the deaths of her children, Anna turned to a group of friends later described in the *Fairplay Flume* as "men and women of doubtful character, to say the least." On Friday evening, April 6, 1894, while Sam was on a freight run to Climax, Anna met her friends at the home of Levi Streeter, long-time Como resident and part-time shoe repairman. Shortly before midnight, the town marshall, A.F. Cook, knocked at Streeter's front door to ask him to hold down the noise of the party, which the *Flume* called a "jollification, quite convivial through partaking of frequent draughts of beer." Throwing open the front door, Streeter fired a revolver at the marshall, hitting him in the head and chest. He fell forward into the room, "his toes resting on the door sill."

Streeter later claimed he thought he was about to be robbed. But Como's townspeople thought otherwise. "There is a strong belief that he suspected his visitor to be Mr. Speas, whose wife was then inside and that, anticipating trouble from the call, he lost no time in taking the initiative."

Word of Marshall Cook's murder spread quickly, even at the quiet hour of midnight. Fearing that a lynch mob would form, Deputy Sheriff Link and Constable Lyons arrested Streeter, hid him in a wagon, and lit out in the dark over the potholed, washboard road for Fairplay.

On Saturday morning, the sheriff and constable also arrested Anna and her friend, Lillian Kennedy Robinson, the only married women at the party without their husbands. In the view of the townspeople, who had insisted on their arrest, this fact made them accessories to murder. Sam pulled into Como later that morning after a seven-hour delay shunting cars at Climax to learn that his wife was in the Fairplay jail, charged with first-degree murder, and that, most likely, he had been the intended victim.

On June 2, in the gray-tone Park County courthouse in Fairplay, Streeter and the two women went on trial for murder. After claiming indigence, Streeter and Lillian were represented by a court-appointed attorney, but Sam hired Webster Ballinger, Park County's most prominent criminal lawyer, to defend Anna. The two women pleaded innocence. They had been in the kitchen when the shots rang out, they said, and had no idea that Streeter intended to shoot anyone. The jury acquitted them, but Streeter was found guilty and sentenced to be hanged at the state penitentiary in Canon City.

On a hot July day four weeks later, Sam returned to Fairplay and, with Webster Ballinger at his side in the same courtroom where Anna had stood trial, requested a divorce. After a short hearing, it was granted. Anna did not appear. Sometime between her acquittal and that July day, she had boarded the passenger train for Denver.

Eighteen months later, Sam was back in the courthouse, this time to marry Ellen O'Leary before the justice of the peace. Like most women who married railroaders, Ellen was part of the railroading world. Her father, Cornelius O'Leary, was among the hordes of Irish immigrants who had laid the track, foot by tedious foot, across the United States. Ellen had been born in Galesburg, Illinois, while Cornelius was laying the Burlington track westward through Illinois. In the early 1880s, the Burlington built into Denver with the tracklayers in the vanguard. By 1883, when Sam arrived in Denver to go to work on the Union Pacific, Cornelius had established his family in the Irish section of west Denver where his children, including Ellen, could go to school.

In the 1890s, Ellen went to work for the Union Pacific as a waitress at Como's Pacific Hotel. Like the famed Harvey Girls, who worked in restaurants along the Santa Fe routes, the women hired by the Union Pacific to work in the railroad's restaurants and hotels were "attractive, intelligent and of good character." Many were daughters of railroaders, and nothing seemed more natural to them than working for the railroad.

At the Pacific Hotel, they scurried about in crisp white aprons over dark serge dresses, waiting tables in the dining room, cooking meals in the kitchen, and cleaning the rooms. They lived in small alcoves tucked under the eaves of the third floor and met suitors in chaperoned parlors. While some may have hoped to attract a railroader with a steady income, which, at the time, made a man seem rich, even the most optimistic young woman probably did not dream of a suitor who had already worked his way up to the lofty position of engineer. But Sam courted Ellen for almost a year, making a point to see her whenever he was in town. After their marriage, she handed in her resignation at the Pacific Hotel and began keeping her own house in the small, clapboard home Sam owned on Broadway. My brother Clarence was born a year later, in 1896. I arrived in 1901, followed by Neil in 1902. With his family growing, Sam moved us into a larger house on the rise overlooking Como, close by the schoolhouse.

Like other wives of railroaders, Ellen found that keeping house in Como was a never-ending job. She hauled buckets of water from the well on washdays—every house had a well on one side and a "chicksale" or outhouse on the other, located so the outhouse wouldn't pollute the well. She stacked coal in the kitchen stove, kept the fire hot, heated the water, and dumped it into a large tin tub. Bending over the washboard hours at a time, she scrubbed the clothes with a vengeance, including Sam's sooty overalls, wrung them by hand, and draped them on lines outdoors to flap dry in the breeze. In winter, she strung the lines through the house and went about her other chores, ducking and weaving through the dripping socks, shirts, and underwear.

Every morning, George Champion, who, with his partner Dave Gwinn, owned Champion-Gwinn Grocery and Market, one of Como's two grocery stores, made his rounds to take orders. In the afternoons, he pulled up in his wagon to deliver the flour, sugar, coffee, and other staple items Ellen usually ordered. Everything else she got through her own efforts. She milked the cow, churned the butter, raised and killed the chickens, tended the vegetable garden during Como's short growing season, and baked a dozen loaves of bread every week, along with our favorite pies and cakes.

As we grew older, we had to help with the chores. We tended to the menagerie of animals we had accumulated—two horses that we rode over South Park, two cows, a henhouse of chickens, and a dog. Each day we filled the kerosene lamps and shined the chimneys until we could see our reflections. We hauled water from the well and brought in the coal and wood for the stoves. The kitchen and dining room stoves burned Baldwin coal which had to be replenished every few hours, but the living room stove burned anthracite, giving off a steady, warm heat days on end. Every day we removed the ashes and dumped them in the ashpit outdoors.

No amount of careful tending of the stoves kept the bedrooms warm during Como's winters. We awoke on dark mornings with the blankets covered by a layer of snow that had sifted through thin cracks in the walls. We jumped out of bed, grabbed the pile of clothing we had carefully set out the night before in anticipation of the icy morning, and ran to the living room to dress in front of the stove. Despite our loud protests, especially in the winter, we took a bath twice a week in the big laundry tub in front of the kitchen stove.

There were times when chores were set aside and Como rolled up its carpets to dance all night. On Saturday nights, everybody in town, along with ranchers from miles around, gathered at the town hall which Sam helped to build in 1908. Someone played the piano, someone else broke out the fiddle, and by 9 p.m., the dance was in full swing while the infants and children slumbered in one corner. At first, oil lanterns lit the hall, but eventually, the Como men installed a sophisticated carbide lighting system. Pencil-thin pipes ran along the walls and ceiling carrying the carbide (acetylene) gas to the lamps. Sooner or later, at every dance, someone would call for a moonlight waltz and turn off the carbide lights. Since they were easier to turn off than on, the rest of the dance was usually by candlelight.

At dawn, the women laid out supper. It was always a feast of baked hams and chickens, roast beef, scalloped potatoes, salads, cakes, and pies. By the time the dance ended, the sun was rising and the dancers could see their way home over the rough wagon roads.

Como's residents also liked to get together at one another's homes. Engineers, who had reached the highest rung on the railroading ladder, socialized mainly with one another, often gathering around our kitchen table to "railroad" and relive their trips and the dangers they had faced. Among my father's close friends were Buddy Schwartz, big and good-natured, with gold coins jangling in his pockets and shoe laces always untied; John Olson, who had fired for Sam in Chalk Creek before being set up to engineer; Walt Parlin, whose family owned Parlin Ranch on the west side of the Alpine Tunnel; Al Kroll, who had worked the helpers out of Schwanders before moving up to a job on the mainline; and George "Jumbo" Miller, second on the seniority list behind Dick O'Herne and one notch above Sam.

One day Sam and his engineer friends met the freight train from Denver and off-loaded a huge crate. After wrestling it onto the wagon, Sam drove the team while the engineers ran alongside, balancing the crate, as the wagon squealed and creaked through town. At our front door, they lifted the crate off the wagon and shoved it into the front room where they peeled it away, revealing a fine Everett piano Sam had ordered from Chicago for Ellen. The arrival of a new piano in any small railroading town was always an important event, and ours was no different. Everyone came to see and hear the new piano. Ellen plunked out the lively tunes she had learned during her schooldays, and the neighbors sang along. Sometimes they rolled up the carpet and danced about the room. The piano became a favorite source of entertainment in Como.

So was J.A. (Al) Zingheim's one-cylinder, one-seater Brush, Como's first automobile. One summer day, Zingheim, who had been set up to engineer at the age of twenty-one, drove into town and roared up and down Como's roads in this new contraption with the engine, located under the seat, connected to the rear wheels by a chain drive. Since there was no muffler, the noise brought everyone outdoors to see what was going on. Soon every kid in town was running alongside.

All that summer, the kids hung around, waiting for Zingheim to back the Brush out of the shed where he kept it and propel it around town. About the farthest it went was the ten-mile trip to Fairplay or Jefferson, and then it was lucky to get back. Even around Como, it had a way of stopping dead in the middle of the road, requiring the kids to push it back into the shed.

Summers were special in Como, with lots of picnics at the old Martin Ranch in the foothills outside town—the grass and trees surrounding the empty ranch house were the closest Como came to a park. Ellen packed the picnic lunches and we walked to the ranch with her friends and their children. Sometimes Ed and Hepsia Pike and their daughters, Ethel and May, pulled up in front of our house in a wagon drawn by two white horses. Then we rode in style alongside Terryall Creek to a shady, grassy picnic spot in the foothills.

The C&S sponsored excursion trains for employees in the summers, even though the all-day trip to Gunnison was a one-time event. Usually, excursions went to Heywood Springs at the foot of Chalk Creek Canon. (Later, it was known as Mount Princeton Hot Springs.) The engines huffed and steamed on the siding while the Como townspeople hiked, picnicked, and swam in the hot springs pool. In September 1908, the C&S ran an excursion train to Pitkin where the Como baseball team was handed a sound defeat by the Pitkin team—90 to 10. Often Sam was the engineer on the excursions, which meant he got to enjoy the fun.

In the rare hours he was free, with an afternoon or summer evening stretching ahead before he had to go on a trip, he would shoulder his Winchester rifle and take us tramping across South Park or into the foothills to hunt rabbits. After years of railroading's hard work and long hours, he was strong and powerful, like the locomotives he ran over the mountains. He could tramp over the rough, broken terrain hours on end while we hurried to keep up. And he was a dead shot, always bringing back enough rabbits for a pot of stew.

The long summer days in Como made up for the winters that descended with a vengeance. It snowed and snowed and snowed in South Park, and when we thought the heavens had emptied it, it snowed some more. Temperatures plunged below zero and stayed there week after week. The winds howled continually, piling snow against our house until, at times, we had to dig our way out the front door and across the porch. But there were days when the sun broke through, bathing the whole town in warmth and turning everything dazzling white.

Like the railroad, life went on as usual, no matter the weather. The railroaders went to work, Champion and Gwinn made their rounds, their wagon sleighs squeaking over the snow, the town hall lit up on Saturday nights, and the kids went to school, even on days when mothers had to prop open the doors and throw their offspring into the storm.

Community affairs went on year-round too. Engineers, who thought of themselves as leading citizens, played an important role in keeping Como an active and interesting town. They helped to organize the volunteer fire department, baseball clubs, and the Como band that performed in the bandshell on summer evenings. They were active in politics. In 1902, Sam was elected town trustee and, in 1904, having had a taste of public office, he was elected to the school board.

Like all railroaders in Como, Sam was a strong booster of the school. With little time or opportunity for school themselves, the railroaders made sure that their children got an education. What's more, Como was a town of immigrants—Nelson and Olson from Sweden, Champion from England, O'Hare from Ireland, and my mother, the daughter of Irish immigrants—people who saw education as a way for their children to better themselves.

Como's one-room schoolhouse was divided by the center coal stove that threw heat to both sides. On one side were the first four grades, taught by Miss Minnie Holthusen. On the other side were grades five through eight, taught by W.C. Myer, who was also the principal. A few fourteen- and fifteen-year-old boys who had finished the eighth grade but were too young or too small to work on the railroad stayed with the older group for "postgraduate" work. Since there was no high school in Como, kids who went to high school usually boarded with railroading families in Buena Vista or Leadville.

When I was in fifth grade, a pitched battle broke out between the principal and two boys in the upper grades, Bruno and Kirk Dittman. We were busy working over our slates when the first angry words flew about the room. The principal took after Bruno with a rubber hose, and ink wells started flying too. Kirk hit a bullseye on the principal's forehead. With ink dripping down his face, the principal took the rubber hose after Kirk and, in a flash, books, overshoes, and everything else not nailed down went sailing around, while the younger kids ducked under the desks out of the way. The principal finally subdued the two brothers and ordered them to pack their books. They were expelled.

Two hours later, down the road they came, with heads bowed. Behind them marched their father, Herman Dittman, a machinist in the shops. Into the school room and straight to the principal's platform they went, while we held our breaths.

"Mister Professor," said Herman, "I bring my boys back, and I want you to put them back in school. My boys apologize to you, Mister Professor, and to the school. Don't you, boys?"

"Yes, father," they said.

"Myself, I left Germany because I was like a slave there. I couldn't go to school. I came to the United States to be free, and so my boys could go to school. They want to be good citizens of our adopted country. Don't you, boys?"

"Yes, father," they said.

"My boys will never give you more trouble," Herman said. "Will you, boys?"

"No, father," they said.

The principal, with ink stains still on his shirt and coat, agreed to let Bruno and Kirk back into school. Years later, the two brothers became engineers on the Union Pacific in Wyoming.

The first Sam Speas was twenty-six years old in 1883 when he boarded the Kansas Pacific passenger train in Kansas City, Missouri, to go railroading in Colorado. *S.F. Speas collection.*

The number 42, a Mason Bogie 2-6-6T with a diamond stack, pauses at Webster in Platte Canon while a Denver, South Park and Pacific freight train rounds Lookout Point on Kenosha Pass. *W.H. Jackson photo. R.A. Ronzio collection.*

The railroads tied together Colorado's remote settlements. A standard gauge Denver, Texas and Gulf passenger train stops for water at Elbert, Colorado, about 1885. *E.J. Haley collection.*

A freight train poses on the ninety-six-foot Devils Gate Viaduct, the highest trestle on the Georgetown Loop. *W.H. Jackson photo. E.J. Haley collection.*

Trains in Clear Creek Canon lumbered uphill at a top speed of fifteen miles per hour and crawled downgrade at five miles per hour. *R.A. Ronzio collection.*

The crew on locomotive number 44. Al Russell, firema; Harvey Greaves, engineer; and John Wale, brakeman, paused for this photograph at the Hidden Treasure Mill near Black Hawk, about 1900. *Mrs. George Lundberg collection.*

In the 1890s, a standard gauge passenger train gets ready to pull out of the Boulder depot at Ninth and Water streets. The third rail in the track was used by the narrow gauge Greeley, Salt Lake and Pacific trains. *J.B. Sturtevant photo. E.J. Haley collection.*

Fireman Sam Speas and Squire Thorne, engineer, are shown on the number 10, "the 10-spot," at Sunset, about 1886. *S.F. Speas collection.*

Sam Speas, *center front,* poses with the rest of the crew and the passengers on an excursion train at Horse Shoe Curve below Sunset on Sunday, August 1, 1886. *J.B. Sturtevant photo. E.J. Haley collection.*

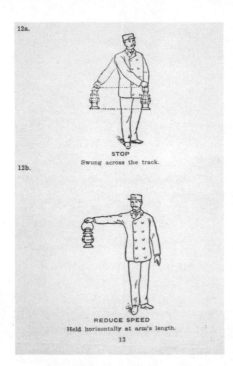

STOP
Swung across the track.

REDUCE SPEED
Held horizontally at arm's length.

13

The locomotive engineer's examination covered hundreds of hand and lamp signals. *S.F. Speas collection.*

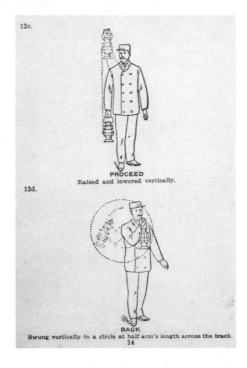

PROCEED
Raised and lowered vertically.

BACK
Swung vertically in a circle at half arm's length across the track.

14

Kenosha Station, almost exactly halfway between Denver and Leadville on the DSP&P, stood at the top of Kenosha Pass. *H.H. Buckwalter photo. R.A. Ronzio collection.*

Denver, Leadville and Gunnison locomotive number 272, with engineer James Duffy in the cab, is shown in 1897 on the "armstrong" turntable, named by the railroaders who said that it took two men with strong arms to turn the table. *Lewis Jewell photo. Marjorie Oshier Garcia collection.*

The number 205 stopped for this photo at Rocky Point Cut on Boreas Pass. *S.F. Speas collection.*

Locomotive 217 waits on a trestle on the Highline, a short distance from Leadville. Brakemen often ran along the top of moving cars to set the brakes. *W.H. Jackson photo. R.A. Ronzio collection.*

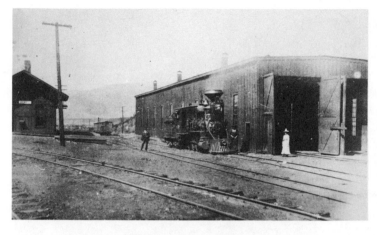

The Dickey station and two-stall engine house around 1901. *R.A. Ronzio collection.*

A Denver, Leadville and Gunnison freight heading toward Kokomo stops in Robinson, the Ten Mile District's largest town, in 1896. *R.A Ronzio collection.*

Coaches on the Denver, Leadville and Gunnison were fine affairs, with wood paneling, red plush seats, green-painted ceilings, ornate lamps, clerestories, and two coal stoves. *M.C. Poor photo. E.J. Haley collection.*

Charlie Girardin, brakeman, and Fatty Johnson, another South Park railroader, pose at Schwanders in 1902. Note the missing finger in Girardin's glove. Railroaders said that you could tell how long a man had been a brakeman by the number of fingers he had left. *George Champion photo*.

The number 36 stops at Hancock on its way to the Alpine Tunnel and Gunnison sometime before 1885. *Joseph Collier photo. R.A. Ronzio collection.*

Locomotive 199 pulls out of the west portal of Alpine Tunnel after the 1895 reopening. *R.A. Ronzio collection.*

The daily eastbound mixed train climbs past the Palisades toward the west portal of the Alpine Tunnel. *Otto Westerman photo. George Champion collection.*

The Colorado and Southern number 9 on the turntable at Como, about 1918. Ernie Anderson, the hostler, leans from the cab. *Left to right:* Brownie Anderson, Tom Gibbony, Joe Delaney, Mike Talbot, John Murray, and John Auers. *George Champion photo.*

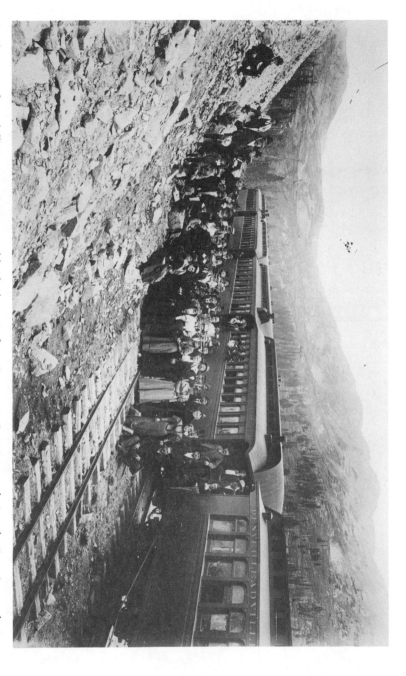

For the sum of ten dollars, excursionists could ride the train from Denver to Gunnison and view the "scenic wonders of mountainside and meadow." These excursionists pose at Atlantic siding, near the east portal of the Alpine Tunnel, in about 1898. *H.H. Buckwalter photo. R.A. Ronzio collection.*

C-1 Pacific Hotel at Como in 1886. Burned Nov. 9, 1896

Some of the white-aproned young women who worked at the Pacific Hotel in Como stand on the veranda in 1886. *George E. Mellon photo. Mary Dyer collection.*

The rotary churns through a cloud of snow as it clears the track at Climax. *Climax Molybdenum Company collection.*

CHAPTER TEN

Wreck on the Line

When the telegraph lines buzzed with the message, "wreck on the line," word spread quickly and everything stopped in Como. Women, children, and those railroaders who happened to be in town hurried to the dispatcher's office for news, hoping their husbands, fathers, sons, and brothers were safe.

Railroaders lived with constant danger. Engineers and firemen operated mobile steam plants with as much as 180 pounds of pressure capable of blowing as high as the mountaintop if not operated properly. Brakemen ran the chance of smashing fingers, hands, arms, and legs every time they coupled or uncoupled a car, or of falling from the top of a train as it rolled along. Equipment could break down at any moment—wheels could crack, brakes fail, and the ball on the rail break—and suddenly, the train would buck off-track and tumble down the mountainside.

Not all wrecks on the narrow gauge were serious, however. Most were minor, resulting in delays and damaged equipment. On one hot July night, Sam was running an extra freight from Como to Denver. At the Eleventh Street yard, he pulled the train onto one of the three-rail tracks built to handle both narrow and broad gauge trains. With the switchman waving him on, he rolled forward slowly. Suddenly, one side of the locomotive

hit the ground beyond the end of the third rail. The wrecking crew had
to jack up the locomotive to pull it back on track, delaying the departure
time for the return trip to Como. Sam was suspended for twenty days.

Not long after the turn of the century, Frank Root, my seven-
teen-year-old cousin who had hired on the C&S as a brakeman in Como,
was working on a freight train to Gunnison. The engineer was a boomer,
unfamiliar with the route, but he was familiar with the new coal chutes
at Pine, Como, Dickey, and Pitkin. To take on coal at these stations, the
engineer ran the locomotive on track alongside the chute and spotted the
tender at one of the chute pockets. Coal was shoveled out of coal cars
and into the chutes from the other side where track ran up an incline as
steep as a 7 percent grade. Locomotives pushed the coal cars into place
for unloading. To do this, they would haul the cars far enough down track,
away from the chute, to get up enough speed to shove the cars up the
incline. The engineer had to judge how fast to go in order to set the cars
exactly in place, without pushing them off the end of the track. As soon
as the cars rolled over the crest, the engineer set the brakes.

Except for the chute at Pitkin, the new C&S chutes were built with
the coaling track on the line grade and the loading track on the elevated
grade. But since the main line ran downhill into Pitkin, the loading track
was not on an incline as steep as the incline at other stations, a fact no
one had thought to tell the boomer engineer. With orders to push two
coal cars onto the loading track, he took the cars down track a distance,
threw open the throttle, and started full blast for a steep incline. The
conductor realized the engineer's mistake and frantically waved the red
lantern to stop. Frank also saw what was happening and jumped from the
tender. The coal cars sailed along the track next to the chute, demolished
the bumper block, flew off the end, and flipped over, spilling coal
everywhere.

"What do you think you're doing?" the conductor yelled to the engineer, who had managed to stop the locomotive before it toppled off the
track.

"Pushing cars up the incline," he yelled back. "Where is it?"

Since the company did not accept excuses for running out of track,
the boomer engineer was fired.

On another occasion, Sam was at the throttle of the number 70, pulling a freight through Blue River valley at fifteen miles per hour, one and
one-half miles above the speed limit. When he pulled into Dickey several
minutes ahead of schedule, the stationmaster wired the dispatcher, who
informed the superintendent, who notified Sam that he was suspended.
Still another time he was suspended for ten days for running engine 40
into the 61 as it was taking on water at Baker's Tank on Boreas Pass. The

fact that railroaders received no pay while suspended gave them powerful incentives to obey the rules and do the best job possible when they got back to work.

Railroads used the "brownie" system—black marks on the railroader's record—to keep track of rules violations. If a railroader accumulated 100 brownies, he was through as a railroader—fired and probably blackballed. The company also gave credit marks for good behavior that offset the brownies. Sam got credits for such things as putting out a fire in a Boreas snowshed and for only one delay of his train in a year.

The company also held railroaders responsible for broken parts. If any part on the locomotive broke down en route, the company considered the engineer at fault. He had not checked it carefully enough before starting out. Repair costs were deducted from the railroader's pay. Sam once had thirty dollars deducted every month for three months to cover the cost of repairing a wheel that happened to crack on his locomotive.

From the company's point of view, carelessness and rules violations led to accidents, and accidents translated into red ink in the financial ledgers. Crumpled locomotives, splintered and twisted cars, delays, and loss of business were unnecessary expenses the company meant to avoid. In the days before workmen's compensation, disability pensions, or pensions of any kind, it was more expensive to replace a wrecked boxcar than a dead engineer or a maimed brakeman.

The company was concerned about its equipment, but the railroaders were concerned about staying alive. Most railroaders in Como had minor accidents at one time or another, but they did everything in their power to avoid major wrecks. They followed a simple rule: watch everything. They also developed a strong sense of danger and played their hunches. On one trip in the winter of 1905, Sam pulled into Dickey late at night with a three-engine freight. After placing the train in the siding, the locomotives took turns at the water tank before backing down to the boardinghouse where the crews were to eat dinner. Sam took the last turn at the tank. He watched the fireman climb onto the tender, pull down the long, heavy spout, fill the tank, and jump off. When he did not climb back into the cab, Sam decided he had walked to the boardinghouse.

Sam released the engine's brakes, moved the Johnson Bar into reverse, and started backing up. Suddenly, a sense of danger came over him. It was so strong, he told me later, that he could feel the hair bristling on the nape of his neck. He set the air, brought the engine to a jerky stop, and jumped from the cab. Walking back alongside the tender, he found the fireman, sprawled unconscious across the track where he had fallen. Sam had stopped the tender only a few inches away.

No matter how sensitive railroaders were to danger, or how careful, things had a way of happening so fast that they had no chance to react. That was the case in 1909 when Sam got a call to run locomotive 55 light to Breckenridge to help push an eastbound freight over Boreas Pass. He pulled out of Como at 1 p.m. Just beyond Peabody's Curve, the ball of the rail snapped under the locomotive, flipping it off-track and down the mountainside. With no time to "join the birds," Sam and the fireman rode the 55 downhill, tumbling end over end in a kind of slow motion. A flying wrench caught Sam in the head, knocking him unconscious. When he came to, he was slumped in a corner of the upended engine, with its sides smashed, stack sheered off, and steam pulsing in the boiler.

Knowing the danger of broken pipes spraying steam around the engine cab, the fireman was frantic to get himself and Sam out of the wreckage, but his finger was wedged in the door and he couldn't free it. In desperation, he took out a pocket knife and cut off his own finger. He helped Sam out of the engine, and the two of them made their way up the mountainside, following the track back to town.

We had just sat down for dinner when the back door opened and Dad walked in, face white except for the blue knot rising on his forehead. Before he could say anything, mother and the three of us boys jumped up and threw our arms around him, sensing he had come close to death.

In 1914, fireman Fred Hunn was trapped when the locomotive on passenger train 70 collided head-on with a Fish Train outside Denver. The engineer managed to crawl free, but Hunn was scalded to death.

The previous year, engineer J.T. Duffy, who worked in the Clear Creek District, met the same fate. He was running engine 69 on the head of a passenger train out of Black Hawk when the ball broke on the rail, pitching the locomotive off-track. It rolled downhill, broken pipes shooting steam into the engine. The fireman jumped. Unable to get out, Duffy was scalded to death.

When a locomotive or cars derailed and rolled down the mountainside on the South Park, it was up to the wrecking boss, Patrick Gibbony, and his crew to set them back on track. Using the power of another locomotive, a pulley, and heavy cables, the crew pulled the derailed cars up the mountainside and maneuvered them back on track. But to get the 55 or any other locomotive up the mountainside, they first had to build a temporary shoofly track downhill. They jacked up the locomotive, pushed it onto the temporary track, and, with the power of the locomotive above, pulled it up to the main track. From there, they pushed it to the shops in Como.

While derailments were sudden, with no time for the railroaders to think, runaways provided moments of sheer terror. Not knowing whether the brakes would grab, engineers faced the challenge of their lives trying to hold a train with sixteen loaded ore cars on the 4.9 percent grades of the South Park.

When they did not grab, the train ran away, pushing the locomotive ahead, faster and faster, until finally it derailed at a curve and pulled the train behind, cars toppling about. There wasn't an engineer on the South Park who didn't have a runaway sometime in his career. Most were lucky to stop the train before it wrecked.

Runaway trains that shot down Kenosha, Fremont, or Boreas passes, or out from the Alpine Tunnel, were like the one I rode out of Black Hawk in 1921 when I was firing C&S narrow gauge steamers in the Clear Creek District. After picking up sixteen loaded ore cars in Black Hawk, the engineer whistled for retainers—or partial—brakes before we started out. Not far from Black Hawk, the train started gathering speed down an almost 4 percent grade. The engineer set the air, but the brakes didn't grab. With the train accelerating, he whistled for the brakemen to set the hand brakes, and hollered to me, "Join the birds. I'll try to stop her."

On the right side, the trees and boulders were close enough to touch, while on the other side, the mountain dropped away. I decided that my best chance lay in helping to slow the galloping train. I climbed onto the tender and jumped to the first ore car, where I wound the brake as tightly as I could. Each car had one hand brake that worked all the wheel brakes. As I jumped to the second car, I could see the conductor and brakemen wobbling on the tops of the rear cars, setting the brakes. By the time I had wound the brake on the third car, they had set the rest, and the train began to slow. They plopped down on the top of the fourth car, legs dangling over the edge, and wiped the sweat from their faces while I made my way back to the engine cab where the engineer was puffing on his pipe, as if nothing had happened.

Not all runaways ended with the engineer puffing on his pipe. Railroaders in Como never stopped talking about the freight that ran away and piled up at the foot of Trout Creek Pass in 1884, killing four railroaders from Como. Nor did they forget the other wrecks that claimed the lives of their friends.

One occurred September 22, 1901, on Kenosha Pass, injuring seventeen passengers and fatally injuring a railroad laborer, W.A. Phillips, and a young engineer, thirty-two-year-old Webster Ballinger, Jr., son of South Park's prominent attorney. Not long before, Ballinger had been set up to engineer after working fourteen years as a fireman, often firing for Sam. He had celebrated the promotion by announcing his engagement to May Pike, his schooldays sweetheart.

Ballinger was at the throttle of the locomotive on mixed train 82, due in Denver at 7 a.m. About 2 a.m., the train ran away on the east slope of

Kenosha Pass. Even though Ballinger set the air and whistled for brakes, the brakes did not hold. The speeding train derailed, piling up nine cars loaded with ore and lumber. It was late the following afternoon before a rescue train from Denver reached the site and brought the injured to a Denver hospital. Ballinger died in the hospital.

In October 1907, engineer Jinx Thomas left Leadville with the 54 on the head of a freight. Engineer Buddy Schwartz, running the 55, had pushed the train to the top of Fremont Pass and into a siding. Since a light engine could go faster than a train, Schwartz started downhill first and Thomas followed. As the train rolled downgrade, it began to pick up speed. Seeing it gaining from behind, Schwartz set the air, holding the 55 to a slow, steady crawl, hoping to slow the train. Instead, the runaway train hit the 55, derailing it. The train then plunged ahead, missed a curve, and turned over. Schwartz was unhurt, but Jinx Thomas was dead. He had lived all his life in Como and was one of five brothers who worked on the railroad.

Two years later, on March 19,1909, Schwartz lost his life in a replay of the accident. This time, he was on the 41 at the head of a freight train pounding down the east side of Boreas Pass with the light engine running ahead. Near Halfway at milepost 93, the center of a seven-mile stretch of sharp curves, some of which were twenty degrees, the train ran away, overtook the light engine, and pushed it off-track. Plummeting downgrade, the 41 sailed off-track at a curve and turned over, with the train piling up behind.

Buddy Schwartz was Sam's close friend. They had fired together as young men on the Clear Creek and had come to the South Park at the same time. He had been set up to engineer in 1888. Shortly before he was killed, Buddy was on a helper engine pushing a freight Sam was running over Boreas Pass. Sam came in from a long, tiring trip, furious with his friend. "I can pull the train," he stormed, "but I can't pull the helper too. I'm through with Buddy," he announced to Ellen, "and I don't want you to see Clara anymore either." Buddy's wife, Clara, and Ellen were also close friends.

"Wait a minute," Ellen replied. "You and Buddy will have to leave your locomotives in the roundhouse. Don't bring them up here in my kitchen. There isn't enough room."

Sam started laughing, and since he could never remember why he was angry with anybody, he and Buddy were soon good friends again.

Everyone in Como attended Buddy's funeral. The Methodist Church overflowed with mourners, and others stood on the outside stoop and gathered under the open windows, silently listening to the services. Afterward, townspeople rode in a long procession of horse-drawn buggies following the hearse with its curtains drawn to the cemetery outside town.

CHAPTER ELEVEN

The Union Men

In 1905, after wrestling freights over the mountains for eighteen years, Sam had enough seniority to take the Leadville passenger run. He left Como every other day at 1:35 p.m. with three coaches and a baggage car and pulled into Leadville five hours later. The next morning he brought the eastbound passenger to Como. Barring sudden blizzards, derailments, or other surprises, he arrived at 1:10 p.m.

He was not through working, however. During the afternoon and evening, and late into the night, he ran the helper engines, pushing freights over Boreas Pass. Often the sun was up and a new day underway before he trudged home, weary from working twenty hours or more and being away from home thirty-six hours.

The long hours railroaders worked did not concern the railroad companies. At the turn of the century, almost every laborer worked from dawn to sunset. In Colorado, it was common for miners, smelterers, bricklayers, brewers, and other laborers to work from seventy-eight to ninety-eight hours each week for thirty-five cents per hour, top wages. Every industry operated under the "natural laws of business," which held that the purchaser of services determined the terms of the job and the pay. It was up to the seller to decide how much or how little he would accept. Under these natural laws, railroaders, like other laborers, had no choices. If they wanted to work, they had to accept the terms and pay offered.

On May 8, 1907, engineer John Olson found out how all-inclusive the terms could be when he was called for a special train. Consisting of two private cars, the train carried President Trumbull and other C&S officials on an inspection tour. From Como, Olson and the fireman ran the train over the Highline to Leadville, returned to Como, and continued to Gunnison. At every station and siding on the route, Trumbull and the officials inspected the facilities. When the train went into sidings for the night, Olson and the fireman slept in the open engine cab. They ate hurried meals in boardinghouses and hotels along the way, while the officials stayed warm and well fed in the private cars. By the time the train pulled into Como, the crew had been gone seven days.

Instead of letting them off duty, the dispatcher ordered Olson and the fireman to stay with the train. Off they went, through South Park, over Kenosha Pass, and down Platte Canon, stopping again at every station. At Waterton, Trumbull told Olson to take the train to Silica, where sand and gravel pits were located. When Trumbull saw two loaded cars on the siding, waiting for a freight to haul them to Denver, he ordered Olson to couple in the cars. Even though Olson protested that it would be dangerous for the locomotive to haul the heavy cars downgrade to Denver, he knew he had to comply or lose his job. He coupled in the cars and the train rolled toward Denver.

When they pulled into Denver Union Station, Olson and the fireman had been on the job two weeks, with only snatches of rest. Finally off duty, they spent the night at a hotel on Seventeenth Street, at their own expense, and caught the morning passenger train to Como.

When engineers protested long hours on duty, they suffered the fate of engineer J.C. Downing. After a thirty-three-hour trip, Downing had just gotten home and sunk into bed when the caller knocked at his door. He refused to take another trip before he had slept a few hours, and for that refusal, he was fired.

More than any other issue, long working hours drove railroaders, along with other laborers, into unions. In Colorado, union membership tripled in the last decade of the nineteenth century. Railroad unions grew from 1,856 members in 1888 to 6,772 members in 1911.

Nineteen different unions represented Colorado's railroaders. Each craft had its own union—track repairmen, mechanics, sleeping car porters, pipe fitters, sheet metal workers, and carpenters. (Eventually craft unions affiliated with the United Transportation Union or with the AFL-CIO.) Switchmen joined the Switchman's Union of North America (SUNA), and conductors belonged to the Order of Railway Conductors.

The Brotherhood of Locomotive Engineers (BLE) represented railroaders who worked only as engineers. Originally called the Brotherhood of the Footboard, it was railroading's oldest union, founded in 1863 after a superintendent on the Michigan Central cut wages and fired anyone who protested. The Brotherhood of Locomotive Firemen and Enginemen, founded in 1873, represented both firemen and those engineers still working occasionally as firemen.

The brotherhoods were modeled on fraternal organizations. Since railroaders could not get insurance because of their hazardous occupation, the first thing the brotherhoods did was set up life insurance programs for their members. They also established welfare funds to help the widows and orphans of railroaders and the members crippled on the job, none of whom received compensation from the railroad companies.

The BLE also negotiated engineers' contracts with companies, covering rights to run and rates of pay, and provided support to engineers who were powerless to deal with the companies on their own. It was the brotherhood that, in the 1880s, forced railroad companies to pay engineers and firemen on the basis of mileage. Before that, first-class engineers had received higher wages than newly promoted engineers, who got two-thirds pay the first year and five-sixths pay the second year. To keep labor costs down, railroad companies routinely fired engineers as soon as they reached first-class status.

Like other railroaders in Colorado, engineers in Como were strong union men. They had belonged to the BLF&E until 1895 when the dues collector left town with the annual dues. At that time, they joined the BLE as the Highline District branch of Denver Lodge 186. Sam was elected the new union dues collector and organizer, a job he held twelve years.

Railroaders wanted the same things as other laborers—shorter working days and safer working conditions. But, unlike other laborers, they pursued their goals with quiet, persistent patience. Between 1893 and 1904, labor strikes erupted in Colorado at the mines in Leadville, Cripple Creek, Victor, Telluride, Idaho Springs, in the coalfields of Fremont, Las Animas, and Huerfano counties, and in the smelters of Denver, Golden, and Colorado City. Yet, there were no railroad strikes in Colorado in that same period.

One reason for peace on the railroads was the conservative nature of the brotherhoods. "Talk, talk, talk" was the unofficial motto of the BLE, which always tried to settle differences by arbitration. Only when railroad officials refused to talk with union leaders would the unions consider calling a strike. From Cleveland, Ohio, the brotherhood's national officers kept in touch with railroad labor problems across the country. At the turn of the century, the grand chief of the BLE was P.M. Arthur, a white-haired, respected engineer who had worked on the New York Central and Hudson River Railroad twenty-two years. Arthur alone held the authority to call a strike of engineers, an authority he used reluctantly.

Part of that reluctance came from the fact that strikes seldom led to the desired results. Companies hired scabs, leaving the strikers unemployed and cooling their heels at the company gates. When Midwestern railroaders went on strike in support of workers at the Pullman plant in Chicago, railroad companies fired the strikers and hired new employees. The Burlington went so far as to import new engineers from England.

In Colorado, strikes brought out the National Guard to "protect the public order." What the troops protected was the right of companies to refuse to negotiate with unions, to fire strikers, and to import new workers. Troops went to Cripple Creek in 1893, to Leadville in 1896, to Telluride in 1904, and back to Cripple Creek that year where they rounded up 238 union ringleaders, put them into boxcars, and sent them to the plains of Kansas. Troops also went to Ludlow in 1914 where they fired on the striking coal miners and their families, killing four men, three women, and eleven children. In the end, strikes were settled in favor of the companies, a fact that strengthened the railroading unions' determination to negotiate.

Each year, the engineers in Como helped to elect a committee to negotiate grievances with company officials in Denver. After the turn of the century, the committee represented engineers in the eight C&S districts —the Wyoming, Fort Collins, Clear Creek, Pueblo, Denver, Trinidad, Canon, and Highline. Committee members laid off their jobs—a risky business that often meant dismissal. In each district, the dues collector took up a collection to help offset the committee's expenses in Denver and the loss of wages.

In July 1900, a committee of level-headed, respected senior engineers arrived in Denver to take up grievances with the newly formed C&S. General chairman was W.W. Hall, an engineer in the Canon District from 1886. George Gray, who had worked in Pueblo since 1891, was the secretary, and Thomas O'Neil, a Trinidad engineer since 1889, was the third committee member.

On July 3 and 4, they met at the Kittredge Building with BLF&E committee members to decide on the joint issues they would discuss with the company. Among those issues were schedule revisions, higher wages for firemen on broad gauge runs, and higher wages for South Park engineers, who made $3.40 per 100 miles compared to $4.00 paid broad gauge engineers.

On July 5, with issues at hand, the committee called upon Charles Dyer, superintendent of the C&S, and requested a meeting. Since negotiations could be costly to railroad companies, officials preferred to avoid them. Knowing that would lead to a strike, they made a practice of stalling union members as long as possible, hoping that heavy expenses would dissuade them and send them home.

Dyer began to stall, explaining he could not see the union men until July 9 at 10 a.m. The committee returned to the Kittredge Building and debated whether to go home or wait in Denver. Even though four days in Denver hotels would run up their costs, it was not long enough for Gray and O'Neil to travel home and return. They voted to stay and map out their strategy.

Promptly at 10 a.m. on July 9, they returned to Dyer's office, but the superintendent was nowhere to be found. His secretary claimed no knowledge of any scheduled meeting, but A.L. Humphrey, superintendent of motive power, agreed to see the committee. "Everything pertaining to his department was settled," Gray reported. Unfortunately, none of the major grievances pertained to his department.

On July 10, Dyer sent a letter to the committee explaining he could not see them before July 13. No mention was made of the missed meeting the day before. By now the union men had been away from home eight days, but they decided to stay in Denver until July 13. In the meantime, they met with the union men from the Colorado Midland and the Denver and Rio Grande to discuss the ways those railroads handled grievances.

On July 13 and 14, Dyer finally met with the committee. After long hours of wrangling, he agreed to minor schedule revisions but refused to grant pay increases. Only Trumbull could grant raises, he claimed, but he promised to take up the matter with the president and let the committee know the decision.

All day July 15, the committee waited for word from Dyer. The next day, they finally heard that Trumbull had refused any pay raises. The committee then trudged to Trumbull's office, past his secretary, and into his presence, only to be told they would have to deal with Dyer. Back they went to see Dyer, who told them he could not meet again until July 23.

By now, officials had stalled the union men nearly three weeks, while conceding minor schedule revisions at no cost to the railroad. With expenses mounting, the union men decided to dig in for a long battle over pay raises. They voted to stay in Denver at their own expense so as not "to work a hardship on the members."

On July 23, the union men traipsed back to Dyer's office to hear him insist that Trumbull alone could grant raises. He promised to bring up the matter again with Trumbull and told the committee to return the next day at 9 a.m.

But the next day, he sent a message that Trumbull "had left Denver and was not expected back until tomorrow." The committee waited two

days for word from Dyer. Finally, in the late afternoon of July 26, they
sent a messenger to Dyer's office. The messenger returned with news that
Dyer had left town that morning. They sent the messenger back to Dyer's
clerk to request a meeting as soon as he returned. The following day the
committee learned that Dyer and Trumbull had gone to Texline and would
not return for several days.

At this point, the committee faced the fact that the company did not
want to negotiate. Aware that the company's refusal would be reason for
the BLE to consider a strike, they decided to give Dyer one more chance
before telegraphing Grand Chief Arthur in Cleveland.

On July 30, Dyer sent word that he would see the committee at 10 a.m.
When they arrived, he told them to return at 2 p.m. At the afternoon meeting, Dyer, probably realizing he had stalled long enough, agreed to discuss wages. The rest of the afternoon and into the evening, he haggled
with the committee over pay raises for the firemen and engineers. Finally,
he agreed to give firemen on the consolidated broad gauge engines a raise
but said he would have to think about raises for the South Park engineers.
He told the committee to return the next day at 10 a.m.

When they came to his office the next morning, he said he was too
busy to see them and suggested they come back in the afternoon. They
returned and, once again, demanded better wages for the South Park engineers. Later that evening, Dyer finally granted what secretary Gray termed
"a slight pay raise of ten cents per 100 miles." After twenty-eight days,
negotiations were closed.

In 1902, another BLE committee spent forty-two days trying to arrange
meetings with Dyer and Trumbull. Refusing to leave Denver until officials
met with them, they were able to negotiate a $7,500 collective raise for
the ninety-seven engineers on the C&S, amounting to seventy-seven dollars
per engineer per year.

In 1903, another grievance committee brought up minor issues that,
if corrected, would make the engineer's life easier. This committee
included two of the C&S's oldest engineers—W.H. Brown, who had gone
to work on the Clear Creek in 1881 and was one of the first engineers
Sam had fired for, and A.H. Scott, a Fort Collins engineer since 1879. They
asked the company to rehire several engineers fired for insubordination
and to rehire J.C. Downing, fired for refusing to make a trip without rest.
They also wanted the engine cabs lined with wood, passes for BLE members, a halt to the practices of giving brownies without investigations,
sending insulting messages to engineers on the road, and pulling engines
out of service without sufficient cause. In the days when engineers had
their own engines, they didn't work when the engines went into the shop.

By now, Dyer had been replaced by Superintendent Dolan who, after going through the usual stalling maneuvers, proved more openhanded. He ordered wood installed on the right side of the cabs to keep ice from building up on the metal walls and ordered boxes built around the Johnson Bars to cut down on drafts. He reinstated the engineers, with the exception of Downing who had refused to go out without rest on several occasions, establishing a pattern the company could not allow. "We can do nothing more about this case," the committee reported.

But, having succeeded with most minor issues, the committee raised the major issue of "long hours on turnarounds and doubling back." Dolan agreed that fourteen hours was long enough for men to be on duty. He issued an order that crew members did not have to "double back"or make "turn arounds" if it would keep them on duty longer than fourteen hours.

Dolan was in the minority of railroad officials who believed there was a limit to the number of hours men should be forced to work. In general, train crews worked as long as necessary to reach a destination. That did not change until March 4, 1907, when Congress, under pressure from the brotherhoods, passed the Hours of Service Act, limiting the number of hours railroaders could work to sixteen in any twenty-four-hour period. Known as the "hog" law, it required ten consecutive hours of rest for men working sixteen consecutive hours, and eight hours rest for men working sixteen non-consecutive hours.

The railroad companies immediately challenged the law in court as limiting their right to make contracts with employees under the natural laws of business. Railroaders called the one-way agreements "yellow-dog contracts," since they recognized no human rights of employees. The Supreme Court upheld the constitutionality of the Hours of Service Act and reminded the railroad companies that the law had come into existence because of the "deplorable casualties resulting from men being required to serve after mental and physical powers had been taxed beyond the limit of human endurance."

While the law had set a maximum limit on the number of hours railroaders could work, the railroad companies interpreted it as normalizing the sixteen-hour work day and made sure every man put in sixteen hours every trip. In 1916, after the railroad unions threatened a nationwide strike, Congress passed the Adamson Law, establishing the eight-hour day for purposes of compensation. One hundred miles equaled an eight-hour day. Railroads could still stretch the working day to sixteen, or send railroaders on trips longer than one hundred miles, but the extra miles and second eight hours were now considered overtime.

The railroad unions were the first labor groups in the nation to demand—and get—political solutions to labor problems. With the backing of a public interested in safe trains, the unions obtained a series of safety laws, beginning with the Safety Appliance Act of 1893, which required railroads engaged in interstate commerce to install air brakes and automatic couplers. While the South Park installed air brakes and Miller couplers on passenger trains, it refused to install safety appliances on freights, arguing they were not engaged in interstate commerce. Not until the early 1900s did the C&S comply with the law by equipping freights with automatic couplers and air brakes.

Congress also passed the Ashpan Act of 1908 that kept firemen from crawling under the engines to dump the ashes; the Electric Headlight Act of 1910, forcing companies to install electric headlights; the Boiler Inspection Act of 1911, requiring companies to keep the boilers in good condition; and the Automatic Firedoor Act, 1911, requiring them to install automatic doors. It even took an act of Congress to get cab curtains on the engines. The Cab Curtain Act was passed in 1928.

Through the quiet persistence of the railroad brotherhoods in Colorado and across the nation, South Park's railroaders gradually began to reap some long-overdue benefits. Revised schedules, slight pay raises, and cabs lined with wood on the engineer's side were small concessions. But the limit on working hours, automatic couplers, and air brakes were large concessions that, for the first time, assured railroaders a measure of safety. More important, they had been won without the loss of jobs.

CHAPTER TWELVE

So Long, Old Friends

The early 1900s were the last of the glory years for the old South Park line. Twenty-seven engineers and thirty-two firemen were working in Como. Freight and passenger trains chugged in and out of town day and night. To handle the steady traffic, six wooden stalls had been added to the roundhouse, bringing the total to nineteen. Work was plentiful and times were good.

Between 1905 and 1910, Sam held one of the passenger runs on train numbers 70 and 71 between Como and Leadville. George "Jumbo" Miller, then senior engineer on the South Park, had the other passenger run. Denver-based "east-end" crews handled the trains between Denver and Como. The west-end engineers and firemen based in Como took the trains to Leadville, but conductors and brakemen out of Denver made the trip all the way to Leadville.

Train number 70, with a baggage car and three coaches, frequently with all seats sold, left Denver Union Station every day at 8 a.m. On the point was one of the 2-6-0 locomotives numbered 7 through 12. The train pulled through Platte Canon, stopping long enough to drop off way passengers and pick up passengers traveling from one mountain town to another. Outside Como, it pulled into the wye, a short stem that had once been part of the track to the King mines, and backed to the depot at 1:20 p.m., giving the passengers a short, backward ride. The engine was now in position to return to Denver. (Freight trains did not turn on the wye. Freight engines were turned on the turntable in front of the roundhouse.)

Como's crews uncoupled the locomotive from train number 70 and moved it to Denver-bound train 71, just in from Leadville. Either passenger engine number 4 or number 6 went on train 70 for the trip to Leadville. Miller ran the number 4, while Sam had the number 6. Both locomotives were 2-6-0s that weighed 58,300 pounds. They were built by Cooke in 1884 and rebuilt by the C&S in 1902 with such precision and soundness they seldom needed repair. They had different personalities, however. The number 6 purred like a kitten under Sam's sure touch, but cantankerous old number 4 purred only for Miller.

The trip over the Highline with the passenger train took five hours, with Sam and Miller working the engines up steep grades and holding them on the downside. But through Blue River valley, past Dickey and into Frisco, they rolled along at twenty miles per hour, almost eight miles above the speed limit for freights. After laying over in Leadville, the crews started back for Como with eastbound train number 71 at 8:30 the next morning.

The position of passenger engineer was the highest rung on the railroading ladder. Passenger engineers, even on the South Park, ran the finest locomotives. Equipment on the train was the most reliable—it would never do to have a wheel crack under a passenger coach. Trains ran on regular schedules, which meant that Sam knew the time he would go out and the time he would come in. Since passenger trains had right of track, he rolled straight through, waving to crews on the freight trains in the sidings.

Engineers with the most seniority drew the passenger runs. For several years, the two runs between Como and Leadville had been held by senior engineer Dick O'Herne and Miller. When poor health forced O'Herne to retire, Miller moved into senior position and Sam claimed the second slot.

Company regulations only required passenger engineers to have one year of experience on freight trains, but Sam had eighteen years of experience before the passenger job opened up. Since there were no retirement plans, and no retirement income, only the direst circumstances forced an engineer to retire. Most were determined to die behind the throttle.

Miller had spent sixteen years running freight trains before he was able to grab the passenger job. Tall, built like a bulldozer, and good-natured about his nickname "Jumbo," he had a reputation for saying exactly what was on his mind. He was oiling the valves on engine number 4 one day when a special train whistled into Como carrying Superintendent J.D. Welsh, who was escorting officials from other railroads over the South Park line. Welsh spotted Miller and herded the officials to meet him. "This is the senior engineer on the South Park, one of our best engineers," the superintendent boasted. "He can buck through snowdrifts as high as thirty feet." "Bull," Miller replied, still oiling around.

While on the Leadville passenger run, Sam found himself with more free time than he had ever known as a railroader. He spent a great deal of it making minor repairs on engine number 6, keeping it in tiptop shape. He still spent afternoons running the helper engines, but he found time to build a barn and put an addition on our house. He and John Olson rode the passenger train to Denver on one occasion, bought two bikes, and pedaled over the bumpy wagon trails to Como. In one corner of the barn, he set up a workshop where he kept every bike in Como in working condition.

On summer days, Clarence, Neil, and I would walk with him to the depot and wait on the platform outside, scuffing our shoes in the dirt while he collected his orders, checked number 6, and got ready for the trip. One day Bill Gallagher, another South Park engineer, noticed us. "How you raising those boys, anyway?" he asked Sam. Gallagher, a widower with two sons and a daughter, was always anxious about the job he was doing rearing his children. Sam thought for a moment and replied, "Can't say exactly. Just go along, day by day, the best I can."

Since he didn't have a great deal of time at home, he took us on the Leadville trip when he could. We would ride in the coach, watching the aspen and ponderosa slip by as the train hauled itself over the passes and through the valleys to Leadville. Once in a while he would let us ride in the engine cab where we would hold onto the door bar, trying to stay upright on the bucking floor, and lean out the window to watch the smoke and steam shoot into the sky as the train curled behind.

One fall day, with summer still in the air, Sam got orders to take a helper to Breckenridge to push a freight over Boreas Pass. He took along Clarence, then ten years old. The engine reached Breckenridge ahead of a sudden storm that dropped four feet of snow and closed the pass. The dispatcher ordered Sam and the fireman, Phil Neuerburg, to tie up at Dickey. They waited three days in the Dickey boardinghouse while the rotary tried to churn through the drifts. With the pass still closed, Sam got orders to take the helper to Leadville. After spending all day battling the snowdrifts on Fremont Pass, they pulled into Leadville where orders were waiting for Neuerburg to return to Como by way of Denver.

Since Sam had no idea when he would get back to Como with the engine, he sent Clarence with Neuerburg. The fireman and boy, who was feeling like a seasoned railroader by now, boarded the Rio Grande train for the all-day trip to Denver, spent the night in a Seventeenth Street hotel near the depot, and caught train number 70 for Como the next morning.

What had started as an afternoon adventure for Clarence had turned into a week's vacation from school.

Even though South Park railroaders were busy during those first years of the new century, the C&S, which was taken over by the Chicago, Burlington and Quincy in 1908, had ledgers that warned of trouble. The fortunes of Colorado railroads were still intertwined with the boom and bust mining industry. At the turn of the century, the mining industry boomed with rich gold deposits in Cripple Creek and the new gold run discovered in Leadville in 1898, but as the decade wore on, the industry declined. The value of gold mined in Colorado dropped from $29 million in 1900 to $20 million in 1910. Silver fell even more, from $12 million to $4 million, and lead went from $7 million to $3 million. In Leadville, the center of the South Park's business, production of gold, silver, and lead fell by half.

With the drop in mining production, the South Park began cutting off freight trains. To make matters worse for the railroad, Leadville's mines, electrified in 1901, no longer used stationary steam engines and coal, and the Mineral Belt Railway, built in 1900, eliminated the need for South Park hay trains that had hauled feed for the horses.

While business was dropping on the South Park, expenses were growing. Running a train on the Highline cost the C&S three times the cost of running a broad gauge train the same distance. A train on the Alpine Tunnel route was five times the cost. At the same time, the South Park had to keep its charges low enough to compete with the Rio Grande for the Leadville and Gunnison traffic. With the company facing new financial challenges, President Trumbull, the financial wizard who had guided the South Park out of bankruptcy and had been at the helm of the C&S since its beginning, retired in 1909. By 1910, the combination of rising costs, diminishing business, and competition brought the South Park to its knees.

In October 1910, the South Park crumbled into three separate, non-connected sections. On October 10, a rockslide blocked part of the Alpine Tunnel, giving C&S officials an excuse to close the costly route, and on October 24, all trains to Gunnison were canceled. About the same time, the waters of Trout Creek rose and flooded the canon, ripping up tracks, scattering ties and rails, and closing the line over Trout Creek Pass. The company also seized upon the decline of the mining industry in Leadville to shut down the Highline. On October 31, the last Leadville-bound train pulled out of Como. The South Park was left with routes between Como and the mines around Alma, between Leadville and Breckenridge, and between Buena Vista and Hancock. It was the end of Como as a busy railroading center.

By 1910, the number of South Park engineers had dropped to twenty-two. That year, fifteen engineers lost their jobs. Thirty firemen were thrown out of work, as well as fifty brakemen and conductors and another fifty roundhouse workers and machinists.

A few engineers kept jobs on the South Park. Sam and Miller were assigned to Leadville to run the passenger trains to Breckenridge. Bill Gallagher took over the freight run between Como and the Alma mines. Pat Colligan took the Buena Vista-Hancock mixed train.

Some engineers found jobs within the C&S system. Andy Nelson went to work as a traveling engineer, supervising engineers on the narrow gauge and in the Denver yards. Art Aichele went to work on the North End in Cheyenne. Some went to work on other railroads. Al Zingheim cranked up the Brush and drove to Denver where he caught on the Moffat Road. Ed Conahan moved to Utah to work for the Rio Grande. Some left railroading altogether. John Olson bought a farm in Wheat Ridge. Ed Haight bought a farm near Morrison. Dave Thomas became a rancher.

Engineers with seniority as firemen, such as Walter Parlin, were set back to firemen's jobs. But Al Kroll, who had started railroading on the Rio Grande and had no seniority as a C&S fireman, bought a small farm in Buena Vista and hired on as watchman in the yards. For two dollars a day, he shoveled coal into the tenders, filled oil cans, shined the windows, and swept the engine cabs and coaches. It was not the same as running a locomotive, but it kept him on the C&S payroll and gave him hope of claiming an engineer's job should one open up. None ever did.

Only women and children stayed in Como that year, waiting for the railroaders to find jobs and send for them. Since almost everyone saw the closings as temporary, and new jobs as stopgaps until the South Park got rolling again, families boarded the Denver-bound passenger train with only small parcels of belongings. Everything else they left at home. Houses were unlocked, furniture still in place, tables set, beds made, clothes in the wardrobes, as if the owners would be coming back soon.

A harsh, dreary winter sank over Como. We didn't see Dad for seven months while he was running the passenger train between Leadville and Breckenridge. He and Mother kept our family together with letters and telegrams. In the spring, rumors spread that the passenger service to Leadville would be restored for the summer only. Dad sent a wire to get ready to move. Mother hired a wagon, and with the help of the kids and the other women still in Como, packed our furniture and belongings, hauled them to the station, and sent them on the freight train to Leadville via Denver. When the first Leadville-bound passenger train chugged out of Como that May in 1911, we were in the coach. Unlike many other railroad families, however, we knew we were riding out of Como for good.

We moved into a house on Leadville's east side, close by the depot at East Seventh Street, in a neighborhood of railroaders. Unlike Como's drafty frame houses, Leadville's houses were tightly constructed with plastered walls, indoor plumbing, bathtubs, and running water. Instead of kerosene lamps and coal stoves, we had electric lights and central heating.

But Leadville had changed from the boom days of the 1880s and 1890s when Sam was running freight trains. Many of Leadville's mines had played out or run out of operating capital, and hundreds of miners and their families had picked up and left town. With them had gone the hustlers, fortune seekers, gamblers, and transients who followed the booms. By 1911, Leadville was a quiet town of about 3,000, mostly miners who still had jobs, railroaders, merchants, schoolteachers, doctors, lawyers, and their families.

In the summer of 1912, the Breckenridge passenger train was abolished, leaving Sam free to bid another job. He could have bid a job in Leadville, but it was unclear at the time which trains would be running out of Leadville and where they would be going, even though the previous year, the C&S had taken the Rio Grande route between Leadville and Dillon and had given the Rio Grande control of the C&S route from Gunnison to Parlins and the Baldwin mines. Sam could have also bid on Gallagher's job running the freights between Como and the Alma mines, which would have taken us back to Como, but Como did not have a high school and he wanted us to attend high school. Clarence was then going to Leadville High School. Deciding that the future looked brighter in Buena Vista, Sam bid the Buena Vista-Hancock run held by Colligan, who went back to Como as a fireman.

On January 20, 1913, after the Breckenridge Chamber of Commerce, represented by attorney Barney Watley, won a court order forcing the C&S to reopen the Highline, passenger service was reinstated between Como and Leadville. Miller returned to Como and his old passenger run, which he now shared with Gallagher. When Miller retired eleven years later, Colligan took over the passenger job.

The court order breathed a faint spark of life into Como. The Denver-Leadville passenger train ran through Como every day, and the mixed train went from Como to the Alma mines six days a week. Other freights chugged between Denver and Leadville when business warranted. With fewer locomotives based in Como, however, the C&S removed ten stalls from the roundhouse. Only a few west-end enginemen, section men, and a skeleton crew of roundhouse workers lived in town with their families. And east-end crews, based in Denver, didn't spend any more time in Como than necessary.

CHAPTER THIRTEEN

Runnin' to Romley

In 1912, Sam started his last decade of railroading and we moved to Buena Vista, a pretty town of broad, tree-lined roads, Victorian houses splashed with gingerbread, and a population of 700. It was the seat of Chaffee County which, along with the Colorado State Reformatory south of town, issued most of the town's pay. It was also the center of the rich Arkansas Valley farming area that produced the lettuce, potatoes, alfalfa, wheat, beans, and barley shipped out of town on the Rio Grande to markets across the state. Every three months the District Court sat in Buena Vista, bringing judges, lawyers, defendants, and witnesses to town for cases ranging from murder to bankruptcy. The District Court gave Buena Vista a touch of sophistication, not to mention entertainment.

But even the most exciting trial paled next to the excitement of Buena Vista's past. In the 1870s and 1880s, 2,000 people had crowded into town—Irishmen laying rails through the Arkansas Valley, goldseekers heading for Chalk Creek, and gamblers and ne'er-do-wells wandering the West. The combination was explosive. Lynchings and gunfights were ordinary occurrences farmers had to look out for when they hitched their wagons and drove to town for supplies.

Davey Bones, who had gone to work on the South Park in 1879, found out how wild and lawless Buena Vista could be when he was running freights to Leadville before the South Park had built the Highline. About 1880, a gang of roughs burst into the boardinghouse where Bones was staying and rousted the snoring engineer from his bed. "Get dressed," they ordered, poking the cold snouts of six-shooters in his ribs. While he pulled overalls over long underwear, they told him he was going to Granite, seventeen miles upgrade. Granite was then the seat of Chaffee County, a fact the roughs intended to change.

As they hustled Bones down Main Street toward the railroad station, he tried to tell them that taking the engine on the main line without notifying the dispatcher could mean a head-on collision. Waving the protests aside, they hoisted Bones into the engine cab and ordered him to couple the engine onto two flatcars.

Away they went uphill to Granite, with one of the roughs firing the boiler, the others on the flatcars, and Bones at the throttle, expecting an oncoming headlight around every curve. At Granite, Bones waited in the engine while the others smashed the courthouse door, hauled out the records, and loaded them onto the flatcars. Backwards they rolled to Buena Vista, the locomotive pushing the flatcars with the roughs spread-eagled on top of the records, trying to hold them down and keep them from blowing away with the smoke. The train pulled into Buena Vista before anyone knew what was going on. Before releasing Bones, the roughs politely thanked him. When morning came, Buena Vista was the new seat of Chaffee County because the records—those that survived—were there.

Davey Bones was still running engines in the tamer days of the early 1920s when I fired for him on the passenger train between Denver and Morrison. His stories about the early days of railroading in Colorado made him popular with the young firemen. On the straightaways, he liked to relax and reminisce about his experiences, including the night the roughs stole Chaffee County. The diamond stickpin that Bones always wore shone like the headlight he had then expected to meet around the curve.

Times were also tamer in 1912 when Sam took over the mixed train number 94 between Buena Vista and Romley. The fireman was Mike Conroy, a promoted engineer set back to shoveling coal. Instead of the loaded freight car and coaches crowded with passengers that once plied Chalk Creek, the number 94 was made up of one passenger coach, a combination baggage and mail car, one or two coal cars, and a few empties heading to the mines to pick up ore. Since the route was isolated from other parts of the C&S system, ore from Chalk Creek was transferred to Rio Grande trains either at Nathrop or at Buena Vista for shipment to Denver.

Still the same, however, were the locomotives—the 57, 62, 65, 67, 69, and 73, built by Rhode Island and Baldwin in the 1880s and 1890s and rotated in pool service out of Leadville and Buena Vista. Every Monday, Wednesday, and Saturday in the summers, train number 94 pulled out of Buena Vista at 8 a.m. It followed the Arkansas River to Nathrop and climbed alongside Chalk Creek to the mines, steaming into St. Elmo at 10:40 a.m. St. Elmo was still the center of the Chalk Creek District and still the destination for most passengers.

From St. Elmo, train 94 whistled upgrade to Romley, the camp that had grown around the Mary Murphy Mine, the district's biggest. In 1912, about 400 men were working at the mine and the mill, which produced lead and zinc concentrate. Other ore from the Mary Murphy went to mills in Leadville and Denver. The miners and mill workers lived in the frame boardinghouses built downhill from the track.

The train crew also had work to do at Romley. Empty ore cars had to be pushed onto sidings for loading. Coal cars were pushed uphill to the loading track alongside the mill's coal bins. Both the mill workers and the railroad crew climbed into the coal cars to shovel coal onto the slide over the bin. Every day the mill's steam engine burned ten tons of coal— or one carload. Keeping the stationary engine supplied was a big part of the C&S business in Chalk Creek.

Sometimes Sam had orders to deliver freight to Hancock or pick up timber there. But even when no cars were destined for Hancock, Sam ran the engine three miles uphill to turn on the Hancock wye. On the return trip, the train, now the number 93, picked up loaded ore cars at Romley, took on passengers and baggage, and lumbered down to St. Elmo where it pulled in at 12:35 p.m. If the crew had not eaten in Romley, they walked down the steep slope to one of the restaurants or hotels fronting St. Elmo's main street. After lunch, they made the easy return trip to Buena Vista, with Sam holding the train at a steady five miles per hour in the mountains and letting it roll at twelve miles per hour through the Chalk Creek and Arkansas valleys.

The best thing about the Buena Vista-Hancock run was its summer schedule of three times a week, even though Sam was on call every day in case business should suddenly pick up. On days he didn't make the trip, he worked on the locomotive. With no shops in Buena Vista, it was up to him to keep the locomotive in good enough condition to take the train to Romley. From time to time, he ran the locomotive light over Denver and Rio Grande track to Leadville for spare parts, repairs he couldn't handle, or annual inspections.

In winter, the mixed train ran almost every day to keep the line open. At times, it took all day to reach Romley, with Sam bucking the drifts with the wedge plow through Chalk Creek Canon. In the winter of 1913, the snow was so heavy that Sam feared train number 94 would plow into a drift and not be found until spring. The dispatcher ordered Walt Parlin to Buena Vista to run a helper. After being thrust back to the ranks of the firemen in Leadville, Parlin was happy to work the throttle again, and Sam was glad for the company of another South Park engineer.

Apart from bucking snow, the Romley run had other moments of excitement. On the winter day of February 21, 1918, engine number 67 pitched off the Romley turntable, giving Sam the fright of his life. In August 1915, the C&S had moved the Gunnison turntable to Romley, eliminating the need for engines to travel to Hancock to turn on the wye. Rather than incur the expense of digging into the rockbound slopes, the company had installed the turntable at the edge of the grade, guaranteeing an accident. Sam ran the 67 onto the table, inching it slowly forward and backward to balance it. When the other crew members and track workers started to turn the table, the iron center casting snapped, tilting the table downhill. The 67 rolled off and crashed through the timber thirty feet down the mountainside. The tender rolled another thirty feet. Just as the table tilted, Sam had jumped from the engine and landed in the turntable pit.

With the 67 downslope in a cloud of steam, Sam, the rest of the crew, and the train were stranded in Romley. Another locomotive would have to come light from Buena Vista to pick up the train. But first, the crew had to get back to Buena Vista. They piled onto a push car—a small, flat car used to move track materials short distances. Push car brakes consisted of oak clubs pushed against the wheels. Carrying the weight of four men, the push car shot down the 4 percent grade with the clubs slowing the wheels only occasionally. It stayed on track, however, finally slowing through the valley into Nathrop. There, the crew sent a telegram to Superintendent E.B. Mitchell in Denver and flagged a Denver and Rio Grande freight for a ride into Buena Vista.

Dad was telling us about the accident later that day when the crank-type telephone rang on the kitchen wall. It was Mitchell calling to find out if Dad had been hurt. "I'm okay," he told them, "but the 67's in bad shape down the mountain." Mitchell was one of those rare railroad officials who thought first of his men and later of profits. "Never mind," he said. "We can afford to lose an engine, but we can't afford to lose an engineer."

Dad went back to Romley the following day to bring the train to Buena Vista, but locomotive 67 spent the winter on the slope at Romley. Not until late spring was the ground solid and dry enough to lay temporary shoofly track downhill. The wrecking crew pulled the 67 up the track and brought it to Denver for repair. It stayed in service until 1927.

Except for the jump into the pit, Sam liked the Romley run. Even though he was responsible for keeping the locomotive in running condition, he still had some free time to fish in Cottonwood Lake, remodel our house, or tend the crops he had planted on the five acres he owned. He found such activities almost as enjoyable as running a locomotive, but not quite.

One day he bought the water tank at Schwanders for twenty-five dollars. It hadn't been used since 1910, when Trout Creek was flooded and the Alpine Tunnel was closed. He and Conroy steamed up locomotive number 73, coupled on two flatcars, and started for Schwanders. Conductor Oscar Perschbacher and his brother, Joe, a brakeman, rode the flatcars with Clarence, Neil, and me. After steaming into Schwanders, we threw cables around the pillars of the tank. It came crashing down. We loaded the redwood onto the flatcars and chugged back to Buena Vista where, not long afterward, Dad transformed the South Park water tank into a porch on our house.

On another day, the passenger train from Denver pulled out of town leaving Peter Heronymous Speas, eighty-three years old, with a white beard and wooden leg, standing on the Buena Vista platform. Sam had not seen his father in the thirty years since he had left Freeman, Missouri, to go railroading in Colorado. But they had corresponded over the years. Peter always closed his letters by wishing he could come West and "be a help to ye, son." When he finally came, he was a connection to the past, a never-ending source of stories about the Missouri-Kansas border wars and Jesse James riding down the road and Cole Younger coming onto the farm. He and Sam spent hours at the kitchen table talking about those days while we gathered around, listening to tales about our father as a boy who dreamed about becoming a railroad engineer.

After two years with us, Peter announced he was leaving. Death was upon him, he said, looking strong and robust, and he intended to die at home. He boarded the Rio Grande for the trip to Denver Union Station, where he caught the train bound for Missouri. Not long afterward, we got a telegram that Peter Heronymous was dead.

In 1915, thirty-two years after Sam had crossed the plains to come to Colorado, he returned to Freeman, retracing the route across the plains where he had watched the coyotes and rabbits, dined on buffalo steak, and wondered about the future. It was a trip to a place that had once been home. Now, home was in the mountains of South Park, and after his father's funeral, Sam hurried back.

CHAPTER FOURTEEN

The Old Engineer

I drew my first pay on the C&S while Sam was running train number 94 from Buena Vista to Romley. But Clarence, Neil, and I had gone railroading in our imaginations during the years we had waited at the Como Depot for Dad to pick up the orders, oil the valves on the locomotive, and get ready for a trip over the Highline or through the Alpine Tunnel. We knew the railroaders' lingo, the meaning of the way the conductor swung the lamp or the engineer blew the whistle before we knew how to read. If there was a more exciting occupation to which a boy could aspire than driving a steam locomotive along two silvery rails, whistle wailing in the night, we didn't have a clue as to what it might be.

Fred Hyde, one of the early engineers on the South Park, offered Neil and me our first jobs on the railroad when we were eleven and twelve years old. He had worked as a hostler in the Leadville yards after poor eyesight forced him to give up a job on the main line. By 1912, he had transferred to Buena Vista as yard watchman, along with Al Kroll.

For Hyde, shoveling four tons of coal each day to keep the locomotives running was the hardest part of the job. He offered Neil and me ten cents a ton to shovel the coal—two cents above what shovelers along the South Park line had made a few years earlier. As soon as school let out, we ran to the station to go to work. After shoveling the coal, we swept the engine cabs and coaches, cleaned the windows, wiped the boilers, and learned how particular old engineers could be about the way their locomotives looked.

The summer when I was fifteen I hired on with the section crew. Like other section crews who walked across the West repairing track and keeping the railroads running, the Buena Vista crew was made up mostly of Italian immigrants. We worked fourteen hours every day replacing cracked ties, tamping ballast, tapping spikes, tightening bolts, cleaning culverts, repairing fences, filling in washed-out ruts, and cutting weeds along the right-of-way. It was a tough job that most of the other crew members spent their lives doing. I considered it another step up the railroading ladder.

By the summer of 1917, I had worked my way into the locomotive. The United States entered World War I that April and Guy Hallack, who was firing for Sam, joined the army. Sam wired the superintendent in Denver: "Fireman quit. Send another." The superintendent wired back: "You crazy? All able-bodied men leaving Denver on troop trains. Hire local."

Since Clarence had caught on firing for the C&S out of Como after graduating from Buena Vista High School, Sam couldn't hire him. But there I was, sixteen years old, willing to work hard, and bursting to get into the engine cab. He hired me.

I worked all summer, firing engines 62 and 57 to Romley and back. Dad had a reputation for expecting firemen to do a good job, and I was intent on proving my worth as a railroader. We worked together without a hitch.

Two years later, after I graduated from Buena Vista High School, I took a job as fireman on the stationary steam engine at Romley Mill. Stationary engines lacked the excitement of locomotives that plummeted downhill and crawled up the sides of mountains, but the job was another step in what I believed to be a steady advancement toward the job of railroad engineer.

That summer of 1919, the future looked dim for both the narrow gauge railroads and the mining industry. With rich lodes still untapped, mining production had slowed throughout Colorado since the turn of the century. Historians have placed blame for the slowdown on labor strikes, the drop in the price of metals, and the greed of mine owners who skimmed profits, leaving nothing for development. Between 1916 and 1919, mining production in Chaffee County dropped from $1.5 million in gold, silver, copper, lead, and zinc to $200,000. In the Chalk Creek District, a few mines around St. Elmo were still operating, but the mines near Romley had closed. Romley Mill was still open, however, rerunning tailings.

I worked the night shift and lived in one of the bunkhouses down-slope from the track. Off hours, I hiked to the top of the surrounding peaks, picking a different one to conquer each day. Often, from a perch high above Romley, I watched train number 94 snake up Chalk Creek Canon with Sam at the throttle of the locomotive, the whistle echoing in the mountain stillness and smoke curling into the sky.

In October, the backsheet of the boiler in the stationary engine cracked. Rather than purchase a new boiler to finish rerunning the tailings, the mining company closed the mill, bringing an end to the mining industry at Romley.

The end of Sam's railroading days was also drawing near, although he didn't know it at the time. Although he survived the hazards of buck-ing snow, holding trains on the steep downgrades, riding a derailed loco-motive down Boreas, and jumping into the Romley pit as the locomotive bolted downhill, he was injured while performing a routine task in 1916. While steam cleaning the locomotive at the Buena Vista coal station, he lost his footing and fell from the top of the boiler, landing on the rails. He suffered three broken ribs and a sprained back, injuries that did not seem serious. But he had other internal injuries to his liver and kidneys, unknown at the time, that eventually ruined his health.

He was no longer the man he had once been, robust and full of energy, capable of riding a bike on the dirt road from Denver to Como, tramping across the high mountains, or putting in thirty hours behind a throttle. His shock of red hair turned white, and he grew worn and tired. He con-tinued to run train 94 to Romley, but the trips were long and hard.

By the time of Sam's fall, company-employee contracts placing the responsibility for safety solely on the shoulders of employees had been outlawed by the Workmen's Compensation Act of 1915. Railroaders injured on the job could sue the company for damages. But the companies protected themselves by requiring an injured employee to sign an agree-ment waiving the right to sue, in return for a small settlement. Sam signed the agreement for compensation of thirty-five dollars. Had he refused to sign, he would have been fired.

In the fall of 1922, he had a slight stroke that forced him to lay off. While he was recuperating, the C&S, under pressure from the unions, adopted its first pension plan, allowing C&S railroaders to retire with a small income. Some of the oldtimers, who had seemed destined to ride out their lives in a locomotive, hastened to take advantage of the pension before the company changed its mind. After four decades as railroaders, oldtimers like Davey Bones, the senior engineer in the Clear Creek Dis-trict, and George Miller, who was still running the passenger from Como to Leadville, hung up their caps and overalls.

Sam decided to join them. He was then sixty-five years old and had spent forty-two years railroading. Thirty-nine of those years had been with the same railroad, even though, in that time, it had been bankrupt, reorganized, and reincorporated, finally becoming the C&S. Sam had never taken a vacation and had laid off only when he was sick, and when he attended his father's funeral. But the company turned down his application for the pension, ruling him ineligible since he was not "in service"—he was still recuperating.

By that time, I was firing for the C&S out of Denver. I came in off a trip one day to find a message that Andy Roach, the master mechanic, wanted to see me. A former engineer on the C&S between Denver and Trinidad, Roach had great understanding and empathy for the men on the road.

"What are we going to do about your father's pension?" he asked. I said I didn't see there was anything we could do.

"You're wrong," he told me. "I've got a plan."

His plan worked like this. Roach temporarily released me from the North End in Denver and sent me to Buena Vista. Sam bid his regular run to Romley. During the next two weeks, train number 94 rolled out of Buena Vista on schedule with the fireman, Bill Gibbony, at the throttle. One of Patrick Gibbony's sons, he was a promoted engineer. I was on the left side of the cab, shoveling coal, taking on water, tending the ashes, and watching the water level in the boiler. Sam was in the coach watching the landscape slip by the familiar route.

The records showed Sam Speas as engineer and Gibbony as fireman. No mention was made of me. Oscar Perschbacher, the conductor, Joe Perschbacher, the brakeman, and every stationmaster, telegrapher, track worker, and other railroader between Buena Vista and Romley knew that the old engineer was in the coach and went along with the scheme to help him get his pension. When Sam reapplied, he was "in service," leaving the company no excuse to deny the application. After a lifetime of railroading, he retired with a pension of sixty-six dollars a month.

That same year, 1922, the C&S filed a petition with the Interstate Commerce Commission to abandon the run between Buena Vista and Romley-Hancock. The drop in mining production had meant losses of $357,576 for the railroad between 1916 and 1921. The number of passengers had declined from 3,711 annually to 725, mostly miners and railroaders still traveling the Chalk Creek road. But enough opposition came from those passengers that the ICC denied the petition. The company reapplied the following year, again citing losses. This time, on September 24, 1923, the ICC granted authority to abandon the line.

Section by section, the old South Park was disappearing. By November 15, 1926, the tracks in Chalk Creek had been torn out under a contract held by Bill Turner, the stepson of Buddy Schwartz. All that remained of the South Park were the passenger and freight runs between Denver and Leadville, the freight between Leadville and Climax, and the mixed train between Como and Alma.

In January 1927, two months after the last of the track had disappeared from the Chalk Creek District, Sam suffered a fatal stroke. Colorado's narrow gauge railroads and one of the men who had made them run were closing out their lives together.

CHAPTER FIFTEEN

A New Day Comin'

In the fall of 1921 I became a full-fledged railroader and considered myself a lucky man. Everyone was hoping to go railroading at that time, it seemed. Crews laid off the narrow gauge routes were streaming into Denver to look for jobs on the broad gauge. Soldiers home from the trenches of France filled the employment lines outside railroad offices. But Colorado was in the throes of a mild postwar depression, and the railroads had few jobs to offer.

I had the inside track to one, however. That September, Clarence, who had started firing for the C&S in Como and had transferred to the North End out of Denver in 1917, heard a rumor that the railroad would be hiring new men. He sent me a telegram in Pueblo where I was working for the telephone company. I quit my job, boarded the first passenger train heading north, and hurried to the C&S roundhouse at Seventh and Water streets in Denver. I was hired as a fireman on the extra board.

Like my father forty years earlier, I had come to Denver to go railroading. In the intervening years, Denver had grown from a frontier town with dusty roads, wooden sidewalks, and horse-drawn carriages to a city of 225,000 people. Model T Fords and clanging trolley cars crowded the downtown streets. Denver's skyscraper, the Daniel's and Fisher Tower, nineteen stories tall, loomed over eight-story office buildings. Beyond the downtown area stretched fine neighborhoods with brick homes on tree-lined streets.

Every day long trains rumbled in and out of Denver Union Station. Corporate consolidations and bankruptcies over the years had left six rail-roads operating into Denver: the Santa Fe, Burlington, Union Pacific, Rio Grande, Denver and Salt Lake (known as the Moffat Road), and the Colorado and Southern. The railroads no longer depended upon mines that produced gold, silver, lead, and zinc, although a few freights still lumbered into the mountains after ore. Since most highways were unpaved roads meandering through the countryside, trucking still was a fledgling industry. Everything moved by train—raw materials, manufactured goods, and people.

C&S trains rolled along the Front Range carrying farm produce, hay, cattle, sheep, sugar beets, limerock, lumber, cement, tools, industrial equipment, household goods, iron ore, gasoline, and coal. By 1920, coal mining had become one of Colorado's most important industries. Mines in Las Animas, Huerfano, and Boulder counties produced 12.5 million tons of coal that year, compared to 437,000 tons produced forty years earlier. The C&S hauled 100 cars of coal out of the Louisville coalfields in Boulder County every day.

On the head of the freight trains were giant broad gauge locomotives that weighed as much as 400,000 pounds and rolled on drivers between fifty-one and sixty-nine inches in diameter. Standing in the yards, they loomed over the biggest narrow gauge engines, the 74, 75, and 76, which weighed 96,000 pounds. The 300 class locomotives, both 4-6-0s and 4-6-2s, hauled passenger trains, while the bigger 2-8-0s—the 400, 500, 600, and 700 class engines—hauled freight. So did the 800-class 2-8-2s, and the biggest C&S locomotives, the 900 class 2-10-2s, the most popular freight locomotives in American railroading. While locomotives had gotten bigger and more powerful over the years, the basic design had not changed since the first steam locomotive rolled out of the factory more than a century before.

The 1923 C&S roster lists fifty-three engineers and forty-six firemen in the Fort Collins District. Known as the North End, the district was made up of the 250-mile section between Denver and Guernsey, Wyoming. Many of the railroaders lucky enough to catch on the C&S at that time would work there for fifty years. Among the young promoted engineers were John Byrne, George Suess, Frank Johnson, Fred Tingle, and Harold Mott. New firemen who eventually became engineers included H. Newcomb, R.J. Sanders, J.O. Peterson, Don Grinstead, Ed Phelan, Tom Gibbony, and Joe Loughry. For a short time after my brother Neil hired on the C&S as a fireman in 1922, Dad and all three of his sons were on the roster. Many of the other new railroaders also came from railroading families. Joe Loughry's father, Pat, had spent years as a section boss on the C&S line near Loveland, and Joe had grown up working around locomotives, sweeping the engines, shining the windows, and shoveling coal. He had come to Denver to work as a fireman after Clarence, passing through on a train, had tipped him that the company was hiring. Tom Gibbony and his brothers, Bill, Frank, and Emmet, had also followed their father railroading, and Ed Phelan's brother, Frank, was a C&S engineer.

The unmarried engineers and firemen roomed at the Cologne Hotel at Fourteenth and Lawrence streets, operated for railroaders by Moffat conductor Cap Wilson and his wife. The caller would telephone the front desk and leave messages which the Wilsons delivered.

Two railroaders could share one single room, since they were never there at the same time. One would crawl out of bed and leave for work before the other got in from a trip. He might pass his roommate in the hall, but some roommates never met. Cap and his wife saw that the bedding was changed weekly.

When we were in town, we gathered at Central Loop Restaurant on Fifteenth Street to eat, drink coffee, and talk about our trips, shouting over the noise of the trolley cars turning in the loop. When we had some time off, we headed for the movie theaters on Curtis Street. Not knowing when we might get another chance to see a movie, we would see four or five in one day. Or we wandered over to Knockers Corner under the jeweler's clock at Sixteenth and Curtis streets to see what was going on. All the railroaders in Denver congregated at Knockers Corner to exchange news. Anyone looking for work went there first to find out which road was hiring. Denver's first traffic light was installed there, and the railroaders liked to entertain themselves by strolling across the street on the red light, causing endless confusion among drivers unused to traffic signals. Finally, two policemen put Knockers Corner on their beat to make sure the railroaders observed the signals.

One afternoon, a Model T, owned by a C&S brakeman, stalled in the intersection. He jumped out, turned the crank, and jumped back into the driver's seat, but the car sputtered and died. He jumped out again, turned the crank, kicked the tires, and swore. Still the car wouldn't start. The railroaders gathered around to offer advice. Anyone who ran a steam locomotive felt competent to run a Model T, but no one could get the car going. In the meantime, trolleys backed up on Sixteenth Street, and cars nosed into the intersection and screeched to a halt, drivers yelling at the brakeman and banging on the cartops. Finally, the brakeman leapt onto the running board and offered the car to the highest bidder. Drivers left their cars, and shoppers and businessmen poured out of the stores. Someone bid a dollar, someone else raised the bid to $2.00, and another offered $2.25. Finally, a conductor yelled $15, a bid no one topped. With the help of other railroaders, the conductor pushed his new car out of the intersection and down the street to the Cologne, while the brakeman pocketed the cash and set out on foot.

Besides visiting Knockers Corner and attending silent films, firemen also occasionally invited another railroader's sister to a movie or church social. But time for courting was limited. We went out on trips not knowing when we would return. On one occasion, I was called to fire a locomotive to Pueblo and back. But in Pueblo, the dispatcher assigned me to the helper engines running to Colorado Springs. I spent ten days on the helpers before catching a trip back to Denver. When we did get in from a long trip, we fell into bed and slept until Cap Wilson hammered at the door shouting the time for the next trip. By the time we found a few hours on our hands and went calling on a lady friend, she could have married someone else.

Before I made my first trip firing, I was required to make one student trip without pay. New firemen usually made several student trips, but the company took into account the fact that I had fired one summer for my father on the narrow gauge. I made my student trip with Clarence on a 600 class locomotive pulling freight train number 41, bound for Cheyenne. The engineer was Charlie Conroe, who had gone railroading in 1902 on the Cripple Creek Short Line. Before the year was out, he had started firing on the C&S North End and was set up to engineer in 1906.

Everything was looking good as we pounded toward Boulder when, suddenly, the train jerked to a stop, brakes squealing, wheels sliding, and cars bumping. We jumped off the engine and hurried back along the train to look for the trouble. Ten cars behind the engine, we found two uncoupled cars. The iron key that held the drawbar in place had jarred loose, causing the bar to drop and uncouple the cars, and throwing the brakes into emergency. The conductor and brakeman, hurrying from the caboose, spotted the drawbar under the train.

It took four of us to wrestle it out, carry it to the uncoupled cars, and put it back into place. After tightening the iron key, we were on our way again, clipping along as if nothing had happened. But we were lucky. Had the drawbar dropped across the rails, it would have derailed the rear cars.

Shortly after my student trip, the C&S was gearing up for the annual beet runs, and I found myself with a temporary firing job. Every September the company ran ten extra freight trains across northern Colorado hauling beets from farms to the Great Western Sugar Company factories in Longmont, Loveland, Greeley, Windsor, and Fort Collins. Along with the beets moved cars of limerock used in the sugar-making process, supplies and equipment, and sheep fattened on the beet pulp. Out of the sugar factories rolled carloads of sugar bound for warehouses in Texas.

During the four months of the beet runs, new men, like myself, moved into regular firing jobs. Promoted engineers still working as firemen the rest of the year got a chance behind the throttle. The few boomers still drifting around the country came to Denver for work, although by the 1920s boomers were a dying breed of railroaders, left behind by company policies of hiring local men for extra boards. When the beet runs ended, the boomers moved on, new engineers went back to shoveling coal, and new firemen slipped back to the extra board.

I was assigned to the switch engines in the Fort Collins yards that first season I worked on the beet runs. Fort Collins was then a quiet town, home of Colorado Agricultural and Mechanical College and center of some of northern Colorado's sprawling farms. Trolley cars rolled down the town's broad, tree-lined streets through neighborhoods of squat, white houses. The C&S had built the streetcar system in 1907 and sold it to the town in 1919. Both the Fort Collins system and the Denver-Boulder Interurban, built by the C&S in 1908, were part of long-range plans that never materialized to run electric passenger trains between Cheyenne and Pueblo.

Rain or shine, seven days a week, I was at work on a switch engine at 5 a.m. The night caller knocked on my door at the Linden Hotel at 3:30 a.m., giving me time to eat breakfast at the only restaurant open that early. The other customers were also railroaders. 200 class engines, built in 1887–88, worked in the yards where they had been retired after years of steaming down the main line.

But I wasn't ready to retire to the yards. Like my father, corralled in the Denver yards forty years earlier, I was eager to roll down the main line instead of making up and breaking up trains and pushing cars from track to track. In the afternoons, after we tied up, I took long walks outside town and read stacks of books from the library. Each night before I fell asleep, I reminded myself, "You're on the railroad, and someday you'll be back on the main line."

In February the beet runs ended and so did my job in the Fort Collins yards. I went back to Denver to work on the extra board.

CHAPTER SIXTEEN

The Extra Board

In the 1920s, ten firemen on the C&S extra board protected twenty-five jobs. When one fireman came in off a trip, he went to the bottom of the call list, eventually working up to first out. Extra board firemen on the North End could choose to work only on the North End or anywhere in the C&S system. I chose the latter, which meant a variety of trips and more of them.

I fired locomotives between Denver and Cheyenne for D.J. Givens, then the senior engineer on the C&S, who had been set up in 1876. I fired for Squire Thorne on the narrow gauge freight train that steamed up Clear Creek Canon to Silver Plume, returning the following day. And I fired for Davey Bones on the narrow gauge mixed train that ran to Morrison and back every Monday, Wednesday, and Saturday.

Sometimes I was called for passenger train 70 and a trip to Como. The Leadville-bound train left Denver Union Station every morning with two coaches and a baggage car and rumbled up Platte Canon, over Kenosha Pass and across South Park, pulling into Como at 1:20 p.m. A west end locomotive went on the point and either Engineer Bill Gallagher or Patrick Colligan got ready to haul the train the rest of the journey to Leadville.

The passenger train was not the only train still rumbling into Como in the 1920s. Unscheduled freights still rolled between Denver and Leadville and between Leadville and the mines near Alma when business warranted, but the sixteen-car ore, hay, and merchandise trains my father had run were part of the past. Since helper engines were no longer stationed at Dickey, the engine house there had been torn down. Helpers ran straight through in the 1920s, with one coupled behind the lead locomotive and two in the middle of the train on the uphill. Downgrade, the helpers ran light.

Only a few west end engineers, firemen, roundhouse helpers, and their families still lived in Como, but many houses were boarded up and tumbleweeds rolled down the streets. One boardinghouse still catered to the railroaders who laid over, and the South Park Hotel was still open. On the way to Como, the passenger train conductor would send a wire to the hotel with the number of passengers planning to eat in the dining room, called the Como Eating House.

Como was isolated. Unlike other sections on the C&S, west end engines and crews did not run into Denver. Most men on the west end had been working for the South Park since its heyday around the turn of the century, and they considered themselves true railroaders, accustomed to brutal weather and work—a cut above the men who worked on the tame broad gauge routes. They took pride in their jobs and in what remained of their town. But the east end men who headed back to Denver with passenger train 71 considered Como and the old South Park the end of the world.

Much of the C&S business on both the narrow gauge and broad gauge was seasonal. Before the beet runs ended, the ice runs had usually begun. Every day in January and February, the narrow gauge ice train steamed up Platte Canon with forty empty cars and two helpers bound for the ice ponds below Grant operated by Maddox Ice Company. I was often called to fire one of the locomotives. We dropped off the empties and picked up forty cars loaded with chunks of ice five feet long and two feet wide that had been sawn out of the ponds by hand and loaded onto a platform. From there, a conveyor belt loaded the chunks into the cars. On the downhill, the helpers steamed ahead, leaving one locomotive to haul the loaded cars to icehouses in Denver. Eventually, the ice went by wagon to the iceboxes of Denver's homes, restaurants, and hotels.

In late summer and fall, C&S trains were busy hauling stock. A mixed train rolled south out of Denver at 3 p.m. every day with one coach, a string of empty stockcars, and a dozen cars loaded with cement, gasoline, and construction materials. On the point was a 300 class engine, 4-6-0, with either Fred Schneider or Bill Stiles at the throttle. On many trips I was on the left side of the cab.

We whistled south to Parker on the Old Line built in 1882 by the Denver and New Orleans Railroad Company. After taking on water at Parker, we started the slow, uphill climb on the 4 percent grade to Hilltop with the engineer working the engine while I shoveled coal as fast as I could. By the 1920s, locomotives were equipped with automatic firebox doors operated by a foot pedal. No longer did the fireman have to jerk an overhead chain to open and close the door while he was shoveling coal into the firebox.

Leaving Hilltop, we rolled along an easy grade to Elizabeth and Elbert, dropping off freight cars at both stations and setting out empty stockcars. At Falcon, we transferred eastbound cars to the Rock Island line and tied up. The C&S maintained two cars on a siding there, a cook car and bunk car. Some of the crew rolled up their sleeves and cooked the batch of groceries we had brought from Denver. Those who didn't cook cleaned up after dinner while others started a game of poker. Most railroaders enjoyed poker, but after finding out how much I disliked losing hard-earned money on the turn of a card, I had given it up. Eventually we dropped onto the cots in the bunk car to catch some sleep before the smell of brewing coffee and sizzling bacon rousted us out for the trip back to Denver.

On the way, we stopped at Elbert and Elizabeth to load cattle from ranches in the area. The cattle had been herded into pens that the C&S built alongside the track. On most trips, we loaded as many as thirty cars of cattle. From Elizabeth, we rumbled along the easy water grade to Denver. The roundtrip paid firemen ten dollars, out of which we bought our groceries. At the time, firemen across the nation averaged about $220 per month, but firemen on the C&S extra board made about $100 per month.

Often extra board firemen were called for trips on the C&S-Santa Fe Joint Line. In 1899, the C&S had abandoned the Old Line as a main line because of the 4 percent grade between Parker and Hilltop, and had reached an agreement with the Santa Fe to use that railroad's track between Denver and Pueblo. In 1918, when the Santa Fe obtained permission to use Rio Grande track south, the C&S also gained access to that track. Under the C&S-Santa Fe agreement, the companies consolidated business between Denver and Pueblo, with the C&S handling Santa Fe business in Denver and the Santa Fe handling C&S business in Pueblo. About 60 percent of the freight business belonged to the C&S while the Santa Fe claimed 40 percent, but passenger business was evenly divided. Passenger trains to Trinidad ran under C&S rules while trains to La Junta were under Santa Fe rules. Each railroad paid for track repairs and maintenance according to its percentage of business.

Once in a while, Santa Fe officials let us know that they didn't appreciate C&S firemen on their locomotives. Before I ran into one of those officials, I had made several trips on Santa Fe passenger train 13 that left Denver at 10:45 p.m., arrived in La Junta about daylight, and returned the following afternoon. The engineer was Frank McCartney. On one return trip, a Santa Fe traveling fireman named Shields boarded the engine at Pueblo. Traveling firemen and engineers could get into a locomotive cab at any point, unannounced, to check on the railroaders. All the way to Colorado Springs, Shields kept after me—I wasn't shoveling fast enough, I put in too much coal, the water level in the boiler was down, the water level was up. I was too lazy. I was too eager. McCartney never said a word, but as soon as he pulled the train into Colorado Springs Depot, he yanked Shields' satchel from the rack, threw it on the gangway, and said, "Get off."

Shields protested. He was a company official and McCartney had no authority to put him off the engine. McCartney squared his shoulders, looked Shields in the eye, and said, "This is my engine and I want you off." Shields grabbed his satchel and jumped down to the platform. "Get back to work," McCartney told me. "You're doing a good job."

Like good engineers, a locomotive that ran the way it was designed to run made trips a pleasure. But a cantakerous locomotive could turn a routine trip into a nightmare. Engineer Frank Wright and I drew one of those engines—the 373—on C&S passenger train 7 to Trinidad. With two chair cars, two Pullmans, a dining car, and six mail cars, the train was going through to Fort Worth. After waiting for the roundhouse crew to finish tuning up the 373, we pulled out of Union Station an hour late, with passengers already disgruntled.

As soon as the train got underway, I knew we had a problem. No matter how fast I shoveled coal, malfunctioning draft appliances in the front end of the smoke box kept the fire from burning hot enough to build a good head of steam. We crept down track, the 373 balking and snorting, and the train getting later. Finally, we pulled into Palmer Lake with steam down and the water in the glass winking at the bottom, showing low water in the boiler. I opened the injector to add more water, shoveled a layer of coal into the firebox, and opened the blower to get the fire burning. Since we were getting later, Wright told me he would shake up the fire and try to get the steam to 200 pounds while I filled the water tank. While I was out on the tank, he got down to oil the valve gear, check the nuts and bolts, and make sure everything was tight and in place. When he found a hot pin—a side rod bearing that had overheated and needed immediate oiling—he promptly forgot the injector pouring water into the boiler. I climbed back into the cab to find the boiler full, steam pressure below 100 pounds, and the brakes in emergency. There we sat with no steam, no air, and brakes set tight while the conductor walked up and down the aisles in the coaches explaining to the passengers why the already late train wasn't moving.

Wright and I worked as fast as we could. We opened the blow-off cocks to drain excess water from the boiler until the water level registered half a glass. Then we shook the fire. Gradually, the steam began rising and the air pump started. Wright opened the throttle, pouring steam into the cylinders. While the thirty-seven-inch drivers on narrow gauge locomotives started rolling with minimum pressure, the sixty-nine-inch wheels on broad gauge passenger engines, such as the 373, required enormous pressure to start up. Slowly, the 373 began moving forward. It picked up speed and by the time we approached Monument, we were thundering down track at seventy miles per hour, making up lost time. Wright hollered, "Watch for the order board." A green board and he meant to keep rolling. If red, he would slow down while I grabbed the orders on the fly. But he didn't want to slow down unless he had to. Even though I was hanging out the side, I didn't see the order board until we sailed by. "Red," I shouted. Wright set the air. With brakes screeching, the train stopped a mile down track. Cursing under his breath, he whistled back to the station. Running the order board meant he had to take time to fill out a report.

When we got underway again, the 373 refused to build another head of steam. We fought the sluggish, balking locomotive to Pueblo, Walsenburg, and Trinidad, pulling into the station four hours late. Since we had committed the most serious sin in the railroading world—bringing in a late passenger train—officials were waiting on the platform. Wright had all he could do to convince them the 373 was at fault, not the crew. He spent still more time filling out a sheaf of reports and answering messages and wires before he finally got to rest. I went straight to the hotel, ate breakfast, and fell into bed, exhausted after shoveling twenty tons of coal.

Not all extra board jobs were on the main line. Sometimes firemen were called for hostlers' jobs at the Seventh Street roundhouse, which the C&S had built in 1900. Main line hostlers ran engines from the roundhouse to Union Station to be coupled onto trains. They also ran incoming engines to the roundhouse yards. Inside hostlers ran the engines in and out of the stalls and prepared them for trips, filling tanks with coal and water, putting supplies in the engine cabs, stirring up the fires, and cleaning the ash pans. Then they ran them to the ready track for the main line hostlers.

As locomotives came in, the inside hostlers moved them onto the ash pits where fire knockers dumped the ashes and fire. Then they ran them onto the 100-foot turntable, built in 1919 to handle the biggest steamers, and into the stalls. Every hostler had a helper who pushed the turntable to the track leading to a vacant stall and opened and closed the heavy stall doors. At least ten engines were usually in line, waiting to have fires knocked out and to be run into the stalls.

On one hostling shift, I was assigned to move the long line of incoming engines. By the time I got to the 353, it had only forty pounds of steam pressure and no air pressure. I ran it onto the turntable and waited while the helper turned the table and gave me the signal to go. When I opened the throttle, the 353 groaned and settled back. Suddenly, it leapt forward and sailed down track into the roundhouse. I set the air, but it kept rolling. The mechanics threw boards under the wheels to slow it. By the time it stopped, the front drawbar was pressing against the far wall. The night foreman yelled, "Get those engines in here while they still have brakes."

That was not an easy task, as Ben Spahn found out when he worked as a hostler several years later. On one shift, Spahn was running the engines into the roundhouse as fast as he could, but by the time he climbed into the cab of the 900, both steam and air pressure were down. When the helper gave Spahn the signal, he opened the throttle. The 900 shot forward into the stalls and kept rolling through the wall at the far end. When it ran aground, part of the roundhouse roof collapsed in heaps of brick and dust over the boiler. The hostlers had to couple on another engine to pull the 900 back into the stall.

Spahn made out official report number 2810, required when equipment was damaged. "At 12:10 a.m.," he wrote, "a large engine punched a small hole in the roundhouse wall in stall 26. Yours truly, Ben Spahn."

One of the clerks in the offices told me later that when master mechanic W.F. Kascal read the report he came out of his seat bellowing. "Get Spahn in here. Right now."

CHAPTER SEVENTEEN

The North End

During the 1920s, even though I was riding the locomotives out of Denver in every direction, I was assigned to the North End. C&S trains chugged up and over the rolling hills between Denver and Cheyenne with sixty and seventy cars of coal, oil, iron ore, lumber, farm produce, cattle, machinery, and manufactured goods. Usually 500 and 600 class locomotives, all hand fired, worked the North End. They weighed about 200,000 pounds and carried ten tons of coal and 8,000 gallons of water in the tenders. Firemen started shoveling coal in Denver and didn't stop until the train pulled into Cheyenne. By then the crew had been on the road sixteen hours and the fireman had shoveled twenty-four tons of coal.

But shoveling coal was only part of the fireman's job. We also climbed onto the tank to take on water three or four times during the trip, and we climbed onto the tank again to take on coal at Fort Collins. We shook the grates and cleaned the fire, dumping ashes into the ash pan. At least four times, usually when we took on water, we opened the ashpan under the boiler to let the ashes and clinkers drop onto a metal plate between the rails. Since there was not enough room to drop the ashes in one pile, the engineer moved the engine forward and backward, leaving rows of

108

enormous ash piles while the fireman breathed the ash dust and sulphurous fumes. Taking on water and dumping the ashes on the broad gauge took at least one hour.

The crew laid over at Cheyenne and walked one mile to a downtown hotel, a long walk for men who had worked sixteen hours. At the prompting of the unions in 1922, the C&S agreed to rent a strip of land near the roundhouse to employees for one dollar a year. Using scraps of lumber from the car repair shops in the Denver yards, the railroaders built eight shacks. Each shack had bunks and a kitchen where the men could rest and cook meals in between trips. The C&S provided the shacks with water and electricity, and the railroaders installed stoves that burned coal from the engines.

Engineers Charlie Conroe, Charlie Lewton, and Jim Bovee built the shack that I stayed in and later purchased with my brothers. Four or five railroaders usually owned one shack, but we had keys to all of them. If one was full, a tired fireman or engineer could bunk in another.

The trip back to Denver also took sixteen hours, with stops along the way to shunt cars into sidings, set out empties, and pick up loaded cars while the fireman shoveled twenty-four tons of coal, took on coal and water, cleaned the fire, and dumped the ashes. The fireman's job on the North End was so tough that eighteen of the twenty men hired in the fall would quit by spring.

One morning, after coming in on a Cheyenne drag, a slow, tonnage train, the heaviest the locomotive could haul, I started walking from the roundhouse to the Cologne Hotel. About halfway, I sat down on the curbing to rest a few minutes. Cars were rolling along Fifteenth Street, and people passed by on their way to work. Before I could start off again, a policeman poked me with his stick. "What's the matter, buddy, you sick or drunk?"

"I'm not drunk," I told him, thinking a shot of whiskey sounded good. "I just put in sixteen hours firing a 600 on the C&S from Cheyenne," I said, "and I'm worn out."

"You staying at the Cologne?" he wanted to know. I nodded. "Come on, I'll walk with you."

"Let me give you some advice," he said, as we walked along Fifteenth Street. "I put in a few trips as a fireman on the C&S before I got smart and quit. You ought to quit too. It's a killer job." Poking me again with his stick, he said, "Say, I could put in a word for you at the police department. It's a lot easier." I thanked him and said I would probably stick with railroading.

Sometimes firemen wondered how they did the job on the C&S. In 1901, when the company ordered the first of the high-wheeled 4-6-0 passenger engines, 323-331, a delegation of firemen went to the round-house to look over the 323. It weighed 169,500 pounds—a monster. In the opinion of the firemen, no man could shovel enough coal to produce the steam needed to drive that giant down track. They demanded that the company put two firemen on the 323. The master mechanic informed the delegation that one man could do the job, if he hustled. And if he didn't hustle, he would be fired.

By the early 1920s, the C&S had purchased the 350 and 370 class pas-senger engines, bigger and faster yet. In fact, the 373, 374, and 375 weighed nearly 300,000 pounds. It also bought six 800 class locomotives that weighed more than 320,000 pounds. Each purchase put locomotives on the roster that were harder to fire than the last, and the 323 no longer seemed like a monster.

Even though locomotives on the North End were hand fired, the C&S ran a few 900 class locomotives with Duplex stokers on the Joint Line. On the 900s, the fireman's main job was to keep the stoker working—making sure the coal moved along the worm drive from the tender to the metal barrels at the rear of the firebox. From there, it moved on elevators into the firebox where steam jets blew it across the firebed. The whole contraption ran on the power of a small steam engine located in the cab near the fireman's seat. When the stoker balked—or if spikes, pieces of iron, or wood jammed the moving parts—the fireman picked up the shovel.

When the stoker jammed during one trip on a 900 class engine, the engineer ordered me to start shoveling. I protested, knowing that once I picked up the shovel, I wouldn't lay it down until the end of the trip. "Give me a minute to find the trouble," I said. With the steam pressure dropping, the engine slowing, and the engineer fussing, I checked the parts of the stoker, finally locating a chunk of concrete in the elevator. As soon as I dislodged it, the stoker started working again. Even though stokers made the job easier for firemen, the C&S did not install stokers on all road locomotives until the early 1940s. The company also replaced Duplex stokers with the more efficient Standard stoker which had a long worm drive that moved the coal from the tank to the firebox. Inside the box, the coal was elevated to a firing plate where steam jets blew it across the fire. It also had a crusher that would crush anything except iron, which meant that the stoker seldom jammed.

Without stokers, the 500 and 600 class engines, 2-8-0s that weighed about 200,000 pounds and hauled most of the North End freights, were a challenge to fire. To make matters worse, engineers could be cranky and hard to work for. Some had been behind the throttle forty years and were beyond tolerating new firemen still learning the job. They could be inconsiderate, demanding, and so impossible to please that firemen called in sick or laid off to avoid them. One engineer on the North End had a reputation for reporting firemen, which meant immediate dismissal. He would watch the fireman during the trip and wait to catch him breaking some rule. When he reported Clarence, the master mechanic held an investigation, cleared Clarence of wrongdoing, and told the engineer the next change in the crew would be on the right side of the cab.

I knew his reputation when I was called to fire for him on freight train 41, rolling north to Cheyenne with a 600 class engine. It was a cold, stormy night, and we had closed the cab windows and curtains in an effort to stay warm. As we approached Longmont, we saw the red order board and the operator, hoop in hand, standing on the platform ready to hand up the orders as we steamed by. I expected the engineer to open his window and grab the hoop, since the operator was on his side.

"Got the orders?" he shouted.

"No," I said. "Didn't you?"

He set the air, stopped the train, and sent the brakeman back for the orders. As soon as the brakeman got off the engine, he turned on me, cursing and calling me every name he could think of. I said nothing, waiting for him to calm down. I knew engineers as a sometimes proud and high-handed lot, but at twenty-two years old, six-feet tall, weighing 175 pounds, with every confidence I could lick my weight in mountain lions, I wasn't easily intimidated. My silence infuriated him, and he continued shouting and cursing. Finally, I grabbed him by the collar, pushed him against the front panel, and said. "Enough. If you had wanted me to get the orders on your side, you should have said so."

"Wait a minute," he stammered. "Let's talk this over." As the years went by, other firemen still complained about his bullying, but when I fired for him, we always talked things over.

On another occasion, I was firing a beet train out of Fort Collins with thirty-five empty cars bound for Wellington and with a hot-tempered engineer no fireman liked. Just out of the west yard, he and the brakeman got into a heated argument. Suddenly, the engineer threw the throttle wide open and pushed down the Johnson Bar, and we took off like a cyclone in Oklahoma with the exhaust tearing up the fire. I was shoveling as fast as I could while coal was blowing out the stack. With the steam pressure dropping, I yelled to the engineer, "Close her down." We hurtled down track with the throttle open and the pressure still dropping. "Close her down," I shouted again, but he was bent over the throttle, holding it wide open.

Finally, I put the clinker hook into the firebox, waited until it was red hot, took it out, and pointed it at the engineer's seat. I had no intention of poking him, but he didn't know that. He glimpsed the hook out of the corner of his eye, jumped up, and fled out the narrow door in front of his seat. I reached over and flipped the lock on the door. Then I closed down the throttle and notched back the Johnson Bar. Back and forth I went between the right and left sides of the engine cab, shoveling coal, checking the water, and running the engine. Gradually, I brought the engine under control, while the engineer was outside on the running board, holding onto the bar.

Three miles down track, I pulled the train into the Giddings beet dump where we had orders to drop empties. When I opened the door, the engineer came at me with blood in his eye, threatening to kill me. First, he was going to report me, he said. "You're through railroading. You'll walk back to Denver," he shouted.

"Let's go make out that report," I told him. "And I'm going to make out a report on the way you were running the locomotive." He folded onto his seat, like a sail that had lost its wind. "You're right," he said. "Let's forget it."

In the days when engineers ran the same locomotive, which they bid along with runs on the basis of seniority and considered their personal property, a fireman could be unlucky enough to draw an irascible engineer and a balky engine trip after trip. Or the fireman could draw a considerate engineer and a locomotive that purred like a contented kitten. When Clarence caught on the broad gauge, he got an assignment on the 643, a locomotive that always steamed the way it had been designed to steam. The engineer was Walter Hayes, a gentleman, always fair and thoughtful toward the firemen. Not until 1920 did the C&S conclude that letting engineers have personal engines was not an efficient way to run a railroad. From then on, broad gauge engineers got the locomotive the dispatcher decided should haul the train. There was no changing things with the narrow gauge engineers, however. They continued to run their personal engines.

Most engineers on the North End respected the firemen and their tough job. Engineer Alvie Pierce, who had been set up in 1910, probably thought about his own days behind a shovel when Ed Phelan and I knocked on the door of the Cheyenne shack one night. We had just come in from firing a doubleheader out of Denver with orders to lay over in Cheyenne. We were both broke. When Alvie opened the door, I told him I was looking for Clarence because I wanted to borrow ten dollars. Alvie grabbed his pocketbook, took out a twenty-dollar bill, and handed it to me. "Clarence is sleeping," he said. "No sense in waking him."

On another trip, I was on a southbound train from Cheyenne, firing for engineer Judy Gowder. We had engine 614 and twenty-five cars of crude oil from Casper, Wyoming. Before pulling out, Gowder got a message we were running a test. If the C&S could move the oil to the Denver refinery in record time, it stood to gain profitable business from the oil company.

As we got underway, Gowder was grinning. "Let's show 'em what we can do," he said. We rocketed down track, whistle blowing in the early dawn. At Fort Collins, we took on enough coal to roar the rest of the way into Denver. After picking up orders on the fly, we crossed La Porte and Mountain avenues with everything looking good for a fast run.

As we steamed past the outskirts of town, a large lump of coal rolled off the top of the tank and hit me in the head. Suddenly, I was sprawled on the deck, blood spurting everywhere. Gowder set the air, stopped the train, and whistled back to the depot. He and the brakeman carried me inside and called Doctor Carey, the railroad doctor in Fort Collins. While we waited for him, Gowder hovered over me as if I were one of his children. "You're going to be okay," he kept assuring me. I wasn't sure he was right. In the meantime, the 614 stood on the track with the train. "What about the test run?" I asked.

"To hell with it," Gowder said.

Doc Carey came padding into the depot in his house slippers, with robe thrown over pajamas. They loaded me out to his car and he took me to the office where he stitched the gash in my head. "If that coal had hit a little closer to your temple," he told me, "they wouldn't have had to wake me. Could have just called the coroner."

By the time Doc Carey took me back to the depot and settled me in the caboose of the next southbound freight, Gowder, an extra fireman, and the 614 were on the way to Denver, bringing in one of the latest test trains on the C&S.

CHAPTER EIGHTEEN

Runnin' on Orders, Messages, and Rules

C&S trains ran on handwritten orders, just as in my father's day. But the narrow gauge trains my father ran had four locomotives that weighed about 60,000 pounds each and pulled sixteen cars at twelve miles per hour. Broad gauge trains roared down track at sixty miles per hour with two locomotives on the point, each weighing about 300,000 pounds, and one hundred cars. Still, they ran according to the orders written on flimsy sheets of paper.

The orders for trains that thundered down the line and darted into sidings moments before another train passed came from the dispatcher's office. In Denver, the chief dispatcher and six assistants worked around the clock in three shifts, seven days a week, to keep the trains moving on the North End and on the narrow gauge. There were no electronic maps to pinpoint moving trains, no computers to print out the exact time a train had to take a siding. The dispatchers figured everything in their heads. By looking at the ledgers, where they copied orders for each train, they calculated the position of trains on the line and wrote orders for new trains, sending them into a maze of main lines and sidings, yards and crossings, up and down the Front Range. Once issued, train orders remained in effect until fulfilled, superceded, or annulled.

114

Orders spelled out the train's destination, which trains would be met along the way, which trains had right of track, and which would take either the siding or low rail—the side rail where trains moved at lower speeds. Clipped to the orders were work messages that specified work to be done en route, such as "pick up coal cars at Louisville, set out empties at Longmont, deliver loaded cars to Fort Collins." The conductor received two copies of ten to twenty different orders and messages and gave one set to the engineer. The double copies provided a back-up system in case either the engineer or conductor misread or forgot the orders.

Forgetting orders, or not following them exactly, could prove fatal. On two occasions, the engineers for whom I was firing misread, misinterpreted, or just plain forgot the orders and nearly got us killed. One incident occurred as we were pulling out of the Denver yards on a northbound freight with orders to stay back of the spring switch at Utah Junction until a southbound passenger train came through. The engineer ran past the switch and out onto the main line, but the conductor pulled the emergency brakes, stopping the train. The engineer realized immediately that he had gone past the switch with the passenger train bearing down the mainline. He threw the reverse lever and backed the train off the main line seconds before the passenger streaked by.

On another occasion, I was firing for Jake Johannbroer on the 627 out of Cheyenne with a tonnage train. Because of a soft spot on the track, we had orders not to exceed ten miles per hour at milepost 103. Johannbroer, an alert engineer usually on top of the job, forgot about the soft spot and we roared past the milepost at thirty-five miles per hour on the downgrade. The 627 rocketed upward, airborne, and landed back on the track, pitching from side to side as Johannbroer set the brakes, trying to bring the train to a stop. After it finally stopped, we climbed out of the engine to assess the damage. The spring hangers on the right side were broken, and the driving springs stood on end, with the top stuck in the boiler jacket. Only luck had kept the unbalanced locomotive from flipping over. Since not even the most mechanically talented engineer could repair the damage on the spot, the engineer and conductor decided to make a slow run for Fort Collins. We crawled down the track, the 627 bucking sideways, holding our breath that it would stay on track.

Not only were crews expected to follow orders, the operators down the line were expected to pass them on correctly. When the dispatcher telegraphed additional orders to a moving train, the operator wrote them on a green form and handed them up on a hoop to the engineer as the train passed the station. If the orders countermanded, or changed previous orders, the operator wrote them on a yellow form and signaled the engineer to stop the train and sign for them. This was done to make sure the engineer understood he had different orders.

One foggy evening in the 1940s, after I had been promoted to engineer, I slowed into Loveland with the 904 on the head of a long freight. As we passed the station, the operator, a new man on the road, handed up the orders. Although he had not signaled me to stop and sign for them, I saw at a glance they were on a yellow form. I set the brake and hollered to the fireman and brakeman to get ready to jump. We were rolling down the main line when we might have lost right of track, and a southbound train could have been bearing down on us in the fog. The train screeched to a stop, and I whistled back to the depot where I read the orders. Instead of countermanding our original orders, as I expected, they were additional instructions that should have been written on a green form. There we sat at the depot, losing time, with the crew shaking at the thought of a head-on collision in the fog. I jumped off the engine, strode into the operator's office, and threw the yellow form on his desk. By then, he had realized I should have signed for the yellow form, and he had covered his mistake by forging my name to his records. "What are you trying to do, kill somebody?" I asked.

"It was a mistake," he shrugged. "It won't happen again."

"You're right," I said, "because you won't be working on this railroad." Not long after I filed a report on the incident, he was fired.

When operators passed on orders correctly and everyone followed them, things ran smoothly.But on one occasion, the conductors decided to "rewrite" orders and bring themselves home early. I was firing the 601 on a freight to Cheyenne with orders giving us right of track over three southbound extras pulled by the 609, 703, and 615. We were to wait at ARA near Boulder until the 609 pulled into the siding. Then we were to run to Longmont and wait for the 703 to go into the sidetrack. From there, we were to head to Berthoud and wait for the 615 to take the siding. The same orders had been telegraphed to stations along the line and given to those trains.

We stopped at ARA, took on water, and waited for the 609. When it pulled into the siding, it was flying a red flag. The brakeman jumped off and ran to our engine with a note from the conductor of the 703, saying the 703 was following the 609 on a flag and ordering us to wait at ARA until both trains passed.

The note contradicted our orders, but we couldn't continue down the main line with the 703 heading toward us. We waited. Finally, the 703 chugged down line and stopped. Another brakeman jumped off, ran to the engine, and handed up a note from the conductor of the 615. It was also coming on a flag, the note said, and we were to wait at ARA until it had passed.

We waited, even though our orders said we should have been in Berthoud by this time and the operators were telegraphing down the line looking for us. By the time the 615 passed and we got underway, we were more than two hours late. But the crews of the first two trains were already home, and the crew of the 615 was on the way.

Several days later, Superintendent E.B. Mitchell called a meeting with the dispatcher, the operators on the line, and crews from all four trains. "What happened to the 601?" he wanted to know. The dispatcher and operators produced orders for the four trains. My engineer produced the two notes from the conductors. Mitchell exploded. "The dispatcher's office sends out the trains on this railroad," he roared. "And since that office never closes, it is never necessary for crews to take over the dispatcher's duty. From now on," he warned, "C&S trains will be dispatched from the dispatcher's office only, not from the caboose."

To avoid any confusion in the orders, the C&S changed some of the old names on the line. Boulder Junction became ARA, which stands for American Railway Association, so engineers would not confuse it with Boulder station three miles away. Louisville Junction, three miles from Louisville station, became Coalton, named for the coal loaded there. Grenfell, a beet loading dock outside Longmont, was named for the C&S treasurer. Names that could not be confused with other places remained the same, such as Utah Junction, a little over three miles from Denver Union Station, named for the Denver, Utah and Pacific crossing of the old Colorado Central. Semper, twelve miles north of the station, had been named for a homestead in the area.

Clear orders were especially important on the C&S, which had no backup system. By the 1920s, both the Union Pacific and the Santa Fe had installed electric block signals that flashed green for trains to proceed and red to stop. An opposing train coming down track automatically activated the red signal. Such a signal would have warned the engineer at Utah Junction not to pull onto the main line. With the exception of block signals between Pueblo and Trinidad, the C&S operated without electric signal systems. Even in later years, when most railroads had installed the Centralized Traffic Control System, which allows the dispatcher's office to activate lights and direct trains on the line, C&S trains still ran on written orders figured out in the dispatcher's head.

While orders changed from train to train, rules under which railroaders worked stayed the same. Every railroader had two rule books, and he knew them from cover to cover. Schedule rules, hammered out over the years by the company and the unions, covered rates of pay, seniority rights, methods of handling grievances, and other rights of the railroaders.

Operating rules covered the standard operating procedures adopted by all Western railroads. Engineers were required to attend classes on the operating rules twice each year, at no pay. The rules spelled out everything railroaders were expected to do during a trip. For example, if a train made an unscheduled stop, one rule required the engineer to "whistle out a flag" with one short blast and three long blasts of the whistle. This meant that the brakeman had to run along the track with his flagging kit, which contained a red flag, fusees, and torpedos. At night, he also carried two hayburner lanterns—a white lantern to cast light for himself and a red lantern to signal an oncoming train. The rule stated that he should light a fusee and set it next to the rail, and lay a torpedo on the rail. Still another rule told the engineer in an oncoming train what to do when he saw a fusee or heard the loud bang as his locomotive rolled over a torpedo. One torpedo explosion meant he should stop immediately. Two torpedos not more than 200 feet apart meant he should slow down and look for danger ahead.

Rules specified such things as the number of whistles the engineer must use to call the brakeman back to the train. No matter how many trains were in an area, each brakeman knew when his engineer was signaling him. If the conductor wanted to make an unscheduled stop on a passenger train—to let off a rancher near his house, for example—rules required him to give three short blasts on the air signal. This signal operated with an air hose that ran the length of the train. The engineer acknowledged the signal with three short blasts of the whistle and stopped the train.

One of the oldest rules was the noise rule, requiring trains to make as much noise as possible when approaching a crossroads or pulling into a station. Left over from the earliest days of railroading, the rule grew out of the necessity to warn folks of the locomotive steaming down track at the giddy speed of five miles per hour. In the 1830s, mounted policemen in New York City led the trains into the station, warning people to get off the track. A century later, engineers were still turning on the bell, blowing the whistle, and letting the steam gust so that people knew the train was coming.

Another rule required engineers to have their twenty-one-jeweled railroad standard watches inspected twice each month. Before starting on a trip, the engineer set his watch in the lighted panel in the engine where he could see it at all times. The watches kept perfect time in any position, despite jarring or vibrations. Any engineer who wore a wristwatch instead of using a railroad standard watch was fired.

The most famous rule was Rule G, prohibiting the use of intoxicants on the job. The penalty was immediate dismissal. While a few conductors and brakemen would sometimes pack a bottle of whiskey in their grips, despite the rule, it was rare for an engineer or fireman to drink on the job.

Railroaders who might tolerate whiskey in the caboose would not tolerate it on the engine. Running a steam locomotive was dangerous enough with the enginemen alert and in top form. No one wanted to ride a speeding train down the main line with a drunken engineer at the throttle, or a drunken fireman keeping an eye on the water level in the boiler. What's more, engineers took a sobriety oath when they joined the BLE, and not drinking was a matter of honor. Not only would the company fire an intoxicated engineer, the BLE would expel him.

Even though it was presumptuous of a fireman to remind an engineer of some rule, sometimes it was necessary. One night I pulled out of Denver on a northbound freight with an 800 class engine and Charlie Conroe, an expert engineer on the North End, at the throttle. The trip went smoothly until we steamed past the Loveland depot and the conductor pulled the air to stop the train. While we waited to start again, Charlie told me to dump the ashes. Taking care of the time-consuming job while we were stopped meant we wouldn't lose more time in Fort Collins. I reminded Charlie of the rule to dump ashes only on iron plates between the rails. There was no iron plate where we sat.

"It'll be okay," he assured me.

I stood on the rule. "The ashes could set the ties on fire," I reminded him. "Besides, I would just get started, the conductor would give us the highball, and I would be responsible for delaying the train."

"Don't worry," Charlie insisted. "I'll take the responsibility."

"But I'll get the brownies," I argued.

We continued arguing, with Charlie insisting I dump the ashes while I insisted on the rule. Finally the conductor gave us the highball. Charlie gave up the argument and opened the throttle.

Years later, after Charlie had retired to an easy chair where he could smoke his pipe and peer at the newspaper through wire-rimmed spectacles, I used to visit him and reminisce about our trips together on the North End. "You were the most stubborn man I ever worked with," he told me. "There was nobody as stubborn as you on the road."

I said, "Sure there was, Charlie. You."

CHAPTER NINETEEN

Those Depression Years

The Depression was lurking on the horizon in the late 1920s, but neither the C&S nor the railroaders saw it. The 1920s were golden years for railroads across the nation. Trains still hauled most of the freight and the travelers. Railroads operated under the assumption that their monopoly on transportation would last forever, despite the fact that highways were being developed, more Americans were purchasing automobiles, and the trucking industry was picking up business. Railroads kept expanding, adding bigger steam locomotives to the rosters and improving tracks and stations. Capital expenditures of railroads in the 1920s equalled the amount spent in the entire previous history of railroading. On the C&S, six 370 class and five 900 class locomotives were added to the roster. The C&S had purchased another five 900 class engines in 1919. The bigger locomotives meant that heavier track had to be laid. Thirty-nine-foot-long steel rails weighing between 90 and 100 pounds per yard gradually replaced lighter rails, including sections of the old thirty-foot-long, 30-pound iron rails.

Every day, sixteen freight trains on the North End rolled out of the C&S yards, and that number did not include extra trains put on from time to time to haul sugar beets, wheat, cattle, coal, and iron ore. Passenger trains 29, 30, 31, and 32 ran every day between Denver and Wendover, Wyoming, while passenger trains 32 and 33 ran between Denver and Fort Collins. It seemed we hardly had time to take off our boots from one trip before setting out on another. But the steady work had given me enough savings to buy a house in north Denver, two miles from the roundhouse in a neighborhood of railroaders. Since the C&S rules required railroaders to live within ten blocks of the roundhouse if they did not have telephones, I put in a phone. My mother moved in to keep house and cook for me. Life was good, and occasionally, I found the time between trips to date Irma, a dark-haired, pretty young woman I had met at a dance.

One Sunday, Irma invited me home for dinner. When we finished the fried chicken, Irma and her mother quietly disappeared, leaving me alone at the dining table with her father, the stocky, bald proprietor of a tire store.

After puffing his cigar and looking me over a few moments, he asked, "What are your plans, young man?"

At first I thought he was referring to my plans for his daughter. I was about to assure him they were honorable when I realized he meant my plans for the future. "As you know, sir," I began, "I'm a railroader."

"Yes, yes," he said, puffing his cigar. "But what are your plans?"

"I plan to be an engineer," I answered. His face brightened. "A railroad engineer," I said, making sure he understood.

"See this house?" he asked, waving his cigar. "And this furniture?"

I looked around the room at the upholstered, straight-back chairs and the buffet with lace doilies and silver candlestick holders. And I looked down the table toward him.

"They're very nice," I said.

"Tell me," he asked, "do you think a railroader could provide a house and furniture like this?"

"I hope so," I answered.

He grunted, shifted, took another puff, and tried another tact. "You're away from home all the time, aren't you?"

I agreed it seemed that way.

"You're comin' and goin' all hours, don't know where you'll be this time tomorrow, right?"

I nodded.

He leaned toward me, and in a fatherly tone, asked, "Now what kind of life is that for a grown man?"

Before I could tell him I considered it a good life, he said, "Since Irma likes you, and you seem to be a fine young man, I'm prepared to make you an offer. The day you and Irma are married, you'll become a partner in my tire store. What do you think?" he prodded.

Not knowing what to think, I blurted, "What would I do in a tire store?"

"Why, sell tires, of course," he answered, slapping his knee as if the matter were settled.

I saw myself streaking down track with whistle blowing and the sun high overhead, not penned behind the counter of a tire store. "Sir," I said, "I'm grateful for your offer, but I'm a railroader."

He stubbed out his cigar, rose from his chair, and announced, "Young man, I will never permit my daughter to marry a railroader."

After saying goodbye to Irma's father, I found Irma in the parlor and said goodbye to her. I never saw them again.

About the time I turned down the partnership in the tire store, confidently looking toward the future on the railroad, the stock market crashed. At first, the crash did not affect the C&S. Scheduled trains still ran on the North End every day, with crews still milling about the roundhouse, coming and going on trips.

But gradually, the Depression gathering in the East began to cast dark shadows over the West. As eastern banks and factories failed, the demand dropped for the raw materials—coal, iron ore, lumber—hauled by western railroads, including the C&S. The railroad business dropped even more as manufactured goods such as steel, cement, tools, machinery, clothing, and furniture grew scarce. To make matters worse, trucks began to siphon off some of the railroad's business. Farmers and manufacturers who could not afford whole carloads of supplies and equipment bought partial carloads shipped by trucks. In 1930, C&S operating income dropped 22 percent below that of the previous year.

The company reacted to the slowdown by abolishing 30 percent of the jobs. Firemen on the extra board who had just caught on the road were the first "cut off," or laid off. Older firemen, men with five and six years seniority,came next. After that, firemen like myself, with eight to ten years seniority and regular jobs,were cut off. New engineers dropped back to firing, and, eventually, engineers with ten years behind the throttle found themselves shoveling coal. Brakemen and conductors were also laid off until only the most senior men remained.

By 1931, the 112 trains that the C&S had run every week on the North End had dropped to eight. Only four trains with five cars each left Denver for Cheyenne twice each week. Mile after mile of boxcars, coal cars, and coaches rusted on sidetracks in the Denver yards. Operating income dropped another 25 percent in 1932, and the following year, those railroaders still holding jobs agreed to a 10 percent cut in wages. Even though the downward trend halted in 1933, business on the C&S would not reach the level of the 1920s until World War II. But business had picked up enough by 1935 that the company rescinded the 10 percent wage cut.

In the bleakest years of the Depression, between 1931 and 1935, I made trips whenever the caller needed an extra fireman. A few of those trips took me back to Como on the passenger train that went to Leadville every other day and returned the next day, carrying an average of sixteen passengers. Or I caught a trip on one of the freight trains still plying the South Park District. On opposite days, the eastbound and westbound freights met in Como on the way to Denver or Leadville, keeping the roundhouse workers busy servicing the four locomotives on each train. But the roundhouse was quiet, with only the passenger locomotive taking on coal and water on days the freights didn't come through. Minor running repairs were still made in the Como shops where Phil Duffy held forth as foreman.

The Depression engulfing the country in the 1930s had hit Como with the 1910 closings and never lifted. There was still no electricity in town, no indoor plumbing. Roads were unpaved, houses boarded up. The last remnant of the weathered, rickety wooden addition to the roundhouse stood until 1935 when a hostler backed engine number 72 into a stall and sparks from the stack ignited a bird's nest, setting the addition on fire. The fire also damaged the wood parts of the numbers 72 and 75, as well as the rotary.

After years of bucking snow and pulling trains over the steep grades, many of the old narrow gauge locomotives spent more time in the shops than on the road. But the steel-framed rolling stock that the C&S had built in the early 1900s was still in good condition. The company began retiring some of the worn-out narrow gauge locomotives and leasing replacements. The Chicago, Burlington and Quincy's number 537, a 2-8-0, came on the roster in 1929, and in 1935, the 343, 345, and 346, also 2-8-0s, were leased from the Denver and Rio Grande Western. The blind drivers on these engines caused frequent derailments, however, until the C&S installed half-flanges on the middle drivers to keep them on track.

Narrow gauge trains were dispatched out of Denver instead of Como, but after twenty years of isolation, South Park railroaders had taken to running trains their own way, with the conductors often sending them down track on flags to suit their own schedules. Like the old fast freight to Leadville, westbound trains usually ran straight through while the eastbound trains switched and shunted cars all the way to Como. This suited the conductors and brakemen, giving them more time at home in Leadville, but it meant a sixteen-hour trip home for the engineers and firemen who lived in Como.

Trips to Como and anywhere else were far apart and unreliable. Since I was cut off most of the time, I picked up odd jobs, hauling bricks from demolished buildings for ten cents an hour, or driving a coal truck twelve hours a day for one dollar. At one point, Clarence, who had also been

cut off, landed a job as stationary fireman at the Hungarian Flour Mills for
five dollars each eight-hour shift, six nights a week. It was the kind of job
that made a man feel like a millionaire in the Depression. One afternoon,
he was getting ready to go to work when he noticed a red rash on his
chest. Since his four children were in bed with the measles, he didn't need
a doctor's diagnosis.

With hundreds of men looking for work, Clarence knew that if he
called in sick, he would lose the job. He called me. I packed my lunch,
walked to the mill, waited until two minutes before the shift started, when
it would be too late for the engineer to call someone else, and walked
into the office. I told the engineer Clarence was sick, but I could handle
the job. He scratched his head, looked me up and down, and said, "Okay."
By the time Clarence got over the measles, the C&S called him back, leaving me with the mill job for several months until the Depression ended
the late shift.

At another point, I hunted up a job with a decorator. After spending
several months learning to paint and hang wallpaper, I bought a set of
tools and went into the business with Clarence, who had been cut off again
from the C&S. When the old engineers and other railroaders who still had
jobs found out about our business, they hired us to redecorate their houses,
whether they needed it or not. They knew we needed the work.

Other railroaders who had been cut off weren't so lucky. They filled
the long unemployment lines each day with hordes of others, hoping to
pick up a few hours work. When they didn't find work, they stood in
lines in downtown Denver for a cup of soup and a piece of pie, their only
meal of the day.

Most days I was too busy scrambling for a living to think about the
Depression, but one afternoon while driving to Montgomery Ward on
South Broadway to buy decorating tools, I was struck by the emptiness
of the city. There were no automobiles in the streets, and no one was walking down the sidewalks. Shops and businesses were shuttered, and everything was quiet, as if Denver had been deserted. I thought, "What terrible
thing has come over this country?"

One snowy night in December 1932, Willard Erway, the caller, banged
on my front door. Since I couldn't afford a telephone, he had walked two
miles from the roundhouse to call me for a trip. "You haven't gone out
in a while," he told me. "Thought you might like the work."

He was right. I needed the work more than at any other time during
the Depression. Despite the fact that I had picked up odd jobs and my
mother had taken in a few railroaders as boarders, I hadn't been able to
save enough money to pay the taxes on the house. For the lack of $200
I was about to lose a $3,000 house. Not long after I mentioned this to

my close friend, Joe Loughry, he called to say his father, Pat, wanted to see me.

I went to the Loughry house and found the old Irishman, retired now from railroading, sitting in an overstuffed chair in the living room. "What about your troubles, lad?" he asked. I told him I couldn't pay the taxes on my house. "And how much would ye be needing?"

"A lot," I said. "Two hundred dollars."

Pat pulled a white sock from the crack between the cushion and arm of the chair. Not believing in banks, he hadn't lost his money when the banks closed. His life savings were in the sock, and he pulled out a wad of bills, counting out $200.

"I can't take your money, Pat," I said.

"And why not?" he asked. "Is it that ye want to lose your house?"

"No," I said, "I sure don't."

"Tis only a borrow," he said, pushing the money toward me. "Give it back when times are good."

I looked at Joe, who was grinning. "That's what Pop wants," he assured me, "and so do I."

Every trip during the Depression made me realize that I was lucky to have work, no matter how sporadic or short-lived. Whole armies of men were on the move, traveling from coast to coast and border to border looking for work. Everyone of them, it seemed, rode the boxcars through Denver, with an estimated 800 to 1,000 coming through town each month. One evening at Prospect station, north of Union Station, I counted fifty hobos getting on the freight train on my side alone.

On another trip, we had orders to drop eight empty boxcars in Fort Collins. As soon as we uncoupled the cars, hobos spilled out like ants and scurried to cars still in the train. When one hobo tried to climb into a box-car, a large, bearded man blocked the door. "This is my car," he said. The man on the ground opened his jacket showing a bottle of wine in the inside pocket. The other man reached down, gave him a hand, and said, "Brother, let me help you into my car."

On another trip to Fort Collins, hobos flew off every car as soon as Engineer Walter Hayes backed the train into the west yard. One ran up to the engine. "What town is this?" he called. Hayes shouted, "Fort Collins."

The hobo said, "How did I get here? I just left here yesterday."

The hobos camped up and down the tracks, waiting to catch on a moving train. They preferred to ride inside boxcars, but they also shoved planks across the truss rods under the boxcars, making platforms where they rode one foot above the rails. The largest hobo jungle on the North End spread alongside the Poudre River under the C&S bridge in Fort

Collins. The trains rumbled over the bridge at night, with campfires flickering below like the lights of a small town.

Riding the rails was dangerous, even though the trains held out hope
to thousands of vagabonds that somewhere down the line they would find
a better place than the place they had left. One day several hobos hopped
a Rio Grande freight train and staked out a place in the end of a boxcar
half filled with scrap iron. When the train stopped suddenly, the scrap
iron slid to the end, crushing two men and mangling the legs of three
others.

In another incident, five young hobos took a near-fatal ride on a northbound C&S freight that I was firing. It was a bitter cold January day, with
temperatures hovering for hours at ten degrees above zero and snow crust-
ing the ground. We left Denver with orders to set out empties at Crouse,
milepost 103. After switching the engine to a sidetrack, we started pushing the empties alongside the train. As we rolled along, I happened to
glimpse five boys lying in an open coal car. I shouted to the engineer to
stop. We jumped out of the engine and ran to the car, calling the brakemen and conductor to help. We picked up the semiconscious boys, who
were about sixteen years old, carried them to the engine, and got them
moving in front of the opened firebox door. After they ate the hot soup,
coffee, and sandwiches we pooled from our lunchboxes, they told us they
were heading to Casper to find jobs, which they needed to help their families. We told them to go back and look for work closer to home. There
weren't any more jobs in Casper than anywhere else, and if they hadn't
frozen to death trying to get there, they were sure to freeze in the Wyoming
winter. The conductor put them in the caboose for the rest of the trip
to Cheyenne and saw to it they got on another caboose for the trip back
to Denver.

By 1936, the wheels of banking and commerce had started slowly turning again, and the Depression began to lift. Crews that had been laid off
for five years were hired back, eventually finding themselves with a regular
schedule. I worked ten months that year, with the growing hope that my
railroading career hadn't been permanently sidetracked after all.

But the narrow gauge sections did not survive the Depression. After
filing several petitions for abandonment, the C&S finally won permission
from the Interstate Commerce Commission to abandon the old routes.
On April 9, 1937, the last South Park train bound for Leadville pulled out
of Union Station. J.F. Farthing was at the throttle of the number 60 and
Robert Terril was the fireman. The conductor was Tom St. John. Roy F.
Hight was the brakeman. At Como, the number 9 went on the point, Engineer Curly Colligan at the throttle, and Conductor St. John still riding the
coaches for the last leg of the trip to Leadville. The following day, the

train made the final run into Denver. Within a year, the track leading in and out of Como was pulled up.

Two years later, the C&S abandoned the old Clear Creek line between Idaho Springs and Silver Plume, once part of the old Colorado Central. It dismantled the Georgetown Loop, selling the steel from Devil's Gate to a mining company for $450. On May 4, 1941, the last narrow gauge train in the Clear Creek chugged to Idaho Springs and Black Hawk.

In the early 1940s, the only C&S narrow gauge trains left ran between Leadville and the molybdenum mine at Climax, with the 74, 75, or 76 on the point. In 1943, the C&S converted the route to a standard gauge, or broad gauge, as the C&S railroaders called it. On August 25, engine number 76 made the final run on a C&S narrow gauge line. That same year, the company removed the third rail from the Denver yards. An era of Colorado railroading had ended.

With business picking up on the broad gauge in 1936, I felt confident enough in the future to ask Margaret McCloskey, a secretary for a Denver architectural firm, to marry me. Her family approved of railroading, possibly because I had been lucky enough to come through the worst of the Depression with a job and house while neighbors and friends all around hadn't been so lucky. Her older brother, Frank, confided to me that his lifelong ambition was to be a railroad engineer, but he had never been able to catch on a road. After Margaret and I were married, my mother, Ellen, lived with us until her death in 1938. Through her father, husband, and sons, she had spent a lifetime railroading.

Over the next few years, it seemed that every time I came in off a trip late at night, I heard a baby crying as soon as I turned the corner half a block from home. I knew that, after shoveling twenty-four tons of coal and working sixteen hours, I was about to take a turn walking the floor with one of my three children. I had become a family man.

We lived near other railroading families. Both Clarence's family and Neil's family were growing up a few blocks away. My brothers had also gotten back on the road and were making regular trips. Even though we were seldom home at the same time, our families got together for dinners and picnics. We joined them when we could.

Often Joe Loughry's family joined Margaret, me, and the kids for a summer outing. We would pile everybody, along with the dogs and luggage, into a Model T Ford and Chevrolet and head for Buena Vista, where we would spend a week hiking the abandoned roadbeds of the old South Park near St. Elmo, Romley, Hancock, and the Alpine Tunnel. By then, rockslides had blocked the tunnel, the winds blew through the abandoned, ramshackle remains of the station buildings and the once-busy stops on the old South Park line had become ghost towns.

A close-up view of the rotary at work on Boreas Pass, with the front blade chopping through the snow. *J.V. Dietz collection.*

Conductor Tom St. John, *right,* and fireman Art Aichell wait at Halfway Tank on Boreas Pass, about 1903. *R.A. Ronzio collection.*

Como in 1895. *S.F. Speas collection.*

The first Sam
Speas, *left*, with
Dave Sullivan,
fireman, and Tom
St. John,
conductor. *S.F.
Speas llection.*

The first Sam Speas is shown on the stoop of the family home in Como in the early 1900s. Speas was a Como town trustee and a member of the Como school board. Railroad engineers considered themselves leading citizens of their towns. *C.E. Speas collection.*

A runaway caused this pile-up in the 1890s on a curve west of Selkirk Tank on Boreas Pass. *S.F. Speas collection.*

Members of the Brotherhood of Locomotive Firemen and Enginemen pose for a portrait in the 1890s. *Top row, left to right:* Ed Conahan, Bill Lyons, Morriss Jordan, Ed Haight. *Bottom row, left to right:* Charles Markle, Ole Westlund, Tom Moore, Bud Mathews, and Webster Ballinger. Ballinger was killed in a runaway on Kenosha Pass in 1901. *George Champion collection.*

The number 6, Sam Speas's personal engine, stands on the track at the Como roundhouse around 1910. *S.F. Speas collection.*

Inside the Boulder Union depot, the office is a study of ordered chaos, with the telegrapher's ledger on the left below the telegraph wire box, a copy press, hoops to hold up orders so that engineers could pick them up "on the fly," an all-cap typewriter for typing orders, dispatchers, phones, and even a spittoon. *Mike Trene collection.*

Clarence Speas is the engineer on this freight train heading north out of Denver on August 14, 1957. *M.C. Trent photo.*

On one of his last runs as an engineer, the senior Sam Speas (with foot on rail) is shown in 1921 with a picnic train he hauled from Buena Vista to Chalk Creek Canon. *C.E. Speas collection.*

Sam Speas, the author, had been firing on the Colorado and Southern (C&S) four years when this photograph was taken at Morrison, in about 1925. *R.A. Ronzio collection.*

The Barnes and Sells-Floto Circus is unloaded from the train in Boulder in 1937. *Boulder Daily Camera collection. Courtesy Lawrence Paddock.*

At Loveland in the 1940s with passenger engine 370 are, *left to right:* master mechanic Frank Gregg, fireman Ed Mortensen, and engineer Clarence Speas. *C.E. Speas collection.*

The crew of the 904 at Longmont, Colorado, July 13, 1957. *Left to right:* Ralph Monahan, conductor; John Dietz, brakeman; George Cheffey, brakeman; Lee Frame, brakeman; Clarence Speas, engineer; John Fenton, fireman. *M.C. Trent collection.*

Finally free of the snowdrifts, the 7020 backs to Fort Collins in January 1949. *S.F. Speas collection.*

The crew of the Pioneer Zephyr during the period that the Zephyr operated in Colorado. *Left to right:* R. Monahan, conductor; George Gwinn, brakeman; Sam Speas (the author), fireman; and Judy Gowder, engineer. *S.F. Speas collection.*

In April 1950, a truck hit the Pioneer Zephyr at a crossing south of Fort Collins, trapping the fireman, Don Grinstead, in the cab. *C.E. Speas collection.*

A tangled pile of wreckage is left after the head-on collision of freight train 77 and passenger train 30 near the Broomfield depot on September 22, 1958.
M.C. Trent photo.

Neil Speas is in the cab, while Clarence Speas stands in the gangway. *S.F. Speas collection.*

The number 807 rolls south past Valmont on February 12, 1959, with Sam Speas at the throttle of a steam locomotive for the last time. *M.C. Trent photo.*

Neil Speas in the cab of the 904, with orders on the clipboard, June 17, 1957. *M.C. Trent photo.*

Steam locomotive number 638 waits for the diesel-powered passenger train in 1958. *M.C. Trent photo.*

Sam Speas was the engineer on this northbound freight train, September 12, 1958. *M.C. Trent photo*.

Sam Speas stops at Boulder on July 3, 1967, the morning of his last trip. *S.F. Speas collection*.

Railroaders kept the trains running in all kinds of weather, such as this blizzard near Boulder on April 11, 1957. *M.C. Trent photo.*

Passenger train number 30 rounds Valmont Lake on June 19, 1966. Sam Speas is the engineer. *M.C. Trent photo.*

CHAPTER TWENTY

Special Trains

By 1940, I had moved up to senior fireman on the C&S, but I was still a fireman. In my father's day, firemen were set up to engineer after three or four years' experience. But firemen who hired on in the 1920s waited twenty years for promotion, partly because of the slowdown in business during the Depression, but also because of the large group of firemen hired after World War I. With two or three more years seniority, they had moved into the available engineers' jobs still young men and had settled behind the throttle expecting to work another thirty years. I wondered, at times, if I would ever get a chance behind the throttle.

That outlook changed with the onset of World War II. Railroads across the nation, including the C&S, geared up for the biggest volume of business in railroading history. At the same time, the national draft had started to create an acute shortage of skilled railroaders.

Despite the obvious need for more engineers, in the early months of the war, Charlie Shaughnessy, the road foreman in charge of promotions, remained confident current engineers could handle the load. Seeing no reason why firemen should be anything but firemen, he refused to give the engineer's exam. Since schedule rules required the C&S to give the exam to firemen with at least eight years seniority before hiring promoted engineers from other railroads, the C&S had no new engineers on the payroll.

After coming in on a drag from Cheyenne one afternoon, I decided I had been a fireman long enough. I walked into Shaughnessy's office at the roundhouse and reminded him that a number of firemen were ready for the engineer's exam. "The company needs new engineers and we need the jobs," I said. Shaughnessy coughed, hemmed, and hawed, but another man I hadn't noticed sitting in a corner spoke up. "Good idea, Shaughnessy. Get on that tomorrow." He was Master Mechanic Frank Gregg, Shaughnessy's boss.

Not much had changed in the engineer's exams since my father's day. They were still oral exams that lasted three days and covered everything an engineer had to know to get the train from one terminal to another—how the steam locomotive worked, how to make repairs en route, what to do if the brakes failed, how to close down a malfunctioning part of the brake system to protect the main system. The exams also covered both operating and schedule rules.

Most C&S firemen could run every class of engine in the roundhouse and recite the rule books backwards. Like the engineers, who were required to attend day-long classes twice each year, firemen also attended a day-long class every year on the locomotive's mechanical systems and the rules. We also got practical experience from engineers like Judy Gowder and Clarence Chapman, who would holler over the clickety-clack of the wheels, the clanking rods, and gusting steam, "Want to run her?" We always jumped at a chance behind the throttle, watching the locomotive hurtle down track while they shoveled coal or ran the stoker.

On May 27, 1940, I passed the exam and was set up to engineer. My seniority date was October 30, 1941, however, because of the rule denying seniority dates to new engineers if engineers ahead of them were still working as firemen. My date was the first day after my promotion that all senior engineers were working as engineers. My brother Clarence had been set up to engineer in 1925, and Neil followed us on the engineer's roster in 1942.

Promotions meant better pay, which was still based on 100 miles, considered an eight-hour day. But by the 1940s, unions had won the concession from companies to base the pay per 100 miles on the class of engine. This gave the railroaders a share in the profits generated by bigger locomotives that hauled more tonnage. For example, the 350 class locomotives paid $8.91 per 100 miles, the 800 class paid $9.25, and the 900 class paid $9.99. A C&S engineer in the 1940s made about $300 per month, putting in at least sixty-hour weeks.

I was called for my first trip as an engineer on July 24, 1940. My fireman was E.W. Hawkins. We pulled out of Denver terminal on the 903, a 2-10-2 locomotive weighing 367,850 pounds, pulling freight train number 45 bound for Fort Collins. I thought about the advice Trainmaster John Bruner had given me after my promotion. "Remember that any fool can start a locomotive," he said. "Your responsibility is to know how and when to stop it. The only other man with that responsibility is the conductor who is 100 cars away."

Even with new men on the roster, C&S engineers put in 100 hours every week during World War II, redballing tanks, guns, ammunition, and troops up and down the Front Range. As a north-south road, the C&S connected to the Burlington, Union Pacific, and Santa Fe trains moving east and west. Ninety-one percent of the military freight and 98 percent of the military personnel moved on the nation's railroads. Since new engineers on the C&S worked off the extra board, I still made occasional trips as a fireman, but enough trains were rolling that I was usually behind the throttle.

On the head of the long freight trains were 800 or 900 class steam locomotives, capable of pulling 1,850 tons each on the ruling grade. One helper engine went on the front, making a "doubleheader" that could haul 100 cars. Every day, a 100-car train of iron ore rolled from Guernsey, Wyoming, to the Colorado Fuel and Iron works in Pueblo, and two trains, each carrying fifty tank cars of oil, moved north from Texas to Wendover, Wyoming. There, they were transferred to the Burlington and hauled to Seattle, where the oil was loaded onto battleships.

The C&S also helped to move troops to the battlefields. Troop trains were usually sixteen cars long, with a diner and cook car in the middle and coaches and Pullmans at both ends. Each train carried 500 army, navy, or marine troops who stayed on the train as it crossed the country, hauled by locomotives and crews of different railroads.

I was at the throttle of a 900 class locomotive on a northbound troop train one evening when we stopped to take on water at Fort Collins. While the fireman was filling the tank, a tall, towheaded soldier came up to the engine. "Where are we?" he hollered.

"Fort Collins," I told him.

He shrugged. "Where's that?"

"Colorado," I said. "Where you from?"

"Hoboken," he replied.

"Where you headed?" I asked.

"San Francisco," he called back.

"You're about halfway there," I told him.

Shaking his head, he said, "I had no idea this country was so big."

Each troop train had a train commander whose authority, at times, even extended over other trains. While hostling in the Denver yards one evening, I had just coupled a locomotive onto a southbound troop train when one of the steam pipes burst. With only an hour before the train's 8 p.m. departure, mechanics were racing about, trying to replace the broken pipe. Suddenly, the train commander appeared on the platform. "Ease up there," he ordered the mechanics. "This train will not depart until 2100 hours." Turning on his heel, he climbed back into the train. While the order gave the mechanics another hour to replace the pipe, it also kept the dispatcher and telegraphers busy notifying the other trains on the line of the change in schedule.

On board the troop trains, the military police enforced the commander's orders, including the order forbidding alcohol. I was oiling the valves and checking the locomotive at Union Station one day, getting ready to move a troop train north, when a six-foot-four soldier, looking as if he had been drafted off the New York Giants' front line, swaggered down the platform. Holding a bottle of whiskey aloft, he shouted, "Nobody's gonna get this." Before he could board the train, a military policeman about half his size stepped in front of him. "Give me the bottle, soldier," he ordered. The soldier meekly handed it over.

Between Denver and Cheyenne, we stopped the troop trains once or twice to let the men exercise. The fireman kept the fire going, and I opened the cock to blow off steam while the train sat on the track and the troops ran through the countryside or down the streets of some small town.

We slowed into Fort Collins with a troop train at noon one day as the soldiers were sitting down to lunch in the dining car, which looked like a mess hall equipped with tin plates and cups. Near the depot, an automobile stalled on the track. I set the emergency brake, almost standing the train on end, and we screeched to a stop inches from the car. Mickey Hansen, the road foreman of engines on the North End, who happened to be traveling with the train, ran up to the engine. "You should see that dining car," he said. "The food is on the ceiling, the coffee's rolling down the aisle, and cups, knives, and forks are scattered everywhere. I got out of there before those soldiers killed me."

Still another time, we were taking on water at Fort Collins when a young soldier hoisted himself into the engine. "This is a nice, smooth ride," he told me. I appreciated the compliment, since he was an engineer on an eastern railroad. The troops on the train were part of a railroad battalion bound for the Philippines and an assignment to run the railroads there.

Following the war years, the C&S converted a few steam locomotives into oil burners, giving the fireman a different set of duties. Among those converted were passenger locomotives 370 to 375, as well as the 353, 531, 646, 647, 648, 800, and 803, and the 900, 902, 903, and 911. On a trip with an oil burner, the fireman had to feed steam from the boiler to the oil in the supply tank which had been set in the coal space. The steam kept the oil hot and liquefied, and it was up to the fireman to judge the right temperature by the feel of the tank. Too much heat and the oil boiled over. Too little, and it could solidify into an asphalt-like substance.

The fireman opened the valve that controlled the flow of oil from the tank to the firebox. At the same time, he let live steam into the firebox, atomizing the oil and causing it to ignite. He regulated the intensity of the fire by the amount of oil injected into the firebox.

If the steam pressure dropped, he knew the oil had clogged the flues. He grabbed his shovel and shoveled sand from the sandbox in the gang-way onto the fire. The exhaust pulled the sand through the flues, cleaning them out, while the smokestack belched black, oily smoke into the air, thick enough to walk across. One tank of oil took a train from Denver to Cheyenne. The fireman did not have to refuel or clean the ash pan en route, saving both time and his energy.

With the end of World War II, the railroads shifted from the high gear of hauling military traffic to a lower gear serving the needs of the civilian population. With gasoline and rubber no longer rationed, trucks, buses, automobiles, and even airplanes began cutting into the railroads' passenger business. But propeller-driven airplanes were small and cramped and flew to only a few cities, while trucks, cars, and buses rolled along two-lane highways or pock-marked dirt roads. C&S passenger trains, on the other hand, streaked up and down the Front Range up to seventy miles per hour. Subsidized by federal mail contracts, passenger trains were still economical for railroads to run. Most mail moved across the country in railway post office cars. Mountains of mail piled up every day at Denver Union Station, waiting to be loaded into the cars. For most Americans, railroads still remained the nation's main form of transportation, a position they would hold only a few more years.

Every evening, passenger train number 29 pulled out of Union Station, destination Billings, and train number 30 returned the next morning. Both trains had five coach cars, a Pullman, and a dining car. Train numbers 31 and 32 with coach cars ran from Denver to Cheyenne and back the same day. On Friday evenings, crowds of university students climbed onto the coaches at Boulder and Fort Collins for weekend visits to their homes throughout Colorado and Wyoming, returning to school on Sunday. Between semesters, out-of-state students shipped their baggage from the local depots to cities across the country and rode the trains to Union Station to catch a passenger train moving east or west.

Some of the old C&S wooden passenger cars still rattled down track in the 1940s, but most had been replaced by steel coaches with double-paned windows and platform coverings. Passengers rode two abreast in plush, red velvet seats on each side of the center aisle. By adjusting the seats, they could face either direction. Drinking faucets and restrooms were located at the end of the cars.

Even more elegant and comfortable were the private cars that carried railroad presidents and industry barons. Only about 2,000 private cars, known as PVs (private varnish—the old term for highly varnished coaches) were built in American railroading history. Resembling sumptuous hotel suites, some were at least forty-two feet long with two bedrooms, a bath, kitchen, paneled dining room, and sitting room that opened onto the observation platform where the passengers watched the countryside slip by from comfortable chairs. The president of the New York Central, for example, could board his private car and travel to California in comfort, paying different railroads to move the car. Coupled onto the end of trains, the private cars were heavy to pull, making slow, difficult trips. Engineers dubbed them "sinkers."

I picked up orders for passenger train 30 at Cheyenne one morning when the operator told me that the private car of Ralph Budd, president of the Burlington since 1932, was on the end of the train. "Give him a smooth ride," he said. I groaned, knowing it would be a slow trip to Denver.

Before the days of *Air Force One,* presidents also crossed the country in private cars. After bringing a passenger train into Union Station one evening during the war, Clarence Chapman was walking alongside the trains toward the station when he spotted the *Ferdinand Magellan,* the private car that carried Franklin Roosevelt 50,000 miles across the country. Built by the Pullman Company in 1928, it was touted as a "mobile security vault" with roof and sides sheathed in five-eighth-inch-thick armor plate, three-inch-thick bulletproof glass in the windows, and a steel platform door that weighed 1,880 pounds. It featured a dining room, four bedrooms, and a sitting area and, at 1,421 tons, was the heaviest private car in the nation.

Sitting on the observation deck of this mobile security vault, cigarette dangling from a long holder, not a secret serviceman or bodyguard in sight, was the president. "Good evening, Mr. President," Chapman blurted out. "Good evening to you, Mr. Railroader," the president said. "What kind of work do you do?"

Chapman told him he was a C&S engineer, just in off a train from Cheyenne. Roosevelt asked if the railroad had enough work, and Chapman replied that, with the war on, railroaders had more work than they needed. The president said he hoped the war would not be on much longer. Chapman tipped his cap and said, "It's been nice talking to you," and continued to the station.

While the war was on, special trains, including circus trains, stayed in the sidetracks, since no railroad had the motive power or crews to haul them. But in the mid-1940s, circus trains started rolling again, white flags on the locomotives, buntings flying from the bright red cars as they had since the first circus train rumbled down track in 1872. Since long trains meant rough rides for the temperamental lions and elephants, a sixty-car circus train was usually divided into two trains of thirty cars each, although in 1947, Ringling Bros. and Barnum and Bailey Circus traveled in two trains totaling 108 cars. One followed the other at a short distance to give yard crews in small towns time to shunt the first train onto sidetracks before the second car arrived.

On one trip with the Ringling Bros. and Barnum and Bailey train, I was at the throttle of engine 528 with a 900 class engine coupled in as a helper. Both locomotives were flying the white flags that all non-scheduled trains flew at the time. We headed north pulling the circus flatcars loaded with wagons, stockcars carrying the most valuable animals, sleepers for the performers, and the pie car—a lounge car where the performers relaxed and ate short-order meals. Main meals were prepared in the cook car and served under a tent where the circus was performing. Thirty minutes after we pulled out of Union Station, the second train left with stockcars carrying the less valuable animals and boxcars loaded with tents, benches, poles, and other equipment. Everything was loaded in such a way that the first things needed to set up the circus could be unloaded first.

When we reached Fort Collins, yard crews began uncoupling and shunting the cars to the sidetracks to make room for the next train. Townspeople had turned out to welcome the circus and watch the performers unload the animals and parade them to the circus grounds. The circus trainmaster hopped into the engine with a fistful of complimentary tickets for the crew. That evening, we watched the performance under the big tent on the edge of town.

The next morning, we pulled the train to Greeley for the next performance, uncoupled it, and returned light to Denver. From Greeley, the circus train would continue its journey on the Union Pacific. About a week later, Master Mechanic Kascal stopped Neil at the roundhouse to tell him he had a letter from the circus officals, thanking the C&S engineer for a smooth ride from Denver to Greeley. Since the circus was an important customer, Kascal said he appreciated the work. "You got the wrong brother," Neil told him, but he promised to pass the compliment to the right one, and he did.

Circus trains were a part of railroading's past, but the new diesel locomotives, introduced on the C&S in the 1940s, pointed to railroading's future. The first diesel on the C&S was the *Texas Zephyr,* which went into service in 1940. Everyday at 12:01 p.m., it rolled out of Denver Union Station pulling a sleek, modern, stainless steel train made up of baggage, mail, and express cars, two chair cars, two or three sleepers, and a diner-observation-lounge car, and carrying 198 passengers.

Diesels did not appear on the North End, however, for several years. I ran one for the first time in the last part of 1944. Fireman J.O. Peterson and I had been called for freight train 78 from Cheyenne to Denver. When we got to the depot, we found Burlington 102, a four-motor Ft diesel on the head of a 100-car freight train. The diesel was making a test run. In the engine were road foremen Mickey Hansen and Harold Mott, both of whom had attended classes on operating diesels at the General Motors Electro-Motive Division in LaGrange, Illinois. Rather than giving engineers formal training on diesels, the company sent trained officials on maiden trips to show the engineers the ropes.

Diesel locomotives of this type were powerful enough to haul 5,000 tons on the ruling grade, nearly three times the tonnage hauled by the largest 900 class steamer. They ran on four large diesel engines which operated electric generators. The generators provided power to traction motors on the driving axles. Diesels rated 33 to 38 percent thermal efficient, compared to steam locomotives which rated 5 to 8 percent thermal efficient. They could run 500 miles without stopping for refueling or servicing, while steam locomotives stopped twice between Denver and Cheyenne to take on water and coal, clean the fire, and dump the ashes. Diesels started up faster than steamers, saving both time and wear on the machinery, but it took longer to stop a diesel-powered train. Their lower center of gravity and lateral springs made for a smoother ride on curves and straightaways, however, and allowed them to plow through snowdrifts.

The main controls—throttle, reverse lever, train and engine brake levers—were located in the same place as on steam locomotives, making the transition from one to the other easier for engineers. Diesels also had instrument panels that indicated speed, air pressure, wheel slippage, and malfunctioning parts. Some had the dead man's control, which meant that the engineer had to keep the foot pedal or throttle lever depressed or the power would automatically shut down. No engineer liked this feature.

Even compared to modern steam locomotives, the diesel's insulated cabs were a model of comfort with heaters and toilets. The windows had windshield wipers and defrosters. No longer did the engineer have to communicate with the crew by hand signals, flags, and whistles. The diesel radio let him talk directly to the conductor 100 cars away.

When I opened the throttle on the 102, the wheels started turning immediately, and the train glided down track like a skater on ice. We hummed past the Cheyenne city limits, heading for Fort Collins at fifty miles per hour. After slowing to pick up a sheaf of orders, we continued toward Longmont without stopping. There was no smoke blowing into the sky, no steam hissing from the cocks. It took all an engineer's skill to "work" a steam locomotive, but the diesel worked itself. I kept the throttle lever down and watched the track ahead, while Peterson watched the track on his side. Instead of tending to the boiler, making sure the steam pressure was up, shaking the fire, and checking the gauges, he had become a mechanic, making sure each engine was functioning. If one developed a problem, the train could continue moving on the other engines while the fireman located and fixed the trouble.

Nearing Longmont, I pulled the brake to slow the train before we entered the yards. Instead of slowing, the cars kept hurtling down track at fifty miles per hour. We were about to blow into the yards like a hurricane and smash into a Burlington engine on the track and a switch engine moving back and forth. If I set the emergency brake on the long train, however, there was a good chance the sudden jar would break the couplers and cause the drawbars to fall across the track, derailing the following cars. Hansen and Mott yelled, "Don't set the emergency."

"I'm still the engineer here," I said, setting the brake and holding my breath. The train held together and we entered the yards under control.

Except for the fact that the train brake had not worked as it should have, the 102 made a successful test run to Denver. Gradually, the C&S began adding diesels to its roster, numbering the days of the steam locomotives. But enough of the dependable steamers stayed on the roster to insure that black smoke would be seen around the curves of C&S track for some time to come.

CHAPTER TWENTY-ONE

Storms

Railroaders moved the freight, delivered the passengers, and fought the weather, all part of the job. Until the late 1920s, working in the cab of a narrow gauge or broad gauge steam locomotive was like working outdoors. Although the door on the engineer's side helped to break the chill winds, canvas curtains were the only protection for the fireman working in the gangway. On most locomotives, curtains were torn and ragged or had disappeared altogether. There was no heat in the cab except for the heat from the boiler. On trips in icy weather, we opened the firebox door and stood in front of the roaring fire to thaw out.

As the 1920s drew to a close, the Cab Curtain Act required railroads to install heavy curtains on each side of the gangway and hood curtains between the cab and tank. Fastened to the cab, they could be rolled up or unrolled and attached to the tank, as the weather dictated. The C&S also installed steam cab heaters near the seats on both sides of the cabs, giving the crew some warmth. Still, engine crews endured winds that blew in the cab windows, shredded the curtains, and blew the coal off the shovel before the fireman could throw it into the firebox, not to mention the snow, rain, and dust swirling about the inside of the cab.

Rainstorms were the least dangerous, but the C&S always took precautions against floods. Both the engineer and fireman on passenger train 29 were killed in the 1920s when C&S locomotive 350 plunged off a washed-out bridge near Casper. Following that accident, the C&S sent motor cars down the line ahead of trains during heavy rainstorms to check the track. On one trip north, I waited two hours at ARA while the section men made sure the track was clear to Longmont.

Fog that swirled across the track, thick as pea soup, cutting visibility to zero, presented greater dangers to trains than rainstorms. In the winter, we often ran into fog between Longmont and Fort Collins, forcing us to figure out where we were by the landmarks and signposts that we spotted next to the track. Near Berthoud one night, an automobile suddenly loomed out of the fog and crossed the track, seconds ahead of the train. Shaken from the close call, Chapman, the engineer, turned to me and said, "This is the kind of weather where we'll hit 'em goin' north and count 'em goin' south."

Winds were often strong enough to stop heavy trains. On a trip to Cheyenne one night, the winds were so strong they stopped the train at milepost 107, near Warrenton, even though we had been hurtling down track with an 800 class engine at full throttle, 200 pounds of steam, and a long, heavy freight train. We waited for the gusts to subside before we could get the train going again.

On another trip about 1925, I was firing a 600 class engine on a southbound freight when the operator at Longmont warned us of high winds near Boulder. We chugged toward Niwot without trouble, but as we started pulling over the hill to ARA, 100-mile-per-hour winds hit us like an oncoming locomotive, stopping the train. There we sat, with the wind pounding the cab and rocking the cars. Slowly, we began backing to Loomis Hole, near the site of the present-day IBM plant, where we set out two heavy cars of iron ore before starting back up the hill. We had gone about halfway when the wind stopped us again. Just as I opened the firedoor to throw in more coal, gusts rushed down the smokestack and blew the fire into the engine cab, setting my overalls, gloves, and cap on fire. I threw myself on the deck and rolled about. Chapman grabbed me and helped to smother the flames, but my face was burned and my eyebrows and eyelashes singed.

We backed downhill a second time, set out two more cars of iron ore, and started out again. This time, we bucked the wind over the top of the hill and dropped into ARA. We had spent four hours going ten miles. With portions of the track between Boulder and Denver under two feet of blowing sand, we got orders to pull into the Boulder freight yards and tie up. We spent twenty-four hours in the caboose waiting for the wind to die down enough for section crews to clear the track so we could continue to Denver.

On a trip in March 1949, we pulled out of Cheyenne in a howling windstorm with nine cars on passenger train 30. I was firing for engineer John Bryne on CB&Q engine 7014. By the time we reached Speer, eight miles south of Cheyenne, the wind was whipping around us at 110 miles per hour. Just as we pulled out of the cut at milepost 103, a gust lifted the seven express and mail cars in back of the engine off track and sent them rolling down the bank like derailed toy cars around a Christmas tree. The derailment threw on the train's emergency brakes, stopping the chair cars and Pullman filled with passengers. We continued down track some distance before Byrne got the locomotive stopped. We climbed down the side ladder with the wind flattening us against the tank and managed to make our way upright alongside the engine. The moment I started down the bank, a gust caught me broadside, blowing me off my feet. I fell backwards and rolled several yards downhill. When I finally stopped, I couldn't stand up in the wind. Byrne was crawling toward the cars, which lay twisted and broken at the bottom of the bank, and I started crawling too. By the time we reached the cars, the conductor, Ike Maymon, had already found the two mail clerks under piles of mail sacks. Neither was hurt.

Huddling together, we crawled and stumbled back to the engine. Since the derailed cars had damaged the track, we were unable to move the engine to the passenger cars. Having no choice but to leave them to the mercies of the wind, we ran the engine three miles down track to Norfolk and telephoned the dispatcher in Denver. After taking the conductor back to wait with the passengers for an engine and crew from Cheyenne, we proceeded to Denver, arriving four hours late with no train.

Not only could high winds stop heavy trains and blow cars off the track, they raised clouds of dust that turned day into night. During the droughts of 1937 and 1938, we would spot dust storms blowing down track miles away. They moved slowly, reaching high into the sky and covering the earth as far as we could see. Running into one was like entering a long, dark tunnel. With headlight on, we couldn't see the track in front of the engine. Nor could we see across the cab. Even though we covered our faces with handkerchiefs, we still breathed and swallowed spoonfuls of dust.

When the wind stopped a train of thirty stockcars south of Louisville in the late 1930s, dust piled around the cars, suffocating the cattle. It took the work crew a full day to dig out the train.

To clear the track of dust, the C&S operated a Jordan spreader which had wings on each side that spread out, pushing the drifting sand off track. Folded in half, the wings could lift and clear the sand out of the cuts.

Like the rotaries used to clear snow, the Jordan spreaders had to be pushed by a locomotive.

Along with dust, the wind blew debris and tumbleweeds over the track, creating dangerous situations and fire hazards. In one windstorm, I was firing for Chapman on passenger train 30 southbound from Cheyenne. At milepost 69, between Fort Collins and Loveland, we approached a cut thirty feet high and as long as a city block filled with tumbleweeds. At sixty miles per hour, we had no time to stop. Chapman opened the throttle and said, "Hold on, we're goin' through." We plowed into the cut at full speed, with tumbleweeds filling the gangway and crashing into the engine cab. We kept moving and shot out the far end, the passenger cars bouncing behind. Had there been a dead animal in the weeds, the train would have derailed, and the combination of dry tumbleweeds and the fire in the firebox would probably have incinerated the train.

Usually snowstorms didn't cause as much havoc on the broad gauge as on the narrow gauge, but in April 1926, with trees budding in the warm weather, a sudden snowstorm closed the main line. I was firing a heavy freight to Cheyenne with Engineer Walter Hayes. We roared northward in lightly falling snow, but by the time we reached Cheyenne early in the morning, thirty inches had covered the ground, and drifts six feet high in places had closed the track. The C&S crews who had managed to get to Cheyenne settled in the shacks to wait out the storm. After three days, we had eaten the groceries we had brought from Denver. Hayes set out in the snow, determined to find a grocery store, but every store in town was closed. Finally, he came upon a wholesale bakery. Banging on the door, he roused the owner and told him of our plight. The baker sold him a stack of apple pies, the only thing he had in stock. For the next two days, we lived on scrambled eggs, coffee, and apple pie while we waited for the rotary, which the C&S kept at Cheyenne, to clear the track.

The snow that closed the line in the winter of 1949 probably rivaled anything the narrow gauge railroaders ever saw. On January 28, I was the engineer on the 370 hauling southbound passenger train 32 with four coaches. The conductor was my cousin Frank Root. Snow was falling when we left Cheyenne in the late afternoon, and by the time we reached Wellington, we were plowing through a heavy snowstorm. At the curve north of Black Hollow Junction, the snow slowed the train, nearly stopping us, but the 370 plowed through, coaches rolling behind. At Fort Collins, snow was falling lightly. Frank and I went into the depot and telegraphed the dispatcher to call out the rotary to clear the track for passenger train 29 scheduled to be coming through in a few hours. The operator glanced out the window and advised the dispatcher not to bother.

Engineer Pete Menninger was at the throttle of the number 29 that night as it rumbled out of Fort Collins toward Cheyenne. Just beyond Norfolk, the train hit a drift and stalled. Throughout the night, snow piled over the engine and coach cars, while the dispatcher wired stations along the line trying to locate the train. The next morning, Clarence was called to take the rotary and work crew to the stranded train. They worked several days digging out the cars by hand and moving them one at a time to Fort Collins.

The storm closed the C&S track north of Fort Collins for almost two weeks. All freight trains were annulled, leaving loaded cars stacked in the Denver yards. Passenger trains 29 and 30 were also annulled, but the 31 and 32 were able to run between Denver and Fort Collins. North of Fort Collins stretched a forbidding white landscape.

When the road reopened, I was called to take one of the first trains to Cheyenne, moving some of the freight backlog. In places alongside the track, snow was four feet deep, pushing against the sides of the train and making it hard to pull. At Norfolk Cut, banks of snow reached thirty feet high. Scattered about were the carcasses of wild deer and stray cattle that had crowded into the cut for protection from the storm and smothered in the deep drifts.

CHAPTER TWENTY-TWO

Wrecks

Accidents on a fast train could happen in the blink of an eye, before the engineer even sensed anything was wrong. A broken rail could derail the train. Water below the safety level in the boiler could cause the locomotive to blow to pieces. Automobiles and trucks could appear out of nowhere and smash into the train at a crossing. Another train could suddenly bear down track. Railroading was just as dangerous as in my father's day. It required alertness and quick thinking to stay alive.

If the engineers and fireman sensed that the locomotive was about to derail or hit another engine head-on, they "joined the birds," although many engineers in Colorado lost their lives trying to bring runaway trains under control. No crew member wanted to be inside a locomotive in a collision or derailment, with broken pipes spouting steam. When engine 802 hit a broken rail north of Longmont in the 1930s, neither Clarence, who was firing, nor Alvie Pierce, the engineer, wanted to ride the locomotive down the bank and take a chance on being scalded. Just before the 802 jumped track, Alvie went out his side, and Clarence went out his, landing unconscious in the tall weeds of a ditch alongside the track. When he came to, he heard Alvie crying and calling his name, certain Clarence had gotten caught in the engine. When Clarence called out, Alvie found him in the weeds and helped him to the caboose. In the meantime, the brakemen had set out fusees and torpedos to warn other trains of the freight stranded on the main line without an engine and were running back toward Longmont to look for a telephone to notify the dispatcher.

Both the engineer and fireman kept close watch on the water gauge, showing the amount of water in the boiler. If the water was winking in the bottom of the glass gauge, they knew that two inches of water still covered the crown sheet above the firebox. If the water disappeared from the gauge, they knew the crown sheet may be exposed and they were in trouble. Cool water hitting the red hot crown sheet would cause an explosion. On the other hand, if the water was too high, it spilled into the cylinders and pistons, causing extensive damage. At the same time, it created a fountain effect, pulling water out of the boiler fast enough to expose the crown sheet. In a steam locomotive, the right amount of water meant the difference between life and death.

On January 26, 1925, engine 603 exploded, killing Engineer Joe Connelly and Fireman Joe Rose. That morning, they had taken a work train with several ballast cars and work crew to Louisville to spread ballast on the track. At the end of the day, they coupled the caboose onto the engine and started for Denver with the crew, leaving the cars at the site. Everything seemed normal as they chugged along the banks of Churches Lake, two miles south of Broomfield, when, suddenly, the boiler of the 603 blew up, shot off the running gear, and landed in the field several hundred feet from the track. The crown sheet, blown out of the boiler, was so hot it set the field grass on fire. Beside the track, the rest of the 603 lay in a heap of tangled rods and axles. Both Connelly and Rose had been blown out of the engine, but the caboose still sat on the track with the stunned and shaken crew.

With engineers and firemen always watching the water gauge, no one knows what happened in the 603. Since water gauges were not standard equipment installed in factories in 1901 when the 603 was built, it is possible that the gauge had been incorrectly installed later in C&S shops and did not register the water level accurately. At any rate, old-timers never relied on water gauges. They always tested the water and steam in the boiler by opening the try-cocks.

Just as in my father's day, railroaders did everything to avoid a wreck. But on a night trip in the 1940s, when my brother, Neil, was firing for Engineer George Suess, they had the misfortune of running into their own train. After making an emergency stop on the hill between Loveland and Berthoud, they were unable to get the train moving again. Broad gauge locomotives, with large driving wheels, started slowly, gradually getting up power to move the train. Going uphill, the high-drivered engine did not have enough tractive effort, so Suess and Neil backed to the foot of Loveland Hill and uncoupled half of the cars. Then they hauled the other half over the hill to Campion, put them in the siding, and returned light for the rest of the train. The brakeman had neglected to set out torpedos ahead of the train or to put red lanterns on the end of the first car. In the darkness, the locomotive crashed into the first car, knocking several cars off track and delaying the trip. The line was tied up while the wrecking crew was called out to set the cars back on the rails. The brakeman lost his job.

Once in a while, locomotives or cars developed minds of their own, causing accidents or near-accidents and giving townspeople on the C&S line the fright of their lives. One night in the early 1920s, a forty-ton car that had been shunted into a siding at Marshall got away. It rolled downhill, gathering speed, and pounded through Boulder at ninety miles per hour. Out past Boulder Junction and down to Longmont it rolled, screaming through town with wheels red hot and smoking. Finally, on the upgrade north of Longmont, it slowed down and stopped.

On another occasion in the 1950s, a flatcar at Ingleside, on the branch line to Rex, north of Fort Collins, got away and sailed down track with a construction worker on the car. He lay down, trying to hold on, as the car whipped through La Porte at 100 miles per hour and sailed into the west yards at Fort Collins. Yard crews ran cars onto the track to slow the runaway, finally bringing it under control. It had covered seventeen miles in sixteen minutes with the construction worker holding on so tight the yard crews had to peel him from the top.

At another time in the 1950s, locomotive 638 "took a walk" out of the Fort Collins engine house where the watchman had been using a torch for some repair work. With the wood in the cab on fire, the engine ran down track toward Cheyenne, a rolling fireball. The hostlers grabbed fire extinguishers, climbed into another locomotive, and followed. Near the Great Western sugar factory, the 638 finally began to slow down. The rescuers caught up, put out the fire, and ran the errant engine back to the engine house.

Sometimes wrecks and other unusual occurrences had nothing to do with broken rails, malfunctioning or willful locomotives and cars, or the way the crew handled the job. A train could be steaming down track with everything going right when an automobile would suddenly appear out of nowhere and smash into it. That happened in Fort Collins about 1922, shortly after I had caught on the road. I was firing the switch engine hauling boxcars through a crossing on a cold, snowy night, with almost zero visibility. Suddenly, a Model T Ford slammed into the side of the locomotive.

The engineer stopped the train and we climbed down and ran to the Ford. The car engine had been sheared off and thrown to one side. Inside the car were a young man and woman. She was too frightened to talk, but he was raving. "Where did that engine come from? How did it get on the street?" Neither was hurt. We stayed with them until the city police arrived. Then we continued hauling the boxcars.

The same kind of accident happened thirty years later when I was firing freight train 77 headed north with Engineer Frank Johnson at the throttle. As we neared a crossing south of Loveland, Johnson saw an automobile coming toward the track. He blew the whistle and set the brakes, but it took almost two miles to stop a long train. We rolled through the crossing just as the automobile glanced off the engine. The driver had seen us in time to turn the wheel, probably saving his life. As soon as the train stopped, we jumped out of the engine and ran back to the car. Inside were a boy and girl about seventeen years old, both in shock. We put them in the engine cab and continued to the Loveland depot where we notified the police and the teenagers' parents. When the girl's mother arrived, she took one look at her daughter's bruised face and started hitting the boy, screaming, "You could have killed her." I jumped between them, pulled the mother into another room, and sat her in a chair. The moment I left her alone, she flew at the boy again, beating him and threatening to kill him. I pulled her into the other room once more, sat her back in the chair, and this time, sat on top of her until the police arrived.

On another trip with Johnson, we had pulled out of Loveland, heading north with a long freight train, and a good head of steam when I saw a truck heading down the road toward the crossing, and hollered to Johnson. He blew the whistle and set the air. The truck crashed into the side of a freight car in the middle of the train. By the time we stopped and ran back to the truck, the driver had climbed from the wreckage and walked away. The C&S later hauled the truck to the yards and telephoned the driver to come and get it. "It's yours," he said. "I come from Russia, and I don't want trouble about running into a train. Keep the truck, and we're even. Yes?"

When automobiles or trucks collided with trains, the driver or the passengers usually did not walk away. In some accidents, neither did the railroaders. A truck slammed into the side of the *Pioneer Zephyr* at a crossing north of Longmont in April 1950. At the time, the C&S had leased the *Pioneer Zephyr*—the nation's first diesel-powered train—from the Burlington for passenger trains 31 and 32. The *Zephyr* ripped the truck in half, carrying the cab down track 170 yards. Inside were a man and his four-year-old daughter, neither seriously injured. The driver said later that his windows were fogged and he had not seen the train. C&S Engineer

Don Grinstead, who happened to be firing that trip for Engineer Clarence Chapman, was trapped in the diesel for more than an hour while rescue workers used blowtorches to cut through the twisted metal. It was the last trip for Grinstead, who had started firing on the C&S in 1922 and had been set up to engineer in 1942. His injuries kept him in the hospital several months and forced him to retire.

Most drivers who found themselves in a crossing with a locomotive bearing down on them had not seen the train. But others tried to beat the trains through the crossings. The engineer could only blow the whistle, making as much noise as possible, and hope the driver would stop. He could not stop the train in time. When Engineer John Byrne was on passenger train 29 in the 1950s, one of the factory workers at the Great Western sugar factory in Fort Collins raced the train every night. "He jams down the gas pedal and heads toward the track," Byrne told me, "but the night he loses the race, he'll be dead. And maybe I'll be dead too."

There was always the chance of a collision at a crossing, but the most bizarre collision I ever had did not involve another vehicle. I had pulled out of Denver Union Station with a diesel locomotive and passenger train 29 on a chilly autumn evening in 1962. My fireman was Jim Chaney. We were going about sixty miles per hour as we crossed the Clear Creek bridge. Just beyond the bridge, I spotted a crowd at a crossing. Near the track was the Flagellante church, lit up like a fireworks display on the Fourth of July, with outdoor lights flooding the track and road. As we rolled toward the crowd, the men surged together, took hold of one man, and threw him in front of the locomotive. I watched his body fly into the air as we hit him. I set the brakes and brought the train to a stop more than a mile down track. "What did you see?" I asked Chaney as we slowed down. "They threw somebody in front of us and we struck him," he replied. Both of us were in shock.

The conductor ran up and clambered on the engine, wanting to know why we had stopped. We told him what had happened and radioed the dispatcher, who gave us orders to back to the church and wait for the police. By the time we reached the church, the lights had been turned out. No one was around. After the police arrived, we walked along the track, explaining what we had seen and searching for the body. But there was no body, and no sign that anything had happened.

Another bizarre event happened on Halloween night in 1955. I had the Burlington steamer 2965, heading into Fort Collins with passenger train 29, unaware that some students at Colorado State University had soaped two miles of rails as a Halloween prank. When I set the brakes to slow into the depot, the wheels stopped turning and the train slid down track like a toboggan down a chute. I knew a southbound freight was due into the depot, and if we didn't slow down, we would hit it head on. I threw open the sand valves to spread sand over the rails. Gradually, the wheels started to turn, the brakes grabbed, and we started to slow, coming to a full stop nose to nose with the freight engine.

On another trip, I was on engine 371 pulling passenger train 29 through the Colorado A&M campus when I saw a Mars oscillating light that looked like the headlight of an oncoming locomotive on the track ahead. I set the air, hollered to the fireman to get ready to jump, and was getting ready to jump myself when I realized the light was not moving down track. As we got closer, I saw it was mounted on a pickup truck parked across the track. Just as we bore down, the truck pulled out of the way. Had we jumped, the passenger train, with an unmanned locomotive, would have plummeted through town and crashed into another train in the yards. When we got to the depot, I called the police, who located the truck and arrested two students. "Those boys cause us more problems than the rest of the students together," the police officer told me later. "They're always up to something. We arrest them every Saturday night, and their fathers bail them out on Sunday."

Sometimes another train was in fact bearing down the track. In the late 1940s, I was firing a freight from Denver to Cheyenne with Engineer H.W. Hultman. At Fort Collins, we got orders to meet a southbound freight at Heston, twenty miles north. Since we had right of track, the southbound was supposed to take the siding. It was a dark night, calm and clear, as we rolled past Bulger. The track ran straight ahead for two miles, then curved through a cut and veered left toward Heston. Just as we passed the cut, I saw the headlight on the track ahead. I yelled to Hultman, "Stop! Here she comes!"

He set the brakes and climbed down the ladder on his side, while I went down on my side, ready to jump. The engineer in the southbound train saw our light and set his brakes, bringing the train to a stop before we crashed. Since the southbound was too heavy to back up on the grade, we uncoupled our engine and used it to push the southbound train into the siding at Heston, where it should have been in the first place. The southbound crew got brownies for pulling out on the main line against orders.

On another trip, I was at the throttle of the 6300, one of the ten freight engines, all 2-10-2s, that the C&S leased from the Burlington from 1927 to 1954. We rolled through Louisville, climbed Burkes Hill, and curved past Good View (later called Fairview), where we could see north to the Valmont power plant and ARA. Suddenly, the fireman and brakeman fell off their seats onto the floor, yelling, "Stop, stop, here comes the train." I set the brakes, ran to the left side, and saw the train about a mile ahead, belching smoke into the sky. The engineer, Bob Sanders, had spotted us at the same time, set his brakes, and sent up the smoke to make sure we saw him. He whistled back to ARA, where he should have been waiting for us to pass.

When two locomotives collided, the crash could be heard a mile away, and the crew was lucky to get out in time. On October 17, 1927, I was called to fire the 612 to Fort Collins and help bring a heavy train of ore and sheep to Denver. The engineer was C.B. Watson, known to the firemen as "Ramrod." The 612 had just been overhauled in the shops and was equipped with outside cylinders, Walschaert valve gears, a first-rate Schmidt superheater, and a new coat of paint. Sleek, shiny, and in peak condition, it was the best engine on the North End at the time.

We pulled into Fort Collins before the southbound had arrived, and Watson and I walked to town for lunch. When we got back to the depot, the freight train stood on the track with engine 643 and Charlie Foster at the throttle. We coupled the 612 ahead of the 643, according to the rules that determined which engine went on the head when two or more were used. But as we started out, the engines uncoupled. A quick check of the couplers showed that the drawbar on the 643 was below standard height. We did not want to move the beautiful 612 to second position where it would be covered with dirt and smoke from the head engine, but we had no choice. Once again, we started out. At Boulder, we got orders to take the siding at Westminster and let the northbound freight with engine 802 proceed on the main line.

From Semper to Westminster, a distance of three miles, we rolled down grade, gathering speed. The first train to arrive at the depot usually opened the switch for the incoming train, even though rules required the crew on the train going into the siding to open the switch. As we approached the depot, we could see that the switch had not been opened and that the 802 was standing on the track ahead. Foster set the brakes, but we were going too fast to stop in time.

Jim Montgomery and John Peterson, the engineer and fireman on the 802, saw us coming and jumped from the engine cab. The crews on the 643 and the 612 also started jumping one by one. We were moving about 25 miles per hour, but it seemed like 100 miles per hour as I climbed down the ladder, saw the ground racing under me, and leaped. I landed in a ditch and rolled away from the track. Just as I sat up, the 643 hit the 802. Both engines reared into the air like bucking broncos and fell to the side. Men lay scattered in the ditch, wherever they had landed, but Peterson had picked himself up, bounded over a fence, and was running across the field. He said later he expected the engines to explode, and he meant to get as far away as possible.

The 643 and 802 lay in a mound of tangled metal, while the beautiful 612 lay upside down in the ditch, its tank ripped off. The 643 was so badly damaged, it had to be scrapped, but both the 612 and 802 were later repaired. Twenty cars had flipped off track, spilling ore everywhere and killing most of the sheep.

During the investigation into the collision, a company official asked the head brakeman on our train, a boomer named Reilly, what he did before the crash. "I saw we were going to hit the 802," he replied, "and I joined the birds. That's all." Because he had not stopped the train, Foster was relieved of his engineer's position for one year.

On a clear morning, September 22, 1958, another head-on collision wrecked two diesel locomotives, injured twenty passengers, and killed three C&S railroaders. Freight train 77 had set out from Denver in the early morning with a four-motor diesel on the head and fifty-one cars. At the throttle was Engineer Fred Tingle, who had started railroading as a fireman on the South Park at the turn of the century and was one of my father's friends, often visiting us on layovers in Como. Tingle had been promoted to engineer in 1922. The fireman was Harry Anderson, and Russell Denery was the conductor.

The number 77 had orders to go into the siding at Semper, five miles south of Broomfield, and wait for southbound passenger train number 30 due to pull out of the Broomfield depot. Instead of taking the siding, however, the number 77 pounded past Semper at fifty miles per hour. Anderson said later that he showed his watch to Tingle, pointing to the hands, and said, "We'll never make it to the Broomfield siding ahead of the passenger." Tingle replied, "We'll make it easy." He was right, but instead of heading into the siding, the number 77 roared past.

I had fired for Tingle many times over the years and knew him to be a first-rate engineer. No one will ever know why he did not pull into the Semper siding according to orders, or why he overshot the Broomfield siding. Nor will anyone know why the conductor or the head brakeman did not pull the emergency brakes when they saw Tingle had overrun both sidings.

At the Broomfield depot, the number 30 had just started moving slowly ahead. In the engine was Frank Johnson, who had been promoted to engineer on the same day as Tingle, thirty-six years before. After hiring out in 1912, Johnson had worked on the switch engine in the Louisville Coal District before transferring to freight on the main line. He had finally moved up to engineer on the passenger run, the top rung of the ladder for C&S engineers. I often fired for Johnson, another fine engineer, and we had managed to escape injury in two minor wrecks.

On that September morning, in 1958, my close friend, Joe Loughry, was firing for Johnson. Joe and I had been railroading together since the 1920s. His father had loaned me the money to save my house during the Depression. Later, my wife and I had introduced Joe to Mamie McAuliffe, the dark-haired, soft-spoken Irish girl he had married. Our families had spent summer vacations together in Buena Vista, hiking the old railbeds to the Alpine Tunnel, exploring the ruins of Romley and Hancock, and talking endlessly about railroading in the generation before us. Joe had been promoted to engineer in 1944, a few years after I got my promotion, but, like all C&S engineers, without enough seniority for a regular engineer's job, he still worked from time to time as a fireman.

He and Johnson could not have seen train 77 bearing down the track that morning until the moment it rounded the curve south of the depot. Johnson set the brakes, but it was too late for them to jump. The 214,000-pound freight diesel number 700D smashed into the smaller passenger diesel, the E7 9936B, breaking it into jagged hunks of steel. Joe Loughry and Frank Johnson died in the wreckage.

On the freight locomotive, Harry Anderson saw the passenger train on the track and stepped into the engine room. Tingle could also have gotten into the room, Anderson said later, "But I guess he wanted to stay with it." After the crash, Anderson stayed with the fatally injured Tingle until a rescue squad got him out of the locomotive. He kept asking about the passenger crew, and when Anderson asked how he was, Tingle replied, "I'm okay." He died in the hospital.

On the passenger train, passengers had been thrown about the sleeper and coaches as brakes squealed and steel crashed against steel. One passenger in the sleeper said he had just gotten dressed and had sat down to enjoy the early morning view of the mountains from the window when the trains hit. He held onto his chair to keep from being thrown across the compartment.

I was laying over in Cheyenne that morning, replacing some shingles on the shack and waiting for the call to head south to Denver with freight train 78. My fireman, Jimmy Tallman, offered to walk to the depot to see when we were scheduled to go out. Within moments, he came running back to the shack, sobbing. I dropped my tools and went to him. "Jimmy, what's the matter?" I asked.

"A terrible wreck," he said. "Tingle, Johnson, Joe Loughry, too. They're all dead."

I sat down beside him and we cried together.

CHAPTER TWENTY-THREE

United We Stand

I n my father's day, railroad engineers often worked twenty- and thirty-hour stretches as long as there was work to be done. Sometimes after a trip on freight over the Highline, he would flop down on the living room sofa, too tired to go to bed. In three or four hours, the caller would rap on the front door, shouting "81's on time," and Sam would be on his way again, without time to eat a hot meal or change his clothes. Had he refused to go out, he would have been fired and blackballed from railroading. As a union organizer, he ran the additional risk of losing his job for some minor infraction of the rules. In the company's view, union men were troublemakers, and company officials looked for opportunities to remove them from the payroll.

Not only did early railroaders have no control over the number of hours they worked, they had no control over working conditions. They worked in open cabs, in rain, wind, and blizzards. They had no assurances that the locomotives were in safe running condition or that the brakes would hold. They received whatever amount of pay the company considered fair compensation, and if they didn't like it, they were free to look for other work.

While individual railroaders had no power, the brotherhoods had the ultimate power to call a strike and shut down the railroad, a fact that drove reluctant companies to the bargaining table. Through negotiations with C&S officials, unions won concessions that generally made the job more tolerable, such as wood lining on the engineer's side of the engine cab, better working schedules, and small raises in pay. On a national level, the brotherhoods won a series of safety laws that helped to protect railroaders. Congress passed some of the laws, such as the Adamson Law, only after the brotherhoods had threatened a nationwide strike.

Other changes championed by the unions came about after President Woodrow Wilson nationalized the railroads during World War I, placing them under the United States Railroad Administration from December 1917 to February 1920. Orders issued by William G. McAdoo, the administration's first general director, revolutionized railroading, set precedents for later federal laws, and strengthened the unions. For example, McAdoo ordered companies to pay overtime at time and a half, instead of leaving the amount up to the companies. Another order forbid discrimination against employees who belonged to unions. Still others set up railroad boards of adjustment to settle disputes over hours, wages, grievances, and discipline. For the first time, railroaders did not have to fear losing their jobs if they joined a union. They also had legally sanctioned methods of protesting unfair company decisions.

In the most controversial order, labeled "featherbedding" by the railroad companies, McAdoo defined the different classes of railroad labor and required crews to make one trip at a time, putting an end to blatant abuses of railroad labor. If a company ordered a main line crew to switch cars in the yard after a trip, it had to pay the crew an extra day's wages. It also had to pay the switching crew that should have done the job but had not been called.

The order prevented railroad companies from using the minimum number of men to move the maximum amount of tonnage, increasing profits at the expense of the railroaders. No longer were crews required to shunt cars in the yard or work on helper engines after coming in from regular trips. The order also stopped companies from taking railroaders from their home bases for long periods, such as the time President Trumbull and other C&S officials kept John Olson and his crew on the job for two weeks hauling a train over the line. Such practices had also been common on the broad gauge. Shortly after Judy Gowder was promoted to engineer in 1910, he got orders to run a freight train from Denver to Cheyenne. There, he got orders to return to Longmont, pick up loaded cars, and haul them to Cheyenne. For ten days, he shuffled trains back and forth between Longmont and Cheyenne with only a few hours rest between trips. Finally, he got orders to go to Westminster. When he pulled into the station, he telegraphed the dispatcher in Denver. "Haven't seen family in ten days. Don't have change of clothes. Am dog tired. Coming to Denver on engine or on foot." The dispatcher cleared him to bring the locomotive back to Denver.

After the railroads returned to private control following World War I, a series of federal laws continued McAdoo's reforms. The Transportation Act of 1920 set up the Railroad Labor Board and established methods of resolving disputes. It also gave the Interstate Commerce Commission authority to change operating rules and to make final decisions on the construction and abandonment of railroads.

But the landmark law was the Railway Labor Act, passed in 1926 and amended in 1934. This act established the National Railroad Board of Adjustment with thirty-six members, half from the railroad companies and half from the unions. Unlike previous boards of adjustment, the decisions of this board applied to railroads across the nation.

Close on the heels of the Railway Labor Act came the Railroad Retirement Act, passed in 1934 and amended in 1937. It set up a separate social security system for railroaders funded by employees and employers. It also required railroad companies to take into account the railroader's total years of service in determining retirement benefits, not just the period of employment with the company from which he retired.

Still other laws and rule changes over the next decade improved working conditions for railroaders. In 1938, the ICC required companies to install stokers on passenger engines weighing 100,000 pounds or more and on freight engines weighing at least 176,000 pounds, a rule that greatly eased the fireman's burden. Another rule change, won by the unions, required the companies to clean the engines. No longer did a fireman have to show up early for a trip to sweep, clean, and shine the locomotive. The C&S installed power washers in the roundhouse to wash the locomotives and passenger cars, but freight cars got a bath only when they went into the shops for repair.

During the brief period from December 27, 1943 to January 18, 1944, when President Roosevelt nationalized the railroads to avert a strike, railroaders won a week's paid vacation, the first vacation in railroading history. Serving as arbitrator between the companies and unions, Roosevelt worked out an agreement that gave the railroaders a raise of four cents per hour along with the vacation.

When engineers and trainmen, demanding rules changes and pay increases, struck the nation's railroads in May 1946, President Truman took over the railroads and placed them under the Office of Defense Transportation. Although Truman asked Congress for authority to draft engineers and firemen into military service, forcing them to return to work, the unions and companies reached an agreement on an eighteen-and-one-half-cents-per-hour raise before any legislation was passed. The railroads were returned to their owners after nine days under federal control.

On the C&S, engineers elected local union chairmen at three terminals, Denver, Cheyenne, and Trinidad. During the time I served as local chairman, from 1945 to 1949, I dealt with the trainmaster or superintendent over such minor disputes as the number of hours an engineer worked, the length of rest periods, or the safety of orders. Any dispute not settled at the local level went to the general chairman, who was elected by the local chairmen. The general chairman had the authority to negotiate with the railroad company president or his representative, and he could appeal decisions to the National Railroad Adjustment Board. Every case had to proceed through the proper channels, from the local chairman to the general chairman to the national board.

During my term as local chairman, George Volleberg, a short, gruff German with a strong determination and stronger sense of fair play, held the office of general chairman on the C&S and the Fort Worth and Denver City, owned by the C&S. Before taking the full-time union job in 1922, Volleberg had worked as an engineer on the North End for seventeen years. The union job kept him on the road as much as when he had been behind the throttle. He traveled between Fort Worth and Casper, stopping at stations on the line to hear the railroaders' grievances and prepare cases to take before management.

Most cases affected only the engineers on the C&S or the FW&DC, but one case involving rates of pay had national consequences. By this time, the rate of pay was determined by the weight of locomotives as well as mileage, a rule that gave engineers a share in profits earned by heavier locomotives capable of hauling more tonnage. Locomotives were weighed on sealed government scales when they left the factory. Company and union representatives were both present at the weighing. Despite the rule, the FW&DC disagreed with the engineers on the rate of pay for the class of diesel locomotives like the 9910 used on the *Texas Zephyr.*

When Volleberg could not settle the dispute with the railroad company, he asked for a hearing before the National Railroad Adjustment Board in Chicago. Working day and night for months, he gathered the information, evidence, and testimony to present the case. He typed the forty-page report himself, pecking it out letter by letter on a dilapidated typewriter in the basement office of his north Denver home. He cranked out thirty-six copies on a hand-turned duplicating machine and stapled them together —one for each board member.

At the same time, a fleet of lawyers, research assistants, and secretaries was at work gathering the company's evidence and testimony. The reports were professionally typed, printed on a fine grade of paper, and bound in handsome covers.

With the date of the hearing at hand, Volleberg boarded the *Denver Zephyr* for Chicago, boxes of reports stacked in the baggage car. In his worn brown suit, he appeared before the board, distributed the duplicated, stapled copies of the report, and argued the case. When he had finished, the smartly tailored railroad lawyers rose, presented the bound copies of the railroad's report, and launched into windy arguments. At the end of the hearing, the board voted for Volleberg and the engineers. Money was not the main issue—less than one dollar per day per engineer was at stake. The issue was whether wages would continue to be based on the weight of locomotives, and the board's decision applied to railroads across the country that operated locomotives similar to the 9910.

When Volleberg retired in 1949, I was elected general chairman on the C&S, a position I held until 1966. During that time, between 150 and 200 C&S engineers belonged to the BLE. I spent one week each month working for the union, which paid me the same wages I would have earned as an engineer. The railroad labor laws made it possible for general chairmen to lay off regular jobs without fear of losing them.

Most of the cases I handled involved engineers who had been disciplined or fired by the company for some rules violation. By law, unions handled all grievance cases, even if the engineer was a "no bill"—a non-union member. Sometimes a dismissed engineer did not get his job back even with union help, but he always got a hearing.

In 1950, the C&S pulled Engineer F.J. Gorney and Fireman Harry Wilson from the main line for running against orders. Gorney had been at the throttle of a diesel on passenger train 29 northbound from Cheyenne to Casper with orders to wait for the southbound passenger train 30 at Wheatland. After unloading the passengers and mail at Wheatland, Gorney headed out on the main line. About two miles down track, he spotted the number 30 coming toward him and set the brake. The other engineer also slammed on the brake before the two trains collided. After the company's official investigation into the incident, Gorney and Wilson were sent to yard jobs that paid less money, and they were lucky not to be fired. After several months, I took up the case with John Walker, the C&S vice-president and general manager. He refused to put the crew back on the main line.

Several days before Christmas, I attended the C&S hospital association meeting in the Johnson Building on Seventeenth Street, where the company offices were located. During a break, I suggested to Larry Madden, general chairman of the firemen, that we go upstairs and ask Walker, once again, to reinstate the Cheyenne crew.

"No way," Madden said, shaking his head. "They cooked their own goose and Walker's gonna let 'em stew in the yards."

I walked up the stairs and started down the hall toward Walker's office just as he came out the door. Then in his sixties, about six feet tall and slightly built with a friendly, pleasant manner, Walker had started railroading as a clerk in the Denver yards years earlier. Before moving into the top management job on the C&S, he had put in several years as superintendent in Trinidad. Having come up through the management ranks, Walker knew most of the C&S railroaders personally, and he had a keen sense of what it was like for the men out on the road.

"Good morning, John," I said. We shook hands and he asked how the hospital meeting was going. Before he could move away, I said, "You know, it's Christmas time, the season of good will, brotherly love, and forgiveness."

"What do you want me to do, Sam? Allow all your cases?" he asked.

"No," I replied. "Just one. That crew in Cheyenne has been working in the yards six months now. You know how hard it is for main line crews to be stuck in the yards. And making less money. They've learned their lesson. Wouldn't it be a wonderful Christmas present for their families if you were to put them back on the passenger?"

Walker rubbed his chin and grinned. "Sam, since I don't have my crying towel with me today, I guess I'll have to do it. Tell them they can go back on the passenger Christmas day."

When I gave Madden the good news, he was flabbergasted. So were Gorney and Wilson, both of whom had expected to spend the rest of their railroading careers riding around the yards on switchers.

When one of the Trinidad engineers was fired, Walker guessed the reason even before he read the report. The engineer had brought passenger train number 7 into Texline one night with a new trainmaster riding one of the coaches. As soon as the train stopped, the trainmaster walked up to the engine and berated the engineer for a rough ride. The engineer, who had a temper like a buzzsaw, bounded off the engine and slugged the trainmaster. A company official pulled the engineer out of service on the spot.

The company dealt directly with railroaders in discipline cases, but railroaders had the right to bring a union representative to the hearing. This engineer, already in his sixties and close to retirement, declined union help. "I'm done for," he told me. "The case is hopeless."

He rode the train to Denver for the hearing and made his way alone to Walker's office. Later, Walker told me he looked up from his desk to see the engineer standing in the doorway, hat in hand and eyes downcast, "the perfect picture of misery."

You've been using your fists to solve problems for forty years now. Isn't that long enough?'' Walker asked. "We can't have you slugging train-masters, or anybody else."

"You gonna fire me?" the engineer asked in a voice barely audible.

"Not if you give me your word it won't happen again," Walker replied.

"You got it," the engineer shouted, rushing over to Walker, grabbing his hand and pumping it. "Thank you, Mr. Walker. Thank you. Thank you."

"Get out," Walker roared, "before I change my mind."

In another case, the union joined with the company to force an engineer to mend his ways. This engineer, who also worked out of Trinidad, had a record of rules violations four pages long. On one trip he was on an SD9, a six-axle, 1,750-horsepower diesel locomotive northbound from Texline with a string of freight cars. He had orders to stop en route where a section gang was repairing the track and to proceed at the direction of the gang foreman.

The train roared into the work area at forty-five miles per hour, with the fireman at the throttle and the engineer sitting on the left side, watching the landscape slip by. Seeing the locomotive bearing down, the track gang threw shovels and bars into the air and jumped out of the way just before the train crashed into the tie tamper. At the later investigation, Superintendent Glen Hoover fired both the engineer and fireman for disobeying orders and damaging railroad property. The $20,000 tie tamper had to be scrapped, while the SD9 went to the shops for major repairs.

After a few weeks, I filed a request to put the engineer back to work on a leniency basis, with no pay for time lost. Several months went by before I got a call to see R.D. Wolfe, who had become C&S vice-president of labor relations after Walker retired. Short and built like the tank of a locomotive, Wolfe had come up through the management ranks of the Burlington. As a young man, he had been riding in a caboose that was overtaken and struck by another train. The injuries had left him walking with a cane for several years.

Wolfe threw a sheaf of papers onto the desk. "This is a sorry record," he said. "We should have fired this man thirty years ago."

I pointed out that in those thirty years, the engineer had long stretches where he had proved himself a competent employee.

"All right," Wolfe said. "It's up to the engineers. You decide what to do about him."

I went to Trinidad and called a meeting with the engineers based there. We went over the engineer's record with him, point by point. The other engineers told him frankly they didn't want him working if he couldn't follow orders—it was too dangerous. He pleaded for another chance, promising to "wake up and become a first class engineer."

I returned to Denver, met with Wolfe again, and told him the other engineers disapproved of the man's record and behavior and that he had sworn to them he would do better. Wolfe agreed to give him another chance, based on the recommendation of the engineers. From then until his retirement several years later, the engineer kept his record clean.

The most difficult cases involved engineers who had suffered heart attacks. Management took the position that, sooner or later, a heart attack victim would have another attack. If it occurred when he was running a locomotive, it could mean a wreck, with other railroaders and passengers endangered and property destroyed. The position was difficult to argue against.

On a trip with passenger train 29 from Cheyenne to Casper, Engineer Tommy Topham, who had started firing on the South Park, rounded a thirty-five-mile-per-hour curve at seventy miles per hour. The conductor pulled the air and stopped the train before it derailed. Tommy told me he did not remember going into the curve. Several days later, before the scheduled investigation into the incident, Tommy had a heart attack and died in his sleep. An autopsy showed several scars on his heart from light attacks, one of which he may have had while running the passenger train.

When an engineer in Trinidad had a heart attack, the company pulled him off the road for six months until I convinced Walker to let him run the night switch engine in the Trinidad yards. I argued that the chances of a wreck were slim should he have another attack since he would be running a steam locomotive with a fireman in the engine cab.

As the weeks went by, the engineer felt better and better. Some of the other railroaders in Trinidad took to asking him why he didn't get off the "sand grinder" and go back on the main line between Trinidad and Texline. The C&S chief surgeon would not hear of it, however.

Finally, the engineer laid off, rode the passenger train to Denver, consulted other doctors, and underwent several tests, all of which showed him to be in the peak condition he believed himself in. With test results in hand, he met with me and asked me to represent him, claiming the C&S doctors had wrongly diagnosed a heart attack. What he had suffered, he was certain, was a bad case of indigestion.

I set up an early morning meeting with Walker for the engineer, the Trinidad local chairman, and myself. We showed Walker the reports and argued that the engineer should be reinstated on the main line. Walker was reluctant to rule against C&S doctors, but finally he gave the engineer his old job, starting the next evening.

The engineer caught the 12:01 passenger train at Denver Union Station, disembarked at Trinidad at 5 p.m., drove home, ate dinner, and told his wife he was going to lie down awhile before getting ready to go to work on the switch engine at 9 p.m. When she went to wake him, he was dead.

A few days later, Walker sent me a letter that must have scorched the mails. I should not have handled the case, he wrote, and from then on, he would rely only on the reports of C&S doctors. Like all cases taken before management, it set a precedent. No C&S engineer who had a heart attack ever went back on the main line.

That included my brother, Neil, who had a heart attack in 1960. At first, I persuaded the company to let him work as a hostler at Denver Union Station. Several months later, an engineer's job opened up in Fort Collins on the branch lines. The company employed three engineers there in the summer and seven engineers for the fall beet runs. Since the trains were shorter than those on the main line, and moved at low speeds, the company agreed to let Neil have the job. Even though he was used to blasting down track at sixty miles per hour—and had earned the nickname "Lightning"—Neil settled into the job, glad to be behind the throttle. He worked there until he retired in 1968.

Sometimes the cases I brought to either Walker's or Wolfe's attention resulted in a more efficient operation. Railroaders on the road often figured out more practical ways of doing things than the dispatchers could figure out in their offices. One example was the order for southbound trains to push empty cars from ARA to Louisville to be picked up by northbound trains. The southbound locomotives had to push the empties up and over a steep hill. On dark nights, it was dangerous to have cars rolling ahead of the locomotive. It was also impractical and time-consuming, since the cars could be picked up at ARA.

The railroaders had tried to tell the dispatcher this, but he refused to change the orders. At a meeting in Walker's office one afternoon, I pulled out a piece of paper and drew a map, illustrating the problem. He reached for the telephone, called the dispatcher, made some harsh remarks about stupid orders, and told him to change them. Both the company and the railroaders benefited.

The most important case I handled during my years as general chairman was not a dispute with the company, but a dispute among BLE members. In 1899, the C&S had entered a joint operating agreement with the Santa Fe allowing C&S trains to use Santa Fe tracks between Denver and Pueblo. The agreement also called for an equal number of engineers from both companies to man the C&S trains between Denver and Trinidad, even though the Santa Fe owned 120 miles of track while the C&S had only 100 miles. The agreement gave C&S engineers an advantage over Santa Fe engineers. In 1950, Santa Fe engineers from Division 734 started an action against C&S engineers to equalize the miles on the Joint Line. We were willing to agree to this, but the Santa Fe engineers also wanted more jobs to make up for mileage lost in the past. Unwilling to give up jobs, we took the position that part of the original agreement could not be changed without changing the entire agreement.

When we couldn't work out a compromise, the BLE sent an assistant grand chief from Cleveland to settle the dispute. He held a two-day hearing, listened to both sides, and ruled in favor of the C&S engineers. But when he returned to Cleveland, he changed his mind and notified me he had found in favor of the Santa Fe engineers. No doubt he had run into a wall of opposition from the twenty-one local chairmen on the Santa Fe, representing engineers from Chicago to Los Angeles, a much larger number than C&S engineers. We were required to give up Joint Line jobs.

In July 1953, I appealed the decision to the national convention of the BLE in Cleveland. The convention delegates, including local and general chairmen from railroads across the country, were divided over the case. Outnumbered by the Santa Fe chairmen, I mounted a one-man political blitzkrieg, buttonholing delegates between meetings, stopping them in the halls, taking every opportunity to argue the C&S case from early morning to late at night. At the same time, Margaret argued our position to the delegates' wives during luncheons and shopping expeditions. When the vote was finally taken, the C&S position won.

But the C&S engineers were not the only engineers affected. The decision by the national convention applied to hundreds of engineers across the country who worked under similar Joint Line agreements.

CHAPTER TWENTY-FOUR

Last Out

On the night of February 10, 1959, I was called for the local, the slow freight that stopped at every station between Denver and Fort Collins. On the point was the number 807, a 2-8-2 oil-fired steamer, one of six locomotives recently purchased from the Burlington and renumbered from the 5500s to 804 through 809. We pulled out of the Denver yards and rolled north at twenty-five miles per hour, whistle blowing and smoke billowing high in the air. The 807 was in peak condition, working like a fine Swiss watch. After stopping at Westminster to drop off and pick up cars, we continued north, stopping again at Longmont, Berthoud, and Loveland to couple new cars into the train and leave others behind.

Twelve hours after leaving Denver, we pulled into Fort Collins in the bright, clear morning. After filling out reports, the crew walked to town, ate breakfast at the Silver Grill, and checked into the Northern Hotel for several hours of rest.

That evening at 11:40 p.m., we left Fort Collins for the return trip to Denver. Along the way we stopped to switch and pick up loaded cars. Twelve hours later, we pulled into Rice yard, the C&S yard in Denver named for company vice-president Robert W. Rice, and uncoupled the train. I ran the 807 to the roundhouse and turned it over to the hostler, who put it in the stall. The 807 had made its last regularly scheduled run, and I had made my final trip at the throttle of a steam locomotive.

The C&S was the last railroad in Colorado, and among the last ten railroads in the nation, to operate standard gauge steam locomotives. Other railroads, such as the Santa Fe, which crossed a 500-mile stretch of desert where water had to be brought in tanks to service the steam locomotives, couldn't ignore the efficiency of the diesel. They began replacing steamers after 1945, sending beautiful, near-new steam locomotives to the scrap yards.

Despite the diesel's efficiency, the C&S phased out steam locomotives over a fifteen-year period, replacing the old steamers as they wore out. In 1950, after using Burlington diesels for several years, the C&S purchased six four-unit diesel locomotives, called the Graybacks by the railroaders because of their coat of gray paint. The numbers 700, 701, and 702 went to work on the C&S while the 750, 751, and 752 ran on the Fort Worth and Denver City. The Graybacks were freight diesels, Model F7, cab-type design, with 1,500 horsepower per unit. Throughout the 1950s, they pulled the long freight trains moving between Wendover, Wyoming, and Fort Worth, Texas.

The C&S also bought several 150 class yard diesels to replace the light-weight 0-6-0 steam locomotives, the numbers 220 through 236, built in 1900 and still working. The 150s were Model NW2, SW7, and SW1200, with 1,000 and 1,200 horsepower, designed for yard work. Gradually the company purchased or leased other diesels for the main line, including additional F models and the larger, six-axle SD models of freight diesels with 1,500 to 3,000 horsepower. It also acquired the streamlined E model passenger diesels with 2,000 horsepower. Passenger diesels had the sleek, cab-type design, while the new hood-type freight diesels resembled heavy, cumbersome boxcars. The mechanical systems were the same, however.

As the C&S added diesels to the roster, it began moving into the yards the dependable 600 class steam locomotives that had hauled much of the freight rolling along the Front Range. By the mid-1950s, steam locomotives pulled a train out of Denver yards only when a diesel wasn't available. But not until 1961, a decade after most railroads had replaced steam locomotives, did the last C&S steamers fall to the cutting torch.

With diesels, railroading entered a new era. Since they pulled longer, heavier trains, heavier rails became necessary. Over the years, the C&S had replaced lighter-weight rails with heavier rails to accommodate heavier trains pulled by bigger steam locomotives. Diesel-powered trains required heavier rails yet, and the company began laying steel rails thirty-nine feet long that weighed 130 pounds per yard. Later, even those rails were replaced in sections by rails one quarter mile long, welded together end to end in solid joints. Eventually, the clickety-clack sound of trains rolling across fishplates that bolted the old rails together would be part of the past.

Longer, nonstop runs made by diesels led to the manufacture of insulated freight cars capable of maintaining the same interior temperature for one week. Frozen foods, fresh meats, and vegetables could be loaded into cars in Colorado, transported across the country, and unloaded a week later, the temperature unchanged.

Old coal cars were replaced by gondola cars that could be filled and emptied as the diesel-powered trains rolled slowly along the track. No longer did laborers have to climb into the cars to empty the coal, shovelful by shovelful.

The biggest change brought by diesels, however, was in the number of crews needed to man the trains. One diesel could haul twice the tonnage hauled by a steam locomotive. In the 1940s, fifteen main line crews worked on the North End. By 1956, with diesels on the roster, the number had dropped to six—four on scheduled freight trains and two on passenger trains 29 and 30, the only C&S passenger trains still running. (Another twenty-five engineers and firemen still worked in the yards.) The six main line crews handled the same tonnage that fifteen crews had handled with steam locomotives.

In 1959, the number of railroaders dropped further when railroad companies won the right to take firemen off freight and yard diesels, arguing that the engineer alone could run a diesel. He could, but if a motor stalled, he had to stop the train while he searched for the problem and tried to fix it. If he couldn't fix it, he had to radio the dispatcher to send out a mechanic. Passenger trains still kept two men in the cab, but the fireman came to be called "assistant engineer." The old railroad fireman who shoveled the coal, shook the fire, and built up the steam to keep the train moving down track no longer existed by 1962.

With fewer trains running, engineers like myself, who had been operating steam locomotives for several years, sometimes worked as firemen in the early 1950s, but by mid-decade, I had one of the four regular runs on freight. The first engineer in from a trip went to the bottom of the call list as "last out," eventually working up to "first out." The system insured adequate rest and an equal amount of work for the four engineers on the jobs, an important feature since we were paid only for trips made. A Grayback was usually on the point of freight trains 77 and 78, but sometimes we were at the throttle of one of the steam locomotives still hauling extra freights.

In the latter part of the 1950s and early 1960s, my brother, Clarence, and George Doyle were at the throttle of passenger diesels on trains 29 and 30, the top running jobs on the C&S. When Clarence retired in 1963, after forty-six years on the C&S—thirty-eight as an engineer—I moved into his slot. Three years later, Doyle retired, leaving me senior engineer on the C&S. Only one out of 100 engineers reached that lofty rung on the railroading ladder, not because of competence or ability, but because of the knack for hanging around the longest.

In my father's day, the senior engineer had his pick of the best little narrow gauge engines running up and down the line. The engine was his personal property, he believed, and the two of them made every trip together. He also had his pick of runs, and he chose the fastest and most direct passenger run.

As senior engineer in 1965, I stayed on the passenger trains, running whatever Model E passenger diesel the dispatcher decided to put on the point. Usually, trains 29 and 30 had two Model E8 9970s, with 2,250 horsepower each, coupled together and powerful enough to pull a train five city blocks long at sixty miles per hour. We left Denver in the evening with two coaches, two sleeping cars, and several baggage-mail cars and streaked down track past the freight trains waiting on the low rail. En route we dropped off mail cars and took on others, varying the consist as the train rolled along. At Cheyenne, another crew took over the locomotive for the trip to Casper, and I returned to Denver at the throttle of another diesel locomotive, pulling southbound passenger train 30.

Trains 29 and 30 were making their last runs in the 1960s. For some time, the C&S had faced tough competition from automobiles, buses, and airlines. Denver had grown to a metropolis of about 500,000, with burgeoning suburbs that added another half million. Many people found it easier to jump into a car and drive to Fort Collins or Cheyenne over the four-lane interstate highways than to drive to Denver Union Station and hop a train. Buses offered several trips each day to cities along the Front Range. And smaller commuter airlines were bidding for passenger business.

In 1966, the C&S bowed to decreasing passenger revenues and discontinued the *Texas Zephyr*. The following year, the last C&S passenger trains, the 29 and 30, were pulled off after the company lost the $300,000 government mail contract that had subsidized passenger service. But even on the final runs, as many as 100 passengers boarded train 29 in Denver on weekends and holidays.

Freight business remained the backbone of the railroad that had been built in Colorado nearly a century before to haul machinery and equipment to the mines and bring out the ore. In 1962, 25 percent of the C&S business still came from the mining industry. Every day, iron ore trains, fifty cars long, with four diesels on the point and three in back, left

Guernsey, Wyoming, on the Burlington and rolled south from Cheyenne on the C&S. The C&S trains also hauled oil and gas until the energy companies constructed giant pipelines to carry oil south from Wyoming. Even then, the railroad moved the heavy pipes, machinery, and men needed to build the line. Long trains hauling Coors beer ran out of Golden every day over the old Colorado Central route, the last section of that railroad still in use. And merchandise trains moved north and south with lumber, cement, tools, industrial equipment, clothing, furniture, newsprint, cattle, and farm products. Over the years, trucks had taken some of the railroad's business, but the fact remains that it takes 300 trucks to haul the same tonnage carried by a single 100-car train.

The railroaders' jobs also changed over the years. The mandatory requirement rule that went into effect in the 1950s required railroaders to hang up their caps and overalls at age seventy and opened top jobs to younger men. Before the retirement rule, railroaders clung to their jobs as long as they could climb into the engine. Even with pension plans, no railroader liked to retire to the front porch to listen to the distant wailing of a locomotive whistle. While some railroads had a policy of pulling engineers off the main line at age sixty-five and putting them in the yards where they could finish their days behind a throttle if they wished, the C&S had let them work as long as they seemed able. One old hog head had worked on the main line when he was nearing eighty years. Finally, the company moved him to the yards, where he showed up hale and hearty every day for the next five years to run the switch engines.

In the 1960s, the length of hours a railroader could work was limited to sixteen. Before the decade ended, the Hours of Service Act was amended to fourteen hours, and another amendment in 1972 dropped the hours to twelve. Unlike my father's day, when companies worked the men until they dropped, modern railroad companies, facing fines as high as $10,000, scrupulously enforced the law. If the time limit ran out with the crew on the road, the engineer stopped the train and waited for the company to send out a new crew to take over. Either the relief crew rode out on another train or arrived by automobile, which the dead crew drove back to the terminal.

Over the years of continuous and persistent struggle, the railroaders had won wages based on mileage and the weight of locomotives that gave them a decent standard of living. In the early 1960s, C&S engineers made about $1,000 a month. They also had retirement and medical benefits and were reimbursed for meals and lodging expenses away from home base. And they had legal methods of handling grievances that let them protest unfair company decisions all the way to a national board, if necessary.

On the job, they had the assurance that the locomotives, trains, and right-of-ways met federal safety standards. And with radios in the engine cab and on the train, they no longer relied on flags and whistles to communicate with the train crew, other trains, or the dispatcher.

Some things remained the same, however. Even though the dispatcher's office was moved from Denver to McCook, Nebraska, in the late 1950s, the dispatcher still sent new trains down the line after studying his ledger and figuring out the position of moving trains, much as in my father's day. Railroaders from other companies with Centralized Traffic Control marveled that the C&S train order system worked, but C&S railroaders accepted it in stride. It was the only system we knew.

Sons still followed their fathers railroading, although nepotism rules adopted by most companies prevented family members from working on the same railroad. By the time my brother Neil retired in 1968, his son Jim had become an engineer on the Southern Pacific, carrying on the family tradition.

On the C&S, railroaders who had caught on the road in the 1940s were carrying on the tradition of a century of Colorado railroading. They had learned their craft from the old engineers like Frank Johnson, Judy Gowder, Charlie Conroe, and Clarence Chapman, who had learned railroading from the engineers of my father's day. One engineer, C.B. Clark, who started railroading in the 1940s, had his career nearly derailed by one of the high-handed, cantankerous old engineers no fireman could please. Not long after Clark had caught on the road, Mickey Hansen called me into his office.

"What do you think of the new man?" he asked.

"He's sharp, quick to learn," I said. "Why do you ask?"

Hansen told me one of the old engineers had reported him and wanted him fired.

"If you do that," I said, "you'll lose a good fireman and future engineer. We both know the C&S needs skilled people. Besides, that engineer wouldn't know a good fireman if he saw one."

"My thought exactly," Hansen said.

Clark was set up to engineer in 1957. When I resigned as general chairman, the C&S engineers elected him to the top union job. Later, he became the senior engineer on the C&S.

Three years before I reached the retirement age of seventy, I decided it was time to hang up my cap and overalls. On July 2, 1967, I climbed into the cab of the Burlington diesel 9946A on the point of passenger train 29. Pat Fondy was the fireman and Clint Colyer was the conductor. We glided out of Denver Union Station and into the clear, beautiful night with a faint tinge of light still outlining the edge of the Rocky Mountains. In between stops to drop off passengers and mail at stations on the way we rolled along at sixty miles per hour, pulling into Cheyenne in the middle of the night. It was still dark when we started back to Denver with passenger train 30 and the Burlington diesel 9944A on the point. As we rounded a curve near Fort Collins, the sun began rising in the east, a red ball of fire. In the early morning light, we rolled south through Loveland, Berthoud, Longmont, Boulder, Broomfield, and Westminster, all the familiar stops on the North End. When we pulled into Denver Union Station on time at 7:15 a.m., my wife, Margaret, our son, Clay, and his family were waiting next to the track. I had made my last trip behind the throttle.

During the Depression, I picked up extra work with a house decorator in between trips on the railroad. One day we were painting the trim on the roof of a house in Westminster when a C&S train chugged down track about a half block away. On the point were two steam locomotives, with whistles blowing and smoke billowing in the air. Behind the locomotives rolled a long line of stock and merchandise cars. It was a beautiful sight. With paint dripping from my brush and running down the roof, I stood watching the train until my boss hollered, "Sam, wake up."

Later, he said, "I hope you get back to railroading soon, because you'll never be good at anything else. You've got too much smoke in your blood."

Bibliographical Notes

In writing this book, especially the chapters on the Denver, South Park and Pacific, we relied upon the data on locomotives and stations supplied by Mac Poor in his definitive study of that railroad, *Denver, South Park and Pacific,* Memorial Edition (1976). F. Hol Wagner, Jr.'s book, *The Colorado Road: History, Motive Power and Equipment of the Colorado and Southern and Fort Worth and Denver Railways* (1970), was a useful source to check the data and statistics on the Colorado and Southern's standard gauge equipment.

Chapters 1 and 2

For a sense of Denver in 1883, when Sam Speas arrived, we are indebted to people who came at the same time and wrote about the experience: Robert Lotta, "Denver in the 1880s," *Colorado Magazine* 18/4 (1941); Rezin H. Constant, "Colorado as Seen by a Visitor of 1880: Diary of Rezin H. Constant," *Colorado Magazine* 12/3 (1935); and W.H. Bergtold, "Denver Fifty Years Ago," *Colorado Magazine* 8/2 (1931).

Microfilms of the *Rocky Mountain News* (1883 and 1884) provided the data on the cost of living in Denver and the quote about the "bunko steerers and sneak thieves."

Other helpful sources were: Jerome C. Smiley's *History of Denver* (1901), Percy Stanley Fritz, *Colorado: The Centennial State* (1941), Frank Hall, *History of the State of Colorado,* 4 volumes (1889–1895), LeRoy R. Hafen, Ed., *Colorado and Its People,* vol. 1 (1948), and Lyle W. Dorsett, *The Queen City, A History of Denver* (1977).

Encyclopedia of North American Railroading (1981) is the source for information on the origins of the four-foot, eight-and-one-half-inch standard gauge, p. 127.

In addition to *Denver, South Park and Pacific,* other useful sources of railroad information included Robert G. Athearn's *Union Pacific Country* (1971), for an overview of the Union Pacific system in the 1880s, and Cornelius W. Hauck's *Narrow Gauge to Central City and Silver Plume,* Colorado Rail Annual Number 10 (1972), for data on the Clear Creek District.

Statistics on Denver's population came from the United States Bureau of the Census, and statistics on mining in Colorado were drawn from Charles W. Henderson's *Mining in Colorado* (U.S. Government Printing Office, 1926).

The description of riding the train in the Clear Creek District is from the diary of Rezin H. Constant, as is the quote in Chapter One that begins, "The city is full of sightseers . . . ." Freight rates charged by wagon companies and railroads are quoted from *Colorado: The Centennial State.*

It can be argued that Colorado's railroads were not the sole cause of the increase in mining production in the 1870s. The Patent Law of 1866 opened mineral lands for exploration, guaranteeing prospectors the title to mines they located and developed to the extent of $1,000. This powerful incentive drove hordes of prospectors to look for gold and silver, since what they found was theirs. They found many new deposits, including the rich silver deposits of Leadville. Also, the development of technically sophisticated mining equipment made it possible to open and work deep mines. And new smelters sprang up. By 1879, there were seventeen smelters in Leadville alone. The fact remains, however, that new discoveries, equipment, and smelters still depended for transportation upon the railroads.

Chapter 3

Several sources were valuable for an understanding of Boulder in the 1880s, including "Boulder in the 80s and 90s as Recalled by Professor W.H. Burger, Native Resident," "Boulder, Colorado in 1883: An Experiment in Local History," "Boulder, Colorado, 1880–1920: The Development from a Frontier Town to a Multifunctional City," by Herbert Pfister, and "A

Municipal History of Boulder, Colorado, 1871–1946," by Lynn I. Perrigo. All four sources are located in the University of Colorado Library, Western History Department.

Another useful source is *History of Clear Creek and Boulder Valley, Colorado,* Chicago: O.L. Baskin and Co., 1880.

The *Boulder County Herald* and the *Boulder News and Courier,* 1883 and 1884, give much information about the town, including articles on the excursion trains. *The Switzerland Trail of America* by Forest Crossen (1962) provides a sound overview of the early history of the Greeley, Salt Lake and Pacific.

The quote about engines likely to lie down on track is from the *Rocky Mountain News,* November 12, 1899.

Chapter 4

Virginia McConnell Simmons' *Bayou Salado* (1966) gives an overview of early day Como and is the source for the statement that 6,000 laborers pitched their tents there (page 164). We have reduced that number to a more realistic 300, as reported in *Railway Age,* June 5, 1879.

The source of information on the railroads' adoption of standard time is *Encyclopedia of North American Railroading: 150 Years of Railroading in the United States and Canada,* by Freeman Hubbard (1981).

W.A. Tuplin's *The Steam Locomotive* (1974) provided the information helpful in explaining the operation of the steam locomotive. Also helpful was *The Steam Locomotive in America: Its Development in the Twentieth Century* (1952) by Alfred W. Bruce, and *This Fascinating Railroad Business* (1942) by Robert Selph Henry.

Mac Poor's *Denver, South Park and Pacific* names the crew on the pay train, on page 326. The old number 2 was changed to the 283 in 1885, according to the roster on page 466.

Tom Gibbony talked about his days as a caller in Como in an interview with the *Rocky Mountain News,* June 19, 1960.

Chapter 5

We are indebted to Mac Poor's *Denver, South Park and Pacific* for the schedule of trains 499 and 488 found in the endpapers, for the data on curves between Como and Leadville, p. 273, and for mileage and information on stations, pp. 446–449. The Dickey anecdote is also from the book, p. 446, as is the quote that begins, "Ruin stared . . . ," p. 449.

Mary Ellen Gilliland's *Summit, A Gold Rush History of Summit County, Colorado* (1980) is the source for some of the information on dredging in

Breckenridge, p. 106.

Muriel V. Sibell's *Cloud Cities of Colorado* (1934) provides valuable information on Robinson and Kokomo, two towns that have disappeared.

We are indebted, again, to Mac Poor for the suggestion that the Denver, Leadville and Gunnison escaped compliance with the Safety Appliance Act because it did not cross state lines, p. 326.

Don L. Griswold and Jean Harvey Griswold are authors of *Carbonate Camp Called Leadville* (1951), the source of the comment that everyone was in Leadville in the 1890s and that the population was 35,000, p. 99. Charles W. Henderson's *Mining in Colorado* put Leadville's peak population at 30,000 in 1879, but Theodore F. Van Wagerner, in *Silver Camps of Colorado* (1919), says the population only reached 14,000.

The statement that freighting was so expensive from Leadville that the ore did not pay for it is from Griswold's book, p. 99.

The number of producing mines in Leadville is from *Leadville: Colorado's Magic City* (1980) by Edward Blair, and from Sibell's *Cloud Cities of Colorado. Cosmopolitan Magazine,* May 1891, is the source for the statement that $160 million had been mined in Leadville.

All the books mentioned proved useful for an understanding of Leadville's booms, but Blair's book is especially good on Leadville's 1893 bust.

Chapter 6

In checking facts for this chapter, Louisa A. Ward's meticulously researched booklet, "Chalk Creek, Colorado" (No. 9, Old West Series, 1940), was invaluable. We are indebted to her for the information on the Spanish treasure, p. 11, the term "the road to everywhere," p. 18, information on the Mount Antero Hotel, p. 22, facts on the Hortense hot springs, p. 11, and on the Alpine Smelting and Ore Co., p. 31, and the Mary Murphy Mine, pp. 40–42. The booklet is available at the Denver Public Library, Western History Division.

Bayou Salado: The Story of the South Park (1966) by Virginia McConnell Simmons also contains information on the Spanish expedition, p. 49.

Mac Poor's *Denver, South Park and Pacific,* with its description of the stations between Como and Chalk Creek, pp. 423–431, proved most helpful in writing this chapter.

Chapter 7

Historic Alpine Tunnel (1963) by Dow Helmers was invaluable as a source of information on construction of the Alpine Tunnel. *The Denver,*

South Park and Pacific has a good account of the tunnel's reopening, pp. 286–87. The newspaper quote on the Pullman Company is also from this book, p. 321, as are the facts on the Woodstock slide, p. 348.

Encyclopedia of Biography of Colorado, vol. I (1901), pp. 347–48, contains biographical information on Frank Trumbull.

Facts on Gunnison came from "Colorado Cities, Their Founding, Origin and Names," *Colorado Magazine* 9/5 (1932), and from "Gunnison in the Early Eighties," by George Root, also in *Colorado Magazine* 9/6 (1932).

Information on upgrading the railroad is from the Colorado and Southern Annual Reports, 1901 and 1902.

Chapter 8

Rules for protecting the rear of the train are found in the *Colorado and Southern Railway Company Rules and Regulations for the Government of Officers and Employees* (1900).

Accounts of the winter of 1898–99 and how it affected the Colorado and Southern narrow gauge can be found in the *Denver Sunday Post* and the *Denver Evening Post,* between January and May 1899. They are also included in *Pictorial Supplement to Denver, South Park and Pacific,* R.H. Kindig, E.J. Haley, and M.C. Poor (1959), pp. 97–107. A reproduction of the Conductor's Register, p. 106, shows Sam Speas on the 211 and John Olson on the 66, bringing the first extra freight into Dickey on April 26, 1899.

Chapter 9

The *Fairplay Flume* frequently carried stories about the day-to-day life in Como. An article on the murder of Marshall Cook appeared on the front page of the *Flume,* April 12, 1894. Other articles on the Como school, picnics, and excursions are in issues published between 1900 and 1910.

Information on the Santa Fe's Harvey Girls, similar to the type of young women hired by the Union Pacific, can be found on page 144 in *The Old West: The Railroaders* (1973) by Keith Wheeler.

Como was not the only small Colorado town with a large number of immigrants around the turn of the century. Many of the towns were filled with people who had come to the United States looking for a better life. In 1890, for example, 30 percent of the population in Leadville was foreign-born, according to *Labor-Management Relations in Colorado* (1961) by Harry Seligson and George E. Bardwell.

Chapter 10

An account of J.T. Duffy's death has been given in other books on early Colorado railroading, including *Narrow Gauge to Central City and Silver Plume: Colorado Rail Annual Number Ten* (1972), p. 143. Pages 111–112 carry the account of the accident that killed Fred Hunn.

The *Fairplay Flume,* October 25, 1907, carried the story of the wreck that killed Jinx Thomas.

The wreck of train 82 that took the life of Webster Ballinger is recorded in the *Denver Times,* September 23, 1901.

Chapter 11

Information on the number of hours laborers worked in Colorado in the nineteenth century, the amount of pay, and the number of unionists is from *Labor Management Relations in Colorado* by Henry Seligson and George E. Bardwell (1961), pp. 37–61. Other works helpful in comparing railroad labor relations with those of other industries in the state were: "Working in Colorado: A Brief History of the Colorado Labor Movement" by Harold V. Knight, published by the University of Colorado Boulder Center for Labor Education and Research (1971) and "A Report on Labor Disturbances in the State of Colorado from 1880 to 1904," 58th Congress, 3d Sess., Senate Doc. No. 122, January 27, 1905.

The Brotherhood of Locomotive Engineers' policies are discussed in "Opening Exercises of the Twenty-Sixth Grand International Convention of the BLE at Denver, October 16, 1889." This document, available at the Denver Public Library, also contains biographical information on Grand Chief Arthur.

Minutes of the grievance committee meetings from 1900 to 1903 are from the "General Board, Colorado and Southern Minute Book, 1899—," which is part of the author's collection.

Chapter 12

Information on the expenses incurred by the South Park in its last glory days is from Mac Poor's *The Denver, South Park and Pacific,* p. 391. The source for the last passenger train from Como to Leadville is *The South Park Line: A Concise History,* Colorado Rail Annual No. 12 (1979) by Gordon S. Chappell, Robert W. Richardson, and Cornelius W. Hauck, p. 122.

Figures on mining production in Colorado are from Charles W. Henderson's *Mining in Colorado* (1926).

Chapter 13

We are indebted to Louisa A. Ward's "Chalk Creek, Colorado" (1940) for information on the Chalk Creek Mining District in the early 1900s.

Sam's experience with the Romley turntable has been written about in *The South Park Line, A Concise History* by Chappell, Richardson, and Hauck, pp. 153–154, although, in this account, Sam is not named as the engineer on the 67.

Chapter 14

The source for the statistics on mining production in Colorado and in Chaffee County is Charles W. Henderson's *Mining in Colorado* (1926).

Again, we are indebted to the scholarship of Mac Poor in *The Denver, South Park and Pacific* for information on the C&S petitions to the ICC to abandon the Buena Vista-Romley-Hancock route, p. 393.

Chapter 15

Mining in Colorado is the source for the statistics on Colorado's coal production between 1880 and 1920.

Information on the Colorado and Southern's locomotives is from F. Hol Wagner, Jr.'s excellent book, *The Colorado Road: History, Motive Power and Equipment of the Colorado and Southern and Fort Worth and Denver Railways* (1970). It is also the source of information on the C&S construction of the Fort Collins trolley system and the Denver and Inter-urban, p. 25.

Chapter 16

The C&S ran regularly scheduled passenger trains to Fort Worth. Denver crews handled the trains to Trinidad, where other crews took over for the trip to Texline on the New Mexico-Texas border. There, Fort Worth and Denver crews took the trains to Fort Worth. Built between 1881 and 1888, the Fort Worth and Denver had long been intertwined with Colorado railroads. When the C&S was formed in December 1898, the Fort Worth and Denver became a subsidiary of the new company. For a clear explanation of the tangled history of the Fort Worth and Denver, see *The Colorado Road,* pp. 191–196.

Chapter 18

The rules referred to in this chapter can be found in the Colorado and

Southern Railway Company's *Standard Code of Train Rules, Block Signal and Interlocking Rules* (1921), issued in accordance with rules adopted by the American Railway Association. Throughout these chapters, we have used the word "class" to designate locomotives, such as "600 class" or "900 class," since this is the way C&S railroaders referred to the locomotives. The reader should not confuse this use of class with the ICC classification of locomotives.

Chapter 19

The Burlington Route: A History of the Burlington Lines by Richard C. Overton (1965) was a valuable reference for the financial condition of the C&S during the 1920s and 1930s. See pp. 357, 368, and 371.

Lyle W. Dorsett, in *The Queen City: A History of Denver* (1977), provides the estimate of 800 to 1,000 men traveling through Denver every month during the Depression on p. 234.

The chronology for the abandonment of the C&S narrow gauge lines is from *The Denver, South Park and Pacific,* pp. 399–413.

Chapter 20

Statistics for the military freight and personnel moved by the nation's railroads during World War II are from *The Burlington Route,* p. 483. That work is also the source of information on the *Texas Zephyr,* p. 458.

The Burlington introduced the first diesel in the United States on a trial run from Denver to Chicago, November 11, 1934. Regular passenger service between the two cities on the *Denver Zephyr* began in 1936, the same year the Union Pacific introduced the *City of Denver Zephyr. The Burlington Route,* beginning on page 393, contains a great deal of factual information on the first diesels and the zephyrs.

The Circus Moves by Rail, by Tom Parkinson and Charles Philip Fox (1978), p. 131, refers to the 108-car Ringling Bros. and Barnum and Bailey Circus train, the longest in the history of that circus. It is also the source of other factual information on circus trains.

Information on the *Ferdinand Magellan* is from *The American Railroad Passenger Car* by John H. White, Jr. (1978), p. 371.

Trains in Transition by Lucius Beebe (1941) is the source for some of the factual details on the diesel locomotive, p. 138.

Chapter 22

Accounts of the accident in which Don Grinstead was involved can be found in the *Denver Post,* April 30, 1950.

The fatal accident at Broomfield was reported in the *Rocky Mountain News,* September 23 and 24, 1958, and in the *Denver Post,* September 23, 1958.

The Westminster accident is reported in the *Denver Post,* October 18, 1927.

Chapter 23

The orders of the general director referred to in the text are Order 17, supplement 4, and Orders 8 through 13. Information on McAdoo's orders can be found in *Burlington Route,* p. 308. That work is also the source of information on Roosevelt's arbitration that resulted in the first vacation for railroaders, p. 486, and for facts on Truman's nationalization of the railroads, pp. 538–39.

Federal legislation pertaining to the railroads can be found in the United States Code (1964), Title 45, sections 52-152. They are summarized in Freeman Hubbard's *Encyclopedia of North American Railroading* (1981), p. 279.

Chapter 24

The C&S Annual Reports for the years 1950 through 1967 show the decline in passenger revenues and the percentages of different kinds of freight hauled.

Information on the size and numbering of diesel locomotives can be found in *The Concise Encyclopedia of World Railway Locomotives,* edited by P. Ransome-Wallis (1959), p. 125 and p. 131.

The Colorado Road, pp. 377–79, is the best authority for the diesel locomotives on the C&S roster.

Bibliography

MANUSCRIPT MATERIALS

Boulder, Colorado

University of Colorado, Western History Division.
  "Boulder, Colorado in 1883. An Experiment in Local History." Pamphlet file.
  "Boulder in the 80s and 90s as Recalled by Professor W.H. Burger, Native Resident." Pamphlet file.
  Perrigo, Lynn I. "A Municipal History of Boulder, Colorado. 1871–1946. Pamphlet file.
  Pfister, Herbert. "Boulder, Colorado 1880–1920: The Development From a Frontier Town to a Multifunctional City." Pamphlet file.
  Smith, Don. "Chalk Creek to the Past," 1958. Pamphlet file.

Denver, Colorado

Denver Public Library, Western History Division.
  Knight, Harold V. "Working in Colorado: A Brief History of the Colorado Labor Movement," University of Colorado Boulder Center for Labor Education and Research (1971).

"Opening Exercises of the Twenty-Sixth Grand International Convention of the
    B of LE at Denver, Colorado, 1889."

GOVERNMENT PUBLICATIONS AND RECORDS

"A Report on Labor Disturbances in the State of Colorado from 1880 to 1904."
    Inclusion with Correspondence Related Thereto. Sen. Doc. 122, 58th Cong.,
    3d sess., January 27, 1905.
"Adamson Law" and "Hours of Service Act," U.S. Code 1964, Title 45, sections
    52-152.

NEWSPAPERS

Boulder County Courier, May 18–April 6, 1883.
Boulder County Herald, 1883–1884.
Boulder News and Courier, May 18, 1883.
Denver Post, 1927, 1950, 1958.
Fairplay Flume, 1894, 1895, 1907, 1912, 1914.
Rocky Mountain News, 1883, 1884, 1902, 1947, 1950, 1958.

BOOKS

Athearn, Robert G. *Rebel of the Rockies: A History of the Denver and Rio Grande
    Western Railroad.* New Haven and London: Yale University Press, 1962.
————. *Union Pacific Country.* Chicago: Rand McNally and Co., 1971.
Beebe, Lucius. *Trains in Transition.* New York: Bonanza Books, 1941.
Blair, Edward. *Leadville: Colorado's Magic City.* Boulder: Pruett Publishing Co.,
    1980.
Brown, Robert L. *Jeep Trails to Colorado Ghost Towns.* Caldwell, Idaho: The
    Caxton Printers, Ltd., 1966.
Bruce, Alfred W. *The Steam Locomotive in America: Its Development in the
    Twentieth Century.* New York: Bonanza Books, 1952.
Chappell, Gordon, Richardson, Robert W., and Hauck, Cornelius W. *The South
    Park Line: A Concise History.* Colorado Rail Annual Number 12. Golden:
    Colorado Railroad Museum, 1974.
Colorado and Southern Railway Company. *Annual Reports.* Denver: Colorado and
    Southern Railway Company, 1901–1967.
————. *Rules and Regulations for the Government of Officers and Employees.*
    Denver: Colorado and Southern Railway Company, 1900.
————. *Standard Code of Train Rules, Block Signal and Interlocking Rules.*
    Denver: Colorado and Southern Railway Company, 1921.
Concise Encyclopedia of World Railway Locomotives, edited by P. Ransome-Wallis.
    London: Hutchinson, 1959.
Crossen, Forest. *The Switzerland Trail of America.* Fort Collins: Robinson Press,
    Inc., 1978.

Dorsett, Lyle W. *The Queen City: A History of Denver.* Vol. I in the Western Urban History Series. Boulder: Pruett Publishing Co., 1977.

Dyer, Mary. *Echoes of Como, Colorado, 1879–1973.* Dillon: D&L Printing, 1974.

Encyclopedia of Biography of Colorado, vol. 1. Chicago: The Century Publishing and Engraving Co., 1901.

Encyclopedia of North American Railroading: 150 Years of Railroading in the United States and Canada, edited by Freeman Hubbard. New York: McGraw Hill, 1981.

Fritz, Percy Stanley. *Colorado: The Centennial State.* New York: Prentice-Hall, 1941.

Gilliland, Mary Ellen. *Summit: A Gold Rush History of Summit County, Colorado.* Silverthorne: Alpenrose Press, 1980.

Greever, William S. *The Bonanza West: The Story of the Western Mining Rushes.* Norman: University of Oklahoma Press, 1963.

Griswold, Don L., and Jean Harvey. *The Carbonate Camp Called Leadville.* Denver: University of Denver Press, 1951.

Hafen, LeRoy R., ed. *Colorado and Its People.* Vols. 1 and 2. New York: Lewis Historical Publishing, 1948.

Hall, Frank. *History of the State of Colorado.* 4 vols. Chicago: Blakely Printing Co., 1889.

Hauck, Cornelius W. *Narrow Gauge to Central and Silver Plume.* Colorado Rail Annual Number 10. Golden: Colorado Railroad Museum, 1972.

Henderson, Charles W. *Mining in Colorado.* U.S. Geological Survey Professional Paper 138. Washington: U.S. Government Printing Office, 1926.

Henry, Robert Selph. *This Fascinating Railroad Business.* 2nd ed. New York: The Bobbs-Merrill Co., 1942.

History of Clear Creek and Boulder Valley, Colorado. Chicago: O.L. Baskin and Co., 1880.

Lathrop, Gilbert A. *Little Engines and Big Men.* Caldwell, Idaho: The Caxton Printers, Ltd., 1955.

Overton, Richard C. *Burlington Route: A History of the Burlington Lines.* Lincoln: University of Nebraska Press, 1965.

Parkinson, Tom, and Fox, Charles Phillip. *The Circus Moves by Rail.* Boulder: Pruett Publishing Co., 1978.

Poor, M.C. *The Denver, South Park and Pacific.* Denver: The Rocky Mountain Railroad Club, 1976.

Seligson, Harry, and Bardwell, George E. *Labor-Management Relations in Colorado.* Denver: Sage Books, 1961.

Sibell, Muriel V. *Cloud Cities of Colorado.* Denver: Smith-Brooks Printing Co., 1934.

Simmons, Virginia McConnell. *Bayou Salado: The History of the South Park.* Colorado Springs: Century One Press, 1966.

Smiley, Jerome C. *History of Denver.* Denver: Denver Times, 1901.

Tuplin, W.A. *The Steam Locomotive.* New York: Charles Scribner's Sons, 1974.

Wagner, F. Hol, Jr. *The Colorado Road: History, Motive Power and Equipment of the Colorado and Southern and Fort Worth and Denver Railways.* Denver: The Intermountain Chapter, National Railway Historical Society, Inc., 1970.

Ward, Louisa A. *Chalk Creek, Colorado.* Denver: John Van Male, 1940.
White, John H., Jr. *The American Railroad Passenger Car.* Baltimore: The Johns Hopkins University Press, 1978.
Young, Otis E., Jr. *Black Powder and Hand Steel: Miners and Machines on the Old Western Frontier.* Norman: The University of Oklahoma Press, 1975.

PERIODICALS

Baer, Everett. "A Journey to Old St. Elmo." *The Denver Brand Book* 14 (1958).
Bauch, Francis Eugene. "Early Days of Central City." *Colorado Magazine* 19 (1942).
Bell, William A. "Mineral Resources of Colorado." *Colorado: A Collection of Thirty-Two Articles* (1919).
Bergtold, W.H. "Denver Fifty Years Ago." *Colorado Magazine* 8 (1931).
"Colorado Cities: Their Founding, Origin and Names." *Colorado Magazine* 9 (1932).
Constant, Rezin H. "Colorado as Seen by a Visitor of 1880." *Colorado Magazine* 12 (1935).
Hafen, LeRoy R. "The Counties of Colorado: A History of Their Creation and the Origin of Their Names." *Colorado Magazine* 8 (1931).
Hagie, E.C. "Gunnison in Early Days." *Colorado Magazine* 8 (1931).
Harvey, Mrs. James, "The Leadville Ice Palace of 1896." *Colorado Magazine* 17 (1940).
Lotta, Robert. "Denver in the 1880s." *Colorado Magazine* 18 (1941).
Root, George A. "Gunnison in the Early Eighties." *Colorado Magazine* 9 (1932).
Van Wagener, Theodore F. "Silver Camps of Colorado." *Colorado: A Collection of Thirty-Two Articles* (1919).

About the Author

Margaret Coel is the award-winning author of *Chief Left Hand: Southern Arapaho*, and many other books and articles that focus on Colorado and the American West. Her articles have appeared in *The New York Times*, *The Christian Science Monitor*, and *The Denver Post*. She is a popular speaker on railroading in Colorado and on the Arapaho Indians. In 1985, *Goin' Railroading* was recipient of the Best Non-Fiction Book award of the Colorado Authors League. The daughter of Sam Speas, Jr., Margaret Coel lives in Boulder, Colorado, with her husband, George.